Teacher Agency in Multilingual Pedagogies

NEW PERSPECTIVES ON LANGUAGE AND EDUCATION

Founding Editor: Viv Edwards, *University of Reading, UK*
Series Editors: Phan Le Ha, *University of Hawaii at Manoa, USA,* Joel Windle, *Monash University, Australia* and Kyle R. McIntosh, *University of Tampa, USA.*

Two decades of research and development in language and literacy education have yielded a broad, multidisciplinary focus. Yet education systems face constant economic and technological change, with attendant issues of identity and power, community and culture. What are the implications for language education of new 'semiotic economies' and communications technologies? Of complex blendings of cultural and linguistic diversity in communities and institutions? Of new cultural, regional and national identities and practices? The New Perspectives on Language and Education series will feature critical and interpretive, disciplinary and multidisciplinary perspectives on teaching and learning, language and literacy in new times. New proposals, particularly for edited volumes, are expected to acknowledge and include perspectives from the Global South. Contributions from scholars from the Global South will be particularly sought out and welcomed, as well as those from marginalized communities within the Global North.

All books in this series are externally peer-reviewed.

Full details of all the books in this series and of all our other publications can be found on http://www.multilingual-matters.com, or by writing to Multilingual Matters, St Nicholas House, 31-34 High Street, Bristol, BS1 2AW, UK.

NEW PERSPECTIVES ON LANGUAGE AND EDUCATION: 129

Teacher Agency in Multilingual Pedagogies

Pedagogical Spaces in the Primary School

Thomas Quehl

MULTILINGUAL MATTERS
Bristol • Jackson

DOI https://doi.org/10.21832/QUEHL6079
Library of Congress Cataloging in Publication Data
A catalog record for this book is available from the Library of Congress.
Names: Quehl, Thomas, author.
Title: Teacher Agency in Multilingual Pedagogies: Pedagogical Spaces in the Primary School/Thomas Quehl.
Description: Bristol; Jackson: Multilingual Matters, [2025] | Series: New Perspectives on Language and Education: 129 | Includes bibliographical references and index. | Summary: 'Through an ethnographic study that took place in highly diverse primary school classrooms in London and the East of England, this book engages with teachers' perspectives and children's descriptions of their plurilingual experiences, as it explores what constitutes, hinders and potentially facilitates teachers' agency in multilingual pedagogies' – Provided by publisher.
Identifiers: LCCN 2024056420 (print) | LCCN 2024056421 (ebook) | ISBN 9781800416079 (hardback) | ISBN 9781800416062 (paperback) | ISBN 9781800416086 (pdf) | ISBN 9781800416093 (epub)
Subjects: LCSH: Multilingual education – Great Britain. | Language teachers – Great Britain. | Language and languages – Study and teaching (Primary) – Great Britain. | Culturally relevant pedagogy – Great Britain.
Classification: LCC LC3736.G6 Q44 2025 (print) | LCC LC3736.G6 (ebook) | DDC 371.829/914041 – dc23/eng/20241213
LC record available at https://lccn.loc.gov/2024056420
LC ebook record available at https://lccn.loc.gov/2024056421

British Library Cataloguing in Publication Data
A catalogue entry for this book is available from the British Library.

ISBN-13: 978-1-80041-607-9 (hbk)
ISBN-13: 978-1-80041-606-2 (pbk)

Multilingual Matters
UK: St Nicholas House, 31-34 High Street, Bristol, BS1 2AW, UK.
USA: Ingram, Jackson, TN, USA.
Authorised Representative: Easy Access System Europe – Mustamäe tee 50, 10621 Tallinn, Estonia, gpsr.requests@easproject.com.

Website: https://www.multilingual-matters.com
X: Multi_Ling_Mat
Bluesky: @multi-ling-mat.bsky.social
Facebook: https://www.facebook.com/multilingualmatters
Blog: https://www.channelviewpublications.wordpress.com

Copyright © 2025 Thomas Quehl.

All rights reserved. No part of this work may be reproduced in any form or by any means without permission in writing from the publisher.

The policy of Multilingual Matters/Channel View Publications is to use papers that are natural, renewable and recyclable products, made from wood grown in sustainable forests. In the manufacturing process of our books, and to further support our policy, preference is given to printers that have FSC and PEFC Chain of Custody certification. The FSC and/or PEFC logos will appear on those books where full certification has been granted to the printer concerned.

Typeset by Riverside Publishing Solutions.

Contents

Acknowledgements		vii
Key to transcripts		ix
Introduction		1
1	Multilingual Pedagogies and Teacher Agency – Mapping Out the Frameworks	6
	1.1 Mapping Out Multilingual Pedagogies	6
	1.2 Mapping Out Teacher Agency	22
	1.3 The Framework for (Researching) Teacher Agency in Multilingual Pedagogies	33
2	Researching Teacher Agency: The Study	37
	2.1 Terminology	37
	2.2 The Schools and the Teachers	41
	2.3 Methodology and Research Design	43
	2.4 Data Collection and Analysis	45
	2.5 Education Policy in England	50
3	Classrooms in Real Schools: Contexts for Teacher Agency	54
	3.1 Ellie's Classroom: Small Choices and the Working Consensus	54
	3.2 Mike's Classroom: Personal Involvement in Writing	62
	3.3 Hira's Classroom: The Everyday Task of Multitasking	65
	3.4 Heather's and Kelly's Classrooms: EAL Responsive Routines and Teaching of Text Genres	68
4	Schools: Contexts for Multilingualism?	76
	4.1 Multilingualism in the Classrooms	76
	4.2 Multilingualism in the Schools	81
	4.3 An EAL Discourse	86
	4.4 A Symbolic Acknowledgement of Multilingualism	94

5	Between the Monolingual Norm and Superdiverse Voices	101
	5.1 The New Monolingual Norm	101
	5.2 Superdiverse Voices	113
	5.3 A Stopover: A 'Pedagogical Space' of Multilingual Pedagogies	129
6	Teachers' Perspectives in Busy Multilingual Classrooms	138
	6.1 'A teacher's life is hard': The Workplace School	138
	6.2 'Knowing the children': Professional Subjectivities	147
	6.3 Language Experiences and Reflexivity: Teachers' Positions	151
7	Towards Possibilities of Multilingual Pedagogies	162
	7.1 'And perhaps, if we had a bit more time, we would be a bit more creative': Teachers' Views on Possibilities	162
	7.2 'Our ideas': Children's Views	177
8	Teacher Agency in Multilingual Pedagogies: No Guarantees	194
	8.1 Achieving and Enhancing Teacher Agency in Multilingual Pedagogies	197
	8.2 Supporting and Empowering Teacher Agency in the Professional Field	200
	References	205
	Index	217

Acknowledgements

A book is a joint endeavour, research in schools is always a dialogue and turning research into a book involves many forms of further collaboration. I would like to thank Jim Anderson, Vally Lytra and Vicky Macleroy for their support, while I found my way into this enquiry, for the critical dialogue they offered throughout and for their advice. Without their generous encouragement, there would have been no PhD research project. I am also very grateful to the headteachers who opened their school gates and to the teachers and children who allowed me into their classrooms, sharing so freely their experiences and time. Without their voices, none of the lines of this book could have been written. I also wish to express my gratitude to the Department of Educational Studies at Goldsmiths University of London for a bursary in support of my research. For including this book into their series, I would like to thank Phan Le Ha, Joel Windle and Kyle R. McIntosh. I am grateful to the anonymous reviewers for their meticulous comments, and to Anna Roderick and everyone at Multilingual Matters for their patience and professionalism. With Ulrike Trapp and Ulrich Schultze, I undertook first curious steps towards exploring teachers' agency in multilingual pedagogies, and I remain grateful to them. Last and most, I would like to thank my mother and late father, Ursel and Jürgen Quehl, who taught me first words and supported my learning ever since; Main Chowdhury, Bettina Fraenkel, Emine Kara, Astrid Schmetterling and Jens Wyrwa, whose talking and listening I cherish, and Andrea Schatz, without whose love for words, there would be neither book nor sunshine.

Key to transcripts

[...] words edited out
. pause 1 sec

Introduction

> Where you know you have got seven, eight, nine different
> languages ... it is pretty inspiring
> Do you know [which] languages the children speak?
> [...] I should do . no .. but I can find that out
> (Mike, class teacher Year 5)

> I haven't really talked about [...] languages and things like that
> and, yeah, you never really get to talk [...] about languages [...]
> you don't really think about languages
> (Brayden, pupil in Mike's class)

These passages are from ethnographic work in a London primary school whose school website stated prominently that the children of its community speak approximately 40 languages apart from English. The diverging perceptions of the teacher and his pupil highlight how challenging it remains for many schools to respond to the normalcy of their students' multilingualism. This book uses the concept of teacher agency to explore the status quo regarding multilingualism in three English primary schools, adapting and developing the notion for an educational setting that constitutes a common context for language education: the classroom, where, on average, pupils speak nine to 10 languages apart from the main language of instruction.

The purpose of this book is twofold: it explores how the concept of teacher agency can shed light on what is (not) occurring in the classroom in relation to children's multilingualism, and it investigates how a detailed understanding of such agency in multilingual pedagogies can advance fresh developments. The ethnographic enquiry takes as its point of departure 'ordinary' classrooms with their day-to-day workings, tracing in detail how they present themselves to the teachers, as it is here that the conceptual power of teacher agency unfolds, allowing for an exploration of the relationship between such agency and possibilities for multilingual pedagogies. The chapters follow the teachers' work and perceptions, along with children's descriptions of their plurilingual repertoires and experiences, before presenting findings relevant to the possibilities of multilingual pedagogies from the perspective of both teachers and children. This approach offers a fresh perspective on how context can be theorised within language education, leading to the conceptualisation of a nuanced framework of interrelated elements that can contribute to the achievement of teacher agency in multilingual pedagogies.

Teacher agency is influenced by myriad personal and contextual factors (Kayi-Aydar *et al.*, 2019: 1). It is, therefore, always individually situated and specific (Priestley *et al.*, 2015). At the same time, it is systematically linked to contexts shaped by both the educational system and society's wider power relations, meaning any exploration of teacher agency necessarily involves a critical examination of the given educational setting and the pedagogical field to which such agency relates. In the study that informs this book, the interwoven examination of teacher agency and multilingual pedagogies required a conceptualisation of teacher agency and an understanding of multilingual pedagogies that are sufficiently flexible to respond to classrooms and pedagogical contexts in which such pedagogies have not yet been officially acknowledged and legitimised. In other words, rather than taking multilingual pedagogies and teacher agency as a given, this enquiry addresses them both as *emerging* phenomena.

'Multilingual pedagogies' is understood here as an umbrella term referring to approaches that *acknowledge, include, use, engage and promote children's plurilingual repertoires* (e.g. Cummins, 2021a: xxxvii; Duarte & Günther-van der Meij, 2018: 29; García & Flores, 2012: 242). Teachers in England – and elsewhere – cannot rely on curriculum guidance or a widely established body of practices, as is the case in other curriculum domains. That is, the situation differs considerably from other classrooms that are, for example, part of bilingual programmes (e.g. García & Kleyn, 2016a; García *et al.*, 2017) or are in bilingual countries/regions where a second official language can serve as a catalyst for plurilingual, more integrated approaches (e.g. Duarte & Günther-van der Meij, 2018; Little & Kirwan, 2019). For this reason, multilingual pedagogies in mainstream primary school education in England might, at most, be expected to 'emerge' and, as such, need to elaborate their own specific profile and shape. It is this constellation that provides an important motivation and rationale for exploring teacher agency and multilingual pedagogies in the mainstream classroom in parallel and in relation to each other.

The two agency models upon which the concept of teacher agency in multilingual pedagogies as developed in this book builds – the subject-centred sociocultural perspective on professional agency (Eteläpelto *et al.*, 2013) and the ecological approach to teacher agency (Priestley *et al.*, 2015) – both foreground the interplay between educators and context. The ecological approach explicitly conceptualises teacher agency as an *emergent* phenomenon (Priestley *et al.*, 2015: 22), encompassing the actors' capacity to make practical and normative judgements among different possible routes of action as they respond to emergent demands and dilemmas in evolving situations

(Emirbayer & Mische, 1998: 971). Thus, the lens of teacher agency enables the identification and exploration of what may form the context for such agency in multilingual pedagogies. The ethnographic lens further supports these explorations in that, by starting with the classroom, it facilitates the examination of its conditions in their interrelation with the institutional context and educators' professional subjectivities.

With this approach, the study links teacher agency to the role and workplace of the *primary school teacher*, the field of *multilingual pedagogies* and the setting of the *primary school classroom*. In this classroom, pupils speak (as teacher Mike put it) 'seven, eight, nine languages', yet (as his student Brayden says) 'you never really get to talk [...] about languages'. The theoretical contribution of the following chapters is to specify teacher agency in relation to this triad, identifying features constitutive for teacher agency in multilingual pedagogies and others which either support or hinder it. Central to the study are four research questions: What constitutes, facilitates and hinders teacher agency in multilingual pedagogies? How can teachers' professional knowledge, experiences and attitudes function as affordances for multilingual pedagogies? How can teacher agency in multilingual pedagogies be achieved and enhanced? And how can possibilities for multilingual pedagogies emerge in mainstream schools?

The findings shed light on the mainstream primary school in England, which forms part of European education systems that have been characterised historically by a 'monolingual habitus' (Gogolin, 1997, 2021) and whose monolingual ideology continues to be well-documented (Cunningham, 2019; Cunningham & Little, 2023; Fashanu *et al.*, 2020; Gundarina & Simpson, 2022). There is, in fact, 'a considerable gap between the state of the art in research [...] and the state of mind prevailing in many teaching contexts' (Duarte & Günther-van der Meij, 2022: 452). Zooming in on this gap, the chapters invite various stakeholders within the professional field in different ways. The features seen as constitutive of, facilitating or hindering teacher agency offer a perspective for *teacher educators* who prepare prospective teachers for work in multilingual classrooms and would like to encourage them to reflect critically on how they can take responsibility for developments in their future educational institutions. *Future teachers, teachers* and *policymakers in schools* are offered a conceptual framework that shows how to strengthen their own or their staff's agency when developing multilingual pedagogies in their respective classrooms. *Researchers* in the field of educational linguistics find a contribution to the growing work on teacher agency in language education, with a fresh focus on how the context for teacher agency can be conceptualised regarding mainstream educational settings.

The mainstream school, financed by the state and attended by the majority of children, is a powerful institution where official knowledge is defined and reproduced via the curriculum (Bernstein, 1971) or potentially contested and transformed. It constitutes an ideologically relevant space situated within wider social, geographical and political contexts. Any analysis of multilingualism in mainstream schools is therefore positioned, as it will engage with and draw on notions that are themselves situated, contested and critiqued. Writing on Southern and Northern epistemologies, Kathleen Heugh (2015, 2018) points out that 'multilingualism, particularly in education, means different things in different contexts' (2015: 280), and she asks, 'Who decides who can use which term to mean what, exactly?' (2018: 181). The concepts in the following chapters are situated within schools in England and relate to European and North American contexts and debates. In European contexts, multilingualism among students is often described as 'normal' or 'increasingly normal'. However, it is important to acknowledge that multilingualism has always been a normalcy in most countries of the Global South (e.g. Heugh, 2021). Therefore, I want to acknowledge the positionality of my own work and will explain my use of certain contested terms in the second chapter. In contemporary European countries significantly characterised by the phenomena of international migration, multilingualism is intertwined with material and symbolic power relations and the ways, in which language can function as a flexible variable within 'natio-racial-culturally coded orders of belonging' (Mecheril, 2018). Thus, disputes about what is considered legitimate language and languaging indicate contested understandings of what is seen as linguistic normality and point to the ways in which powerful political and media discourses link multilingualism to imaginaries of 'us' and 'them' that reproduce dichotomies and risk discriminatory and racist divides (e.g. Badwan, 2021a; Blackledge, 2004; Dirim & Mecheril, 2010). Exploring how it may be possible to normalise multilingualism and multilingual pedagogies in schools is linked to hope and the quest to repel those divisive discourses and their consequences in educational settings.

The ethnographic approach encouraged and facilitated research that allowed teachers' and children's voices to be heard and also enabled the development of a line of enquiry that simultaneously sheds light on the status quo and evolving possibilities of multilingual pedagogies. Importantly, for a critical enquiry and the counter-hegemonic potential of ethnographic work (Blommaert, 2018), this approach could trace the small facets, tensions and emerging possibilities related to teacher agency and multilingual pedagogies in the five classrooms. My intent was to keep the enquiry's character of listening to educators and children alive when drawing on their voices in the analysis and writing of these chapters. All names have been anonymised.

A brief look at the chapters: Chapter 1 maps out the conceptual contexts of multilingual pedagogies and teacher agency and presents the framework for teacher agency in multilingual pedagogies developed for the enquiry. Chapter 2 addresses the study's methodology and research design, and some key features of education policy in England. Chapter 3 looks at the classrooms of the participating teachers as a context for their general teacher agency. In Chapter 4, I focus on how the teachers react on the classroom level to their pupils' multilingualism and how schools respond on the institutional level. Chapter 5 zooms in on the conditions of mono- and multilingualism in the classrooms: its first part addresses how the dominance of monolingualism takes shape, and its second part presents insights from the participatory activities with the children, exploring their 'superdiverse' voices. The last part of this chapter is a stopover, where I discuss the conceptual implications of these findings for multilingual pedagogies in the primary school. Chapter 6 consists of three parts: it addresses teacher agency in relation to the workplace school, then turns to educators' professional subjectivities and finally explores how teachers thematise facets of multilingualism in school. In Chapter 7, I present findings relevant for possibilities of multilingual pedagogies as seen from the perspective of the teachers. The chapter's second part draws on the participatory activities with the children, exploring how pupils' and teachers' experiences can come together for further developments. Chapter 8 provides an overview of features identified throughout the book as constituting, hindering and potentially facilitating teacher agency in multilingual pedagogies. It addresses how such agency can emerge in every primary school classroom, and the implications for developments in teacher professionalisation.

1 Multilingual Pedagogies and Teacher Agency – Mapping Out the Frameworks

This chapter describes the frameworks used to explore teacher agency in multilingual pedagogies within five classrooms in three urban primary schools in London and the East of England. The first part addresses the multilayered field of multilingual pedagogies. The second section outlines two (teacher) agency models – the subject-centred sociocultural framework of professional agency (Eteläpelto et al., 2013) and the ecological approach to teacher agency (Priestley et al., 2015) – on which this study was building, when developing a framework of four interconnected elements that can contribute to the achievement of teacher agency in multilingual pedagogies. This framework, which guided data collection and their analysis, is described in the third part of the chapter.

1.1 Mapping Out Multilingual Pedagogies

'[O]ne of the difficulties in speaking about multilingual pedagogies is that it always has to be done in the plural' (García & Flores, 2012: 232), and, in addition, teachers need an environment and a pedagogical context that allows them to speak about and practice them.

213	TQ:	What do you think are the moments or the situations or the parts of
214		lessons or the lessons where you acknowledge their multilingualism, that they
215		are speakers of more than one language?
216	Ellie:	. Hm
217	TQ:	are there any, or…?
218	Ellie:	Not particularly. … I don't think we do encourage it that much in lessons.
219		I can't say we do…

(Interview Ellie, 24 March 2017)

This interview passage from a Year 4 teacher, including my cautious move from 'moments' and 'situations' through 'parts of lessons' to 'lessons' when phrasing the question, points to the challenges involved when exploring what has been described in the introduction as two emergent phenomena: multilingual pedagogies and teacher agency. Where could multilingual pedagogies start in Ellie's classroom, and where would an exploration of teacher agency begin? Moreover, what might be considered as *context* for Ellie's teacher agency in multilingual pedagogies regarding both the conceptualisation of such agency and the very classroom, where she teaches? That is, where the teacher works every day with a group of 30 children, who are recorded in the school's statistical system with 10 languages besides English.

The notion of multilingual pedagogies has been established over the last decade in Northern and Southern contexts of schooling as an umbrella term that increasingly questions monolingual ideologies and practices (Mary & Hélot, 2022: 100), which are the legacy of nation building in the 18th and 19th centuries in Northern contexts and those nations' colonial rule in Southern contexts. Thus, debates in education and applied linguistics around inclusive and more dynamic multilingual pedagogies are a global concern but need to refer to specific political and language ideological contexts, and therefore to various experiences of multilingualism. In European educational systems, this means addressing the widely persisting myth 'that a nation state is monolingual not by its creation, but "by mere nature", and that individual monolingualism in the national language is the "natural" result of being born and growing up in the respective state' (Gogolin, 2021: 298).

Multilingual pedagogies are pedagogical approaches that *acknowledge, include, use, engage* and *promote* students' plurilingual repertoires. This description draws on three sources: García and Flores (2012: 242) suggest that to build on pupils' linguistic and cultural strengths and to develop multilingual awareness and tolerance, 'educators plan carefully the ways in which all the students' home languages and their language practices are acknowledged, included and used in the classroom'. A similar distinction between *acknowledgement* and *use* in instruction, seen as located on a continuum, features in the conceptual model developed for schools in the bilingual region of Fryslân/Netherlands (Duarte & Günther-van der Meij, 2018: 29). Cummins (2021a: xxxvii) also describes various approaches where instruction *acknowledges, engages* and *promotes* the multilingual repertoire of students. The explicit acknowledgement of *pedagogies* draws attention to the important interplay between teaching/learning practices and associated (socio-)linguistic and pedagogical reasonings and values. Pedagogy 'is what one needs to know, and the skills one needs to command, in order to make and justify the many different kinds of decision of which teaching is constituted' (Alexander, 2008: 47).

Building on this, multilingual pedagogies can be described as *what one needs to know about multilingualism, multilingual learning and learners, along with the skills one needs to command to make and justify the many different kinds of decisions by which teaching is constituted when it acknowledges, includes, uses, engages and promotes languages other than the main language of instruction.*

The differentiation between four types of socioeducational contexts for multilingual pedagogies – foreign language teaching, second language teaching, bilingual/monoglossic instruction and plurilingual/heteroglossic instruction (García & Flores, 2012: 233) – helps trace the debate and the ongoing paradigmatic shift in multilingual pedagogies. García and Flores identify ideological assumptions and the underlying language uses and orientations on which these teaching contexts are based. They view long-established foreign language instruction as anchored in the monoglossic paradigm, which assumes that the acquisition of a new language is linear and sequential. Second-language teaching traditionally relied on similar suppositions, namely the expectation that second-language speakers would behave like first-language speakers. This perspective leads to the dominant approach of subtractive bilingualism and considerable neglect of pupils' first languages in second-language pedagogy. In various versions of bilingual programmes, a primarily monoglossic approach has also been adopted. As García and Flores (2012: 234–239) argue, although such programmes use two languages for instruction aiming to equalise power disparities between minoritised and majority languages, they traditionally operate with a monoglossic understanding of languages and language arrangements, maintaining separation of the languages. To further advance, plurilingual instruction requires a shift to a dynamic and heteroglossic orientation. Such approaches encourage students to draw on their various linguistic skills and complex, fluid practices they use in out-of-lesson contexts, challenging the concept of autonomous languages. They are intentionally designed and carefully planned by their teachers.

Such a paradigmatic shift – the 'multilingual turn' (Conteh & Meier, 2014; May, 2014), as widely described in applied linguistics and sociolinguistics – replaces the monoglossic with a heteroglossic language orientation, which conceptualises languages as social practices (Heller, 2007). Put forward as a general term in two edited volumes about language education (Conteh & Meier, 2014) and second language acquisition (SLA), teaching English to speakers of other languages (TESOL) and bilingual education (May, 2014), the 'multilingual turn' was meant to mark the momentum gained once the monolingual lens is replaced by a multilingual lens in theoretical perspectives of the various sub-disciplines and their practices. Cummins (2017: 105) traces the evolution of the multilingual turn – in the broad sense of researching cross-language transfer and its facilitation in education.

This evolution spans from the common underlying proficiency hypothesis (Cummins, 1979) through the critique of the monolingual bias, which views bilinguals as two monolinguals in one person (Grosjean, 1989), to the concept of 'multicompetence' (Cook, 1995). It further extends to dynamic system concepts of multilingualism (e.g. Herdina & Jessner, 2002) and culminates in the conceptualisations of dynamic bilingualism and translanguaging (e.g. García & Kleyn, 2016a).

The concept of heteroglossia accentuates the social dimension of linguistic signs and their sociohistorical associations, approaching multilingualism as participation in a historical flow of relations, struggles and meanings, contrary to a view of linguistic systems as discrete and ahistorical. The perspective of heteroglossia incorporates intra-language varieties like dialects or professional registers (Bailey, 2012: 499–500). Tensions are generally perceived as inherent in language, and multilingualism is considered part of this complex normality: '[f]rom the perspective of heteroglossia, multilingual speech is simply one way of negotiating social and communicative worlds' (Bailey, 2012: 504). In a sense, primary school pedagogy that starts to incorporate multilingual pedagogies joins and connects to the flow of language experiences that children have as plurilingual speakers in their everyday lives.

The paradigmatic shift in multilingual pedagogies has been prominently, but not exclusively, propelled and pedagogically shaped by the translanguaging approach (and debates about it), which explicitly thematises and embraces language practices that form part of many societies. As Jason Anderson reminds us, for example, 'in India, as in so many complex multilingual countries around the world, translanguaging is as old as pedagogy, as old as communication, and as old as humanity' (2024: 80). In the US context, translanguaging has been defined,

> as a process by which students and teachers engage in complex discursive practices that include *all* the language practices of students in order to develop new language practices and sustain old ones, communicate [and] appropriate knowledge, and give voice to new sociopolitical realities by interrogating linguistic inequality. (García & Kano, 2014: 261, emphasis in original)

This description encapsulates the crucial and explicit combination of pedagogical and sociolinguistic perspectives in translanguaging theory and pedagogy, rendering it significant for exploring teacher agency in multilingual pedagogies. In various educational contexts and often in close cooperation between researchers and educators, translanguaging has proved an effective practice in settings where the language of instruction differs from the languages of the students (Li & Lin, 2019: 211). These settings include US *bilingual programmes* or *mainly bilingual settings* (e.g. García & Kleyn, 2016a), *complementary schools* in England (Creese & Blackledge, 2010), *preschool settings* (e.g. Kirsch,

2021), *primary schools* in officially bi-/multilingual regions or countries (e.g. Duarte & Günther-van der Meij, 2018; Little & Kirwan, 2019; Makalela, 2019), officially monolingual contexts (e.g. Carbonara & Scibetta, 2022) and in *secondary classrooms* in officially bi-/multilingual regions (e.g. Probyn, 2019) or officially monolingual countries (e.g. Duarte, 2019). However, the concept requires further clarification in relation to other educational settings (Leung & Valdés, 2019: 365–366), and it needs to be linked to the logic of their respective context – that is, in the case of the present enquiry into teacher agency, to the working of the primary school under linguistically very diverse conditions.

García and Li (2014: 120–121) build on the definition quoted above when delineating three sets of goals and possible strategies. The first set relates to the *communication and appropriation of knowledge* (e.g. multilingual listening, reading multilingual texts and project learning). The second set focuses on the *development of new language practices* and the *sustainment of existing ones*, including metalinguistic awareness (e.g. via multilingual vocabulary enquiry and translating). The third set of goals seeks 'identity investment and positionality; that is, to engage learners' and '[t]o interrogate linguistic inequality and disrupt linguistic hierarchies and social structures' (García & Li, 2014: 121). All the strategies mentioned here are oriented towards 'giving voice and shaping new sociopolitical realities by interrogating linguistic inequality' (García & Li, 2014: 121). Finally, they suggest using translanguaging strategies in mainstream and bilingual education.

1.1.1 Anchor points from the translanguaging framework for studying teacher agency

For the enquiry into teacher agency in multilingual pedagogies, three anchor points from the translanguaging framework proved particularly helpful during the data analysis precisely because the framework operates on the level of both theory and pedagogical practices (García & Kleyn, 2016a):

(1) the *thematisation* of dominance and power relations;
(2) the *strategical* use of translanguaging;
(3) the inclusion of the position of the *bi/plurilingual speaker* and their voice.

These three anchor points are characteristic of the wider paradigmatic shift outlined above. They align with language awareness pedagogy (Hélot *et al.*, 2018a), the multilingual turn in education (e.g. Meier, 2017) and speaker-centred approaches in multilingualism research (Busch, 2017b; chapters in Purkarthofer & Flubacher, 2022). By drawing on these points, we can not only enquire about what is happening in a given classroom situation or an interview passage but also consider what might be required to support the teacher's agency in that respective context. The three points are interrelated, as the following episode from Ellie's Year 4 classroom shows.

> *'Miss said, she needs to write in English'*
> The children are asked, in a cross-curricular topic lesson, to choose from three different locations a place to build a Roman village. They must write down a rationale, considering factors such as whether the place is appropriate for agriculture or near a river. The lesson is taught by a supply teacher, and Adriana, Bianca and Norman work in a group of three. Adriana was new to English when joining the class approximately five months before this episode, having attended primary school in Romania beforehand. Bianca has Romanian in her linguistic repertoire and is one of the most confident and articulate pupils in the class.
>
> | 140 | | Adriana talks with Bianca in Romanian. After a while [...] |
> |---|---|---|
> | 142 | TQ: | What are you talking about? |
> | 143 | Bianca: | She wants to know what to write. |
> | 144 | | I get a small whiteboard, 'Maybe you could write in Romanian?' |
> | 145 | B.: | She is not allowed. |
> | 146 | TQ: | What is she not allowed? |
> | 147 | B.: | Miss said, she needs to write in English. |
> | 148 | | Children continue to work together on the task. Bianca writes. |
>
> (Fieldnotes Y4, Castle Primary, 24 January 2017)

The classroom's monolingual norm appears to hinder more active participation in the group's learning on Adriana's part, and it was this observation that triggered my question about the use of Romanian for writing (Line 144). Bianca's response, 'She is not allowed' (Line 145) and 'Miss said, she needs to write in English' (Line 147), can be seen as a declaration of the norm. As such, the episode illustrates how the norm affects not only children who have arrived recently in the English-speaking classroom but also other plurilingual pupils, albeit differently. The monolingual norm has major consequences for Adriana's learning because she does not have the opportunity to participate more actively in the task at hand. However, there is also

> an implication for Bianca, who, by repeating the teacher's instruction that her peer 'needs to write in English' (Line 147), presents herself as someone who cares about or at least acknowledges the teacher's rule. Stating the rule directed at Adriana, Bianca is simultaneously – and inevitably – being subjected to it, taking up the position available to herself in relation to 'English is the only official language for learning'. Her subject position – as a child who uses her Romanian sometimes, as she does in this episode (Line 140) and other more private spaces in school, but does not depend on it for learning – can be described as the position of 'the bilingual child who is a monolingual pupil'; a position that corresponds to the norm 'English is the only official language for learning'.

In this episode, the three anchor points are conspicuous by their absence: (1) wider societal and linguistic power relations affect the classroom. Yet, they are *not* thematised but rather naturalised in formulating a rule that allows children to communicate in another language than English but prohibits using Romanian for the more visible and 'official' purpose of writing. (2) There is *no* strategy in place that would enable Adriana or Bianca to leverage their Romanian for learning. (3) Thus, the children are *not* included as bi-/plurilingual speakers, with various consequences for their learning. Bianca is taught that Romanian is not a legitimate and useful part of learning, just as – having been previously the only Romanian-speaking child in the class – she could have the opportunity to expand her knowledge of Romanian, e.g. into the realm of some academic language through engaging with someone who was schooled in Romanian before. At the same time, the monolingual norm makes it difficult for Adriana to envision for herself the position of a successful learner. In her case, the monolingual norm prevents her from taking advantage of the fortuitous fact that there is a successful learner in her class who can speak Romanian. While it might not be hard to name these missed opportunities and to envision steps supporting the teacher's agency to bridge the gaps in her pedagogical approaches in this episode, the three anchor points need to be linked more systematically to the logic and pedagogy of the specific educational setting – in this case, the linguistically very diverse primary school. I will turn to this task now.

(1) It is relevant for the primary school and its pedagogy to thematise the relationship between school and society's linguistic power relations. This allows for an explicit consideration of how dominance is realised in the institution and how discourses on language use and monolingual practices become naturalised. The school is, historically, in a dialectical relation with the labour market, the site where the recognition of legitimate language is imposed or reproduced (Bourdieu, 1991: Ch. 1). However, the association of 'one language' with a given, supposedly

monolingual nation-state 'has consequences for the hierarchisation of languages in society – accepting monolingualism as the rule implies that multilingual forms of practice, particularly those that are migration-induced, acquire the status of deviant or "illegitimate" practices' (Duarte & Gogolin, 2013: 6). As Hélot *et al.* assert:

> [W]hat is at stake in multilingual classrooms where LA [language awareness] activities are implemented with minoritized language speakers is the issue of power: a process of empowerment happens when students see their languages becoming legitimate at school, when they are free to use them to acquire school knowledge and when they can showcase their plurilingual competence. (2018b: 9–10)

For the linguistically very diverse primary school, the question arises: What kind of pedagogical practices can be envisioned if multilingualism and multilingual forms of practice are legitimised and considered as 'the rule'? Following the assertion that translanguaging pedagogy is 'an action to transform classroom discourses, including both the discourses by the participants of the classroom activities and the discourses about the classroom' (Li & Lin, 2019: 211), it is important to identify the specific task, responsibility and contribution of the primary school during a phase of schooling that lays the foundations for learning itself and explores themes of individual and societal significance.

To understand teacher agency, it is relevant to consider how social and linguistic power relations operate at the macro, meso and micro levels within the institution of school, which constitutes the context for such agency. Perhaps the best-known conceptualisation of this constellation is Jim Cummins's 'intervention framework for collaborative empowerment', originally developed in the context of bilingual learners' educational achievement (Cummins, 2000, 2021a; Cummins *et al.*, 2011a). It serves as a very fruitful point of departure for examining teacher agency, as it conceptualises the teacher's position neither as independent from societal power relations between linguistically diverse groups and the resulting consequences for the structures of schooling nor as solely defined by them:

> Educational structures, together with educator role definitions, determine the patterns of interactions between educators, students, and communities. These interactions form an interpersonal space within which the acquisition of knowledge and formation of identity are negotiated. (Cummins *et al.*, 2011a: 25)

While teacher agency is only very briefly mentioned to highlight the fact that educators have opportunities to make choices in their teaching (Cummins *et al.*, 2011b: 156), the intervention framework is important for research on teacher agency in multilingual pedagogies. It explicitly draws attention to the teacher's role within the context of *school and multilingualism*, pointing to a location of agency that is worthwhile to explore in its own right. Without explicitly stating such a reference, Cummins uses the notion of 'power' in a Foucauldian sense, that is, both repressive and productive (e.g. Foucault, 1971) and, therefore, as a force that generates identities and subjectivities. Framing the overall constellation for multilingual students and their teachers in this way can provide a sustainable background against which issues around teacher agency, multilingualism and pedagogy in the institution of school can be examined.

The following episode sheds light on the relevance of the next two anchor points:

> '*Reading in French*'
>
> In the participatory activities, the children were asked to use the language portrait template as a mind map, writing down what they would like to do or think they could do with their languages in school. When talking about their ideas, Maimouna, a girl in a Year 3 class, did not respond initially but had written 'fairy tales' and 'book', among other suggestions (Figure 1.1).
>
>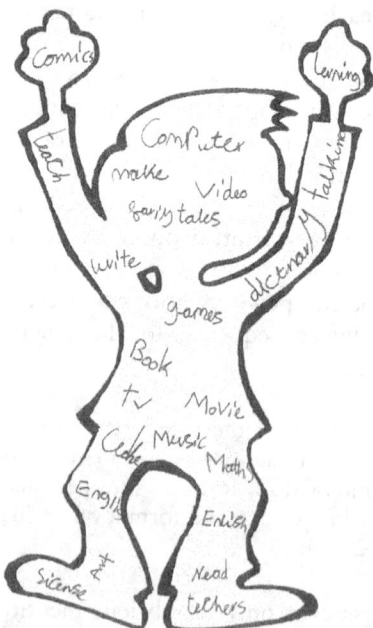
>
> **Figure 1.1** Maimouna's mind map
> Source: Österreichisches Sprachen-Kompetenz-Zentrum (ed.) (2010). Reprinted with permission.

74	TQ:	What would you like to do?
75	Maimouna:	Reading in French.
76	TQ:	Do you read in French at home?
77	M.:	Yes.
78	TQ:	[…] Which kind of stories do you read in French?
79	M.:	Fairy tales.
80	TQ:	Fairy tales. Did you bring them once to school?
81	M.:	No.

(Activities 2, Bird Primary Y3/1-2, 29 January 2017)

According to her teacher, Maimouna has been a very quiet child throughout her primary school years so far. She speaks French at home and said that she is 'not sure' whether the French teacher is aware of this – an uncertainty shared by her classmate Hamza regarding his French. Maimouna typically participates very timidly in classroom talk, and her hesitation to present her ideas here appears to mirror this situation. In *Reading in French* (Line 75), she expresses a wish that can be understood either as the desire to showcase her French reading skills in school or simply to do what she does at home, namely, read in a language other than English.

(2) 'Whether translanguaging as pedagogy is used as an active teaching practice, or as a student learning process, it is always used *strategically* and is never random' (García, 2014: 4, emphasis in original). Here, García describes one of the tenets of translanguaging pedagogy, underscoring the goal-oriented use of languages in school. The concept of translanguaging originally emerged from classrooms in which the presence of two languages was legitimate – or at least negotiable – such as Welsh schools (Lewis *et al.*, 2012a, 2012b), complementary schools (Creese & Blackledge, 2010) and chiefly bilingual settings and classes for newly arrived pupils in the US (García & Kleyn, 2016a). However, in primary schools like those involved in this study, where children might speak 40 or so languages between them, bilingual education is not realistically feasible (Hélot *et al.*, 2018b: 9; Sneddon, 2014: 122). Therefore, it is worth considering whether some strategies specified by García and Li (2014: 10, 120–121) can also be understood in such classrooms as working towards broader goals like learner engagement and addressing linguistic inequality and hierarchies. From this angle, the strategic use of translanguaging implies an active, planned teaching approach on the part of educators. For instance, Maimouna and the other children taking part in the activities did not recall bringing their

non-English books or other reading resources to school. Thus, in a linguistically very diverse primary school, strategic use might also involve educators taking responsibility and planning pedagogically for activities that *strategically* do not accept monolingualism as the rule and address hierarchisations in the sense formulated above by Duarte and Gogolin (2013) and Hélot *et al.* (2018b).

(3) A third conceptual anchor point from the translanguaging framework relevant to the primary school and the exploration of teacher agency in multilingual pedagogies is the inclusion of the perspective of the bilingual or plurilingual speaker and their voice. The translanguaging stance 'takes *the point of view of the bilingual speaker himself or herself* for whom the concept of two linguistic systems does not apply, for he or she has one complex and dynamic linguistic system [...]' (García & Kleyn, 2016b: 12, emphasis in original). The concept of translanguaging has developed into an extensive field, allowing – separately or simultaneously – its application as a theoretical framework, a language political position, a lens for analysis or a pedagogical stance (Vallejo & Dooly, 2020: 6). Some claims within the field have been critiqued. While there is generally broad agreement regarding its practical implications for learning and teaching (Cummins, 2021b: 29), the controversy about the proposed unitary view of bilinguals' linguistic system, as contended in the quotation above, is ongoing (e.g. Cummins, 2021b; Li, 2018; chapters in MacSwan, 2022; Otheguy *et al.*, 2019). Furthermore, attention is drawn to the imperative to consider the respective linguistic power relations of different contexts when working with the translanguaging concept. For example, this applies to schools involving regional minority languages (Cenoz & Gorter, 2017) or Indigenous language education (May, 2022a: 347–348). It is highlighted that in countries in Africa, the realities of code switching in classrooms and the constellations and epistemologies of southern multilingualism need to be considered to pursue the overall goal of social justice under conditions of postcoloniality (Heugh, 2021).

In the context of European multilingual mainstream classrooms, however, 'there is no doubt that the concept offers an enormous contribution to redefining language pedagogy that "draws attention to the speakers' agentive behaviour and creative practices" (Kirsch, [2021: 16])' (Duarte & Kirsch, 2021: 5). On the whole, the perspective offered by the concept of translanguaging on the plurilingual speaker aligns with the status that the first-person perspective acquires in biographical and speaker-centred research on multilingualism. As Busch (2017b: 341) highlights when using the notion of 'the lived experience of language', the first-person perspective on language focuses on how someone lives language as a subjective experience, interdependent with how they become constituted as speaking subjects through language (second-person perspective) and how they interact by means of the language (third-person perspective).

Against this background, Maimouna's experience is relevant for the broader pedagogical framing of multilingual pedagogies within the primary school. She is a learner for whom it is important to develop her confidence and, literally, her audibility – to find her voice in the classroom. How a child finds their voice in the classroom is both a genuine general pedagogical question and a specific concern for multilingual pedagogies. Dell Hymes conjoins 'two kinds of freedom in the notion of *voice*: freedom to have one's voice heard, freedom to develop a voice worth hearing' (Hymes, 1996: 64, emphasis in original). Pedagogically, the perspective of *voices* and *voices being heard* also helps to understand the status quo of multilingualism in classrooms, drawing attention to the processes that enable every pupil to find their voice for classroom interactions and learning to be successful. It allows for the exploration of the ways in which pupils negotiate the audibility of their plurilingual voices and, by extension, the relevance that various elements of their linguistic repertoire can have for them in school.

'Voices being heard' does not only emerge regarding the use of different languages; it is a general aspect of a classroom's pedagogical practices that define who is in what situations considered a legitimate speaker and what constitutes legitimate language practice (Bourdieu, 1991). This applies irrespective of whether plurilingual speakers are involved or not. In fact, this concept interconnects various concerns in education more generally – for example, children's opportunities for decision making (Alexander, 2010: Ch. 10) or pedagogical traditions that emphasise dialogic teaching and the joint construction of knowledge (Alexander, 2017; Barnes, 1976; Mercer, 2019) – and research on and approaches to multilingual pedagogies (e.g. Macleroy, 2021; Miller, 1999, 2003; Norton, 2013). For the enquiry into teacher agency in multilingual pedagogies, the lens of 'voice' also encompasses the voice of the teacher and the relationship and power differential between their voice and the pupils' voices.

For each of the three children featured in the two episodes presented so far, aspects of voice, audibility and confidence as learners come together in different ways. However, their experiences point to a crucial question for the broader pedagogical framing of multilingual pedagogies: How is a child's 'lived experience of language' (Busch, 2017b) shaped in school? To develop such pedagogies in the linguistically very diverse classroom, the perspective of 'language-as-a-resource' – originally introduced as an orientation for language policy to overcome the impasse between the language-as-problem and language-as-right dichotomy (Ruiz, 1984/2017: 24) – is vital. Those pedagogical approaches must create affordances that enable plurilingual children to *experience* language as a resource for 'doing something' and learning *in school*. The emphasis here is on *in school*, as children already know from their daily lives that using their entire linguistic repertoires allows them to constantly enlarge the scope of the world within which they act and interact with.

1.1.2 The school as a place for multilingual pedagogies

The three anchor points from the translanguaging framework and the paradigmatic shift in multilingual pedagogies more generally point to connected sociolinguistic and pedagogical concerns. The importance of the teachers' agency involved in this encounter is often emphasised: educators' translanguaging stance is understood as driving pedagogical responses that see the language repertoires of bilingual children as resources, thereby overcoming deficit perspectives (García *et al.*, 2017). Teacher agency is described as an important factor in advancing multilingual approaches in European mainstream schools (Kirsch *et al.*, 2021), and as taking centre stage in the processes of transformation in the schooling of plurilingual learners (Cummins, 2021a). Thus, 'teacher agency' is frequently emphasised in intervention studies and school development programmes that entail the very prerequisite still missing elsewhere in mainstream settings: the legitimisation of multilingual pedagogies. For the exploration of the classroom and teacher agency under such circumstances, a conceptual compass that highlights the following interrelated aspects of *the school as a place for multilingual pedagogies* proved helpful:

(1) the school as a place of language experience;
(2) the school as a place where linguistic repertoires and language ideologies come in contact;
(3) the school as a place where the actors negotiate the meanings of linguistic repertoires and language ideologies (Figure 1.2).

While these aspects are relevant to every school, they are particularly important for schools where multilingual pedagogies have not yet been legitimised. Emerging from the study of five classrooms where multilingual activities were not observable in the official teaching/learning processes

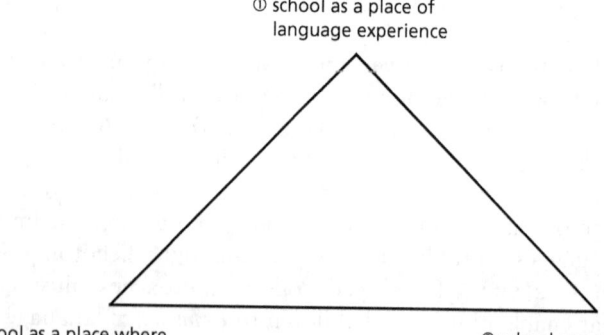

Figure 1.2 Three aspects of the school as a place for multilingual pedagogies

(apart from modern foreign language lessons), the triangle provides a conceptual background that can structure and guide explorations of the current situation and insights into possible new pedagogical developments. In the two episodes, Adriana could not use any learning resources or her literacy skills in Romanian for language or content learning. Maimouna had never showcased her French reading skills in school. Pedagogies that acknowledge, include, use, engage and promote children's plurilingual repertoires, and teachers who want to become agentic in these pedagogies need to connect to the respective status quo, and when educators implement elements of multilingual approaches, the conditions at each of the triangle's vertices will be rearranged.

(1) *School as a place of language experience* relates to the question formulated in the last section as highly important for the wider pedagogical framing of multilingual pedagogies: How is a child's 'lived experience of language' shaped in school? In the context of biographical and speaker-centred research on multilingualism, Busch (2012, 2017a, 2017b) introduced the concept of the 'lived experience of language' and its crucial role in mediating between discourses about language and a speaker's linguistic repertoire (Busch, 2017a: 53). Building on the concept of the 'repertoire' as including all the accepted ways of articulating messages (Gumperz, 1964), attention is drawn to the fact that a speaker's linguistic choices are not simply determined by interactions in specific situations and by grammatical and social rules, but also by historical-political and biographical dimensions. Thus, the meanings that someone ascribes to linguistic practices and languages are linked to their life trajectories and experiences, especially to how linguistic resources are experienced within discursive constructions of national, ethnic and social affiliation or non-affiliation (Busch, 2012: 520). Moreover, '[t]he concept of lived experience of language [...] stands for affective and interpersonal relations that render languages and language use meaningful across the lifespan' (Purkarthofer, 2022: 27).

Against this background, *school as a place of language experience* was initially associated with pupils. However, as indicated in the teacher interviews, the school also needs to be understood as a place of and for the language experience of educators – as evident in this extract from Mike, the Year 5 teacher already quoted at the start of the introduction.

'I never got to the point where I could enthusiastically commit to another language'
When he is asked about instances when he would acknowledge the children's multilingualism, Mike replies:

153   [...] I never got to the point where I could
154   enthusiastically commit to another language, I don't know, I wished I would

155	have would have. Yeah, so I mention that the whole time to the children, the
156	fact that out of my two regrets the language thing is my most pertinent
157	regret I have. [...] I hope they, they take it on board.
158	I think if the teacher speaks candidly like that and almost like in a personal way
159	I think the children do take that on board and they do notice that.
160	So hopefully that raises the profile of learning another language in the school –
161	which yeah they all, they all have their languages anyway. So I think they do
162	get some element of esteem, self-esteem from the fact that I'm standing there
163	as an adult saying *[laughs]* 'I wish, I wish I could...' [...]

(Interview, 20 March 2017)

Mike describes that he had learnt some French but 'never got to the point...' (Lines 153–154) of experiencing this as successful. He then explains how he expresses his regrets and tells children about his language experience 'candidly like that and almost like in a personal way' (Line 158). In line 160, the teacher links multilingualism to foreign language learning: 'So hopefully that raises the profile of learning another language in the school'. This is followed – almost as an afterthought – by a mention of the children's multilingualism: 'they all have their languages anyway' (Line 161). Finally, Mike connects this with children's self-esteem due to being multilingual while their teacher points out his monolingualism.

This extract exemplifies how the teachers mentioned – importantly, without any prompting – their own experiences with languages when talking about their plurilingual pupils. This will be discussed in Chapter 6.

(2) *School as a place where linguistic repertoires and language ideologies come into contact* brings together the perspectives of the speaking subject – the student and their entire linguistic repertoire, as well as teachers and other actors in school – and the school as a space constituted and framed by language ideologies and discourses around multilingualism that exist in wider society. As Busch argues (2017a),

> Language ideologies or discourses on language and language use, on linguistic normativity, appropriateness, hierarchies, taboos, etc., translate

into attitudes, into the ways in which we perceive ourselves and others as speakers, and into the ways in which these perceptions are enacted in language practices that confirm, subvert or transform categorisations, norms and rules. (2017a: 52)

The school is a powerful production site for these ideologies and discourses, where they are not simply *imposed* but *(re-)produced* (e.g. Apple, 1982), and where a microculture conveys pedagogical messages beyond those of the single classroom (Alexander, 2008: 48). In other words, schools are places where meanings around languages, language hierarchies and multilingualism are – implicitly or explicitly – mediated, learnt and naturalised. From the cluster concept of language ideologies (Kroskrity, 2010), the following dimensions are particularly relevant for the encounter between pupils' linguistic repertoires and the school's language ideologies regarding multilingualism: language ideologies are not neutral but formed in the interests of a specific social/cultural group (Kroskrity, 2010: 195). They are multiple and contested due to the ways in which various axes of difference and inequality intersect: language ideologies 'are thus grounded in social experience which is never uniformly distributed throughout polities of any scale' (Kroskrity, 2010: 197). Moreover, within the 'natio-racial-culturally coded orders of belonging' (Mecheril, 2018) in Western societies characterised by phenomena of international migration, the tropes 'language' and 'multilingualism' feature in debates and contestations about the very character of the democratic polity. In fact, in political and media discourses, they become a proxy for 'immigration' or 'otherness', entangled with debates on 'the nation', multiculturalism, racism and social cohesion (Blackledge, 2004). An analysis of the UK's right-leaning press, for example, found a media narrative that problematises, and 'others' non-native speakers of English in ways that promote 'linguistic xenophobia' (Wright & Brookes, 2019: 79).

Another dimension of language ideologies that is relevant for the institution of school is the fact that members of society can show different degrees of awareness of such ideologies, varying between a high level of awareness, active disputation of ideologies and a 'practical consciousness with relatively unchallenged, highly naturalized, and definitively dominant ideologies' (Kroskrity, 2010: 198). Different sites where language ideologies are generated and commented upon contribute to those varying degrees of awareness, and the school was historically (and continues to be) at the forefront of these processes.

(3) *The school as a place where the actors negotiate the meanings of linguistic repertoires and language ideologies*: this aspect refers to a twofold understanding of 'meaning'. First, pupils and teachers may negotiate the significance that the children's repertoires can have in school. Second – as became evident in the participatory activities with the children reported in Chapter 5 – children and educators

(would need to) build on a diversity of meanings that 'speaking a language' has for the children in these linguistically very diverse classrooms. In contrast to the previous aspect, this foregrounds that language ideologies, as described before, are never completely dominant, and that examining frictions or negotiations can help explore the space between the current situation and future developments, which is crucial for teacher agency.

This conceptual compass for understanding the school as a place for multilingual pedagogies relates to an overall situation in England, where the dominance of monolingualism has been documented for the mainstream primary school (e.g. Bourne, 2001; Cunningham, 2019; Fashanu *et al.*, 2020). Kenner and Ruby (2012) and Welply (2017), for example, describe the monolingual norm as implicitly expected rather than explicitly stated, while others mention practices and policies that explicitly ban the use of non-English languages (e.g. Foley *et al.*, 2022; Gundarina & Simpson, 2022; Pearce, 2012). At the same time, research in complementary schools in England shows how pupils *negotiate* the meanings that speaking a certain language or being plurilingual has for them (e.g. Blackledge & Creese, 2010; Li, 2014; Lytra, 2011). Thus, educators need to be cautious not to make rash assumptions about their pupils' linguistic repertoires and avoid essentialisation when considering students' language practices and affiliations, or those of their families (e.g. Foley, 2022; Harris, 1997; Rampton, 2005).

Approaching the 'ordinary' classroom with such a compass – as a place where all children and educators experience languages, where these experiences are mediated, and where meanings attributed to different language practices are learnt and negotiated – can support the analysis of multilingual pedagogies in mainstream primary schools, i.e. in contexts where teachers cannot rely on the settings of bilingual programmes or schools in officially bilingual countries/regions. The compass helps examine how teachers' agency is embedded in classrooms and wider contexts, where teachers need to shape their own multilingual pedagogies.

1.2 Mapping Out Teacher Agency

The present research in the English primary school is based on two assumptions. First, multilingual pedagogies have not yet materialised into a well-established body of approaches recognised and legitimised by the curriculum or related education policy texts. Thus, considerable creativity and willingness are required from teachers in this pedagogical field. Second, the nexus between dominant language ideologies and the surrounding discourses on language use, immigration and the general education policy indicates the importance of addressing multilingualism in formal education institutions by considering society's power relations. How this nexus affects schools constitutes the structure(s) within and against which teacher agency in multilingual pedagogies may or may not develop.

Concepts of teacher agency are empowering and hopeful precisely because they focus on the position of the agentic educator between larger structures and the decisions they make in the daily workings of their classrooms. This is perhaps most prominently outlined in Cummins's (2000) intervention framework, in García *et al.*'s (2017) advocacy of the teachers' transformational role when taking a translanguaging stance, and in the assertion that 'there is typically space for policy negotiation in classroom practice, as it is ultimately educators – particularly classroom teachers – who are the final arbiters of language policy implementation' (Menken & García, 2010: 1). Overall, research on teacher agency always involves a projective, future-oriented perspective, either to transform a current situation or to feed back into teacher education. School education always works within complex sociopolitical constellations, in which various stakeholders can legitimately claim their 'stake' and where the challenge exists to strike a balance between them, namely students, parents, the state, employers and organisations from the public sphere (Priestley *et al.*, 2015: 4–5). Thus, the elaboration of teacher agency foregrounds 'that teachers are stakeholders as well [...], not least because they possess unique professional expertise and experience of the everyday realities of education' (Priestley *et al.*, 2015: 5).

The growing field of studies on teacher agency is characterised by the following prevalent themes (Toom *et al.*, 2015: 618–620):

- the relation between agency and professional identity as two aspects linked via ideals, goals, commitments and ethics;
- the key feature of the (pedagogical) action;
- the essentiality of context factors on the micro, meso and macro levels that influence professional agency, comprising explicit or implicit structures and professional discourses, among others.

Eteläpelto *et al.* (2015), for example, examined how novice teachers in Finland perceive their professional agency on the levels of classroom practices, school community and school organisation, drawing on a subject-centred sociocultural framework for professional agency (Eteläpelto *et al.*, 2013). Pantić (2015, 2017) has developed a model for the study of teacher agency for social justice with four components: (1) a sense of purpose (belief that a certain practice is worthwhile for realising a particular outcome, and belief about the role of teachers as agents for social justice); (2) competence (knowledge of ways to influence practically a desired goal); (3) scope of autonomy (power to make a difference to the respective structural environment and to collaborate with others); and (4) reflexivity (teachers' capacity to monitor and evaluate their own practices and institutional settings). Kayi-Aydar (2015, 2019a) explored the relationship between agency and the developing professional identities of language teachers. Her model combines the interrelatedness of individual and collective agency with professional identities and emotions and proposes a context structure at the micro level (classroom), meso level (school environment) and macro level (language policies and ideologies, political and educational discourses). Teachers' linguistic history and language learning experiences are explicitly included as an aspect of agency (Kayi-Aydar, 2019b).

In developing a framework for examining and conceptualising teacher agency in multilingual pedagogies, I drew substantially on the subject-centred sociocultural framework of professional agency (Eteläpelto et al., 2013) and the ecological approach to teacher agency (Priestley et al., 2015). These two are congruent regarding their overall understanding of agency: first, as emerging from the interplay between the professional subject and the social and institutional context, and second, as characterised by the individual's practice of making choices in their work.

However, the research presented in the following chapters diverges from both Eteläpelto et al.'s (2015) study on the agency of novice teachers and Priestley et al.'s (2015) study in the context of Scottish curriculum reform as my enquiry takes the classroom – through an ethnographic process – as a point of departure. In addition to the numerous aspects where the two models overlap, they provide different accentuations that proved instructive for exploring teacher agency in multilingual pedagogies. Thus, the subject-centred sociocultural framework allows for a more detailed conceptualisation of the classroom as a sociocultural context for teacher agency that also includes, more explicitly, the workplace. The overall importance of the workplace and its demands was evident throughout the enquiry, as exemplified in these passages from an interview with Hira, a Year 3 teacher:

'Sometimes I feel I would need to rip myself in half'		
49 50	TQ:	[…] I find it amazing for how many needs you actually – being one person – for how many needs you actually cater.
51	Hira:	Sometimes I feel
52		I would need to rip myself in half to be there – at the same time you have to
53		challenge the Gifted and Talented and in one way you have to support the
54		lowest and in another to support the EAL children who don't understand
55		anything. And in another way, you have to support the SEN children
558		It is difficult because the curriculum is so jam-packed […]
561		[…] if we ever have a bit of

562	spare time, we are doing something that they, you know, giving them some
563	free time sometimes if they have behaved well. But given the jam-packed
564	curriculum [...]
	(Interview, 27 June 2017)

Ultimately, the classroom is always both a sociocultural context for teaching and a workplace. The differentiation between them, along with their entanglements, is relevant to understanding teacher agency in the 'ordinary' classroom, especially regarding a pedagogical domain not acknowledged in the curriculum, like multilingual pedagogies.

The ecological approach to teacher agency, like various other studies (e.g. Fones, 2019; Kayi-Aydar, 2019b; Tao & Gao, 2021), differentiates between layers of context, providing an additional lens for identifying factors that support the achievement of agency in the classroom. While Priestley *et al.* (2015: 152–153) distinguish between macro, meso and micro levels, which they link to policy formation, its interpretation and its enactment, these levels were adapted for the present study. Societal conditions around mono- and multilingualism, as manifested in dominant language ideologies and resulting in a lack of policy formation, are seen as comprising the macro level. Notwithstanding this absence, it is helpful to conceptualise (following Priestley *et al.*, 2015: 157–158) a meso level that can provide guidance, which defines, resources and supports processes around multilingual pedagogies and increases teachers' potential to achieve agency in this domain. What has been described regarding curriculum innovation as 'additional guidance' can be understood for multilingual pedagogies as 'conceptual guidance' and resourcing. Such a function may be assigned to knowledgeable meso-level actors, such as educational organisations and institutions or actors at the school level. Finally, in this enquiry, the individual school and the classroom are seen as at the micro level, although it is not always possible to distinguish neatly between meso and micro levels (e.g. a knowledgeable meso actor might be part of an individual school). Figure 1.3 shows how the two models were combined for the subsequent development of the framework for (researching) teacher agency in multilingual pedagogies (see Section 1.3).

1.2.1 The subject-centred sociocultural perspective on professional agency

Eteläpelto *et al.* (2013) proposed a concept of professional agency within a subject-centred sociocultural framework after reviewing a wide

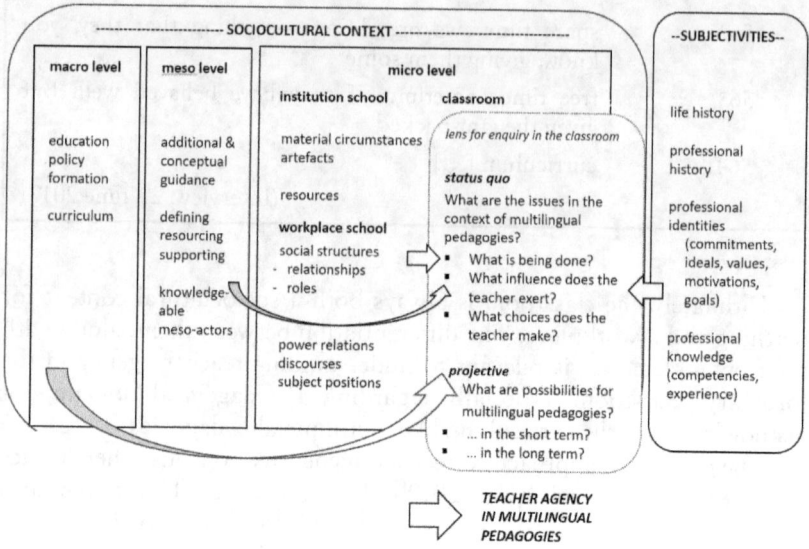

Figure 1.3 Merged models of teacher agency employed for the development of the framework for (researching) teacher agency in multilingual pedagogies

range of social science traditions, post-structural and sociocultural perspectives and life-course approaches. While a detailed description of these strands is not intended here, a few theoretical markers help trace how the subject-centred sociocultural perspective on professional agency arrives at those aspects that are central to the framework for (researching) teacher agency in multilingual pedagogies.

Within the classic sociological structure–agency debate, the power of the individual to bring something about (Giddens, 1984) is important as a prerequisite for professional agency. It facilitates consideration of how different manifestations of power are closely connected with agency: 'official power' relations – as established in workplace structures or managerial practices – but also 'unofficial power' displayed in workplace games and passive resistance are both features of professional agency in the workplace (Eteläpelto et al., 2013: 50). Such ambiguities appear in studies when teachers' actions are in agreement with policy changes, and also when their actions resist changing requirements (e.g. Buchanan, 2015; Lasky, 2005). Moreover, within sociology's concern about stratification, agency is, for Archer (2000: 261), always understood as collective, an emphasis that helps, in teacher agency research, to highlight aspects of collaboration in the school as an organisation (Pantić, 2017).

For a conceptualisation of professional agency at work and its aspects of professional learning and identity negotiations, it is crucial to include post-structural feminist perspectives that allow for discourses, subject positions and subjectivities. '[P]rofessional identities and subjectivities [...] are central for professional learning; this is especially the case in domains such as education, health care, and creative work, where employees need to act as whole human persons, containing emotions and ethical commitments' (Eteläpelto et al., 2013: 51). In particular, Eteläpelto et al. point to post-structural perspectives that offer an enhanced repertoire for working towards changing social practices through the inclusion of selfhood, reflexivity and experience. Drawing on gender studies and the status of experience as socially positioned, they contend that this:

> provides a way of placing a socially and culturally relational subject at the center of any elaboration of agency, without attributing to agency some kind of naïve personalist or 'substantialist illusion' – something that would reduce agency to nothing more than the representation of individual actors. (Eteläpelto et al., 2013: 54)

Agency, then, emerges from people's lived experience within their social relations and their capacity for action, including importantly self-reflection and self-evaluation. Thematising the individual's sense of self, and hence of identity, in this way allows Eteläpelto et al. to infer that agency needs to be considered from a subject-centred perspective, which conceptualises professional identity:

> as a work history-based constellation of teachers' perceptions of themselves as professional actors – perceptions that encompass the teacher's current professional ideals, goals, interests, and values (including their views on teaching and on the students' learning), their ethical standards and commitments, and their own future prospects. (Eteläpelto et al., 2015: 664)

Moving to the sociocultural component of their model, Eteläpelto and colleagues foreground approaches that focus on the workplace and workplace learning as social practices. Within a framework of 'relational interdependence', two sets of continuities are negotiated:

> Social practices such as workplaces, educational institutions, and community groupings provide opportunities directed toward advancing their goals and practices or interests within them [...] However, individuals' participation in social practice is also mediated by their intentions for continuity and development, albeit shaped by subjectivities about cultural and occupational identity. (Billet, 2006: 61–62)

This interplay and its degree of consonance or contestation constitute the parameters for reproducing specific social practices. Therefore, enquiries into professional agency need to consider the person's interests, identities and subjectivities alongside the aims and continuities of the practice. Agency encompasses the option of an active role in modifying the practice. Individuals exercise agency when they decide which problems to engage with and to what degree (Eteläpelto et al., 2013: 56–57).

Sociocultural understandings of the relationship between educators and the context of schools or communities underpin many studies on teacher agency (e.g. Fones, 2019; Lasky, 2005; Pantić, 2015, 2017), drawing in various ways on the key concept of mediated agency (Wertsch et al., 1993). For the present enquiry, it is crucial to understand how the classroom becomes the sociocultural context for teachers' general agency and, by extension, their agency in multilingual pedagogies. According to Wertsch et al. (1993), two aspects are fundamental for a sociocultural approach to agency. First, agency should not be understood solely as the property of an individual; rather, it should be seen as socially distributed or shared (Wertsch et al., 1993: 352). If the teacher's agency 'is highly relational and thus embedded in professional interactions between teachers, pupils and their parents as well as with other members of the school community' (Pyhältö et al., 2014: 307), then the classroom becomes the salient sphere where interactions between teachers and pupils occur. The second aspect follows from Vygotsky's (1981) central tenet that human action is mediated by tools, signs or other human beings.

> [T]he appropriate unit of analysis for understanding agency is an individual or individuals functioning *together with mediational means*. In this view the individual(s) involved certainly continues to bear the major responsibility for initiating and carrying out an action, but the possibilities for formulating certain problems, let alone the possibilities for following certain paths of action are shaped by the mediational means employed. (Wertsch et al., 1993: 342, emphasis added)

This perspective of agency as 'individual(s)-operating-with-mediational-means' – or 'mediated agency' (Wertsch et al., 1993: 342) – helps us to understand the relationship between the classroom and the teacher's general agency. It allows for a conceptualisation of the classroom not only as a space where teacher agency is practised but also as a means that mediates this agency, simultaneously situated within wider sociocultural contexts.

Here, I would like to briefly spell out in more detail how the classroom will be conceptualised as a mediational means for teacher agency (particularly in Chapter 3, where teachers' general agency is explored). Following the cultural-historical school and socioculturally oriented perspectives, a classroom consists of artefacts. Primary artefacts include items like pencils and small or interactive whiteboards, while secondary artefacts, which 'play a central role in preserving and transmitting modes of action and belief' (Cole, 1996: 121), may include, for example, educational concepts and teaching approaches. Additional mediators are individuals (Kozulin, 1998: 62–65) within the classroom, using their linguistic and other semiotic repertoires to make meaning and interact with teaching/learning processes. While all these elements of 'the classroom' can play a mediating role, two sides of these processes appear particularly relevant to teacher agency. First, the elements might mediate what the teacher perceives as 'the classroom', and how it is equipped materially and shaped conceptually as a place of pedagogical practice. In this sense, the classroom is a means that is both material and ideal. Second, its artefacts/elements mediate how the teacher understands teaching and the broader activity of 'running a classroom'. These mediated actions and activities of teaching and running a classroom can be understood, in turn, as principal points of reference for the teacher's general agency. In other words, the teacher who achieves or practises such agency is responding to routines and making choices based on a specific classroom context – even if this situated practice may also be influenced by previous or prospective classrooms. Furthermore, the wider contexts in which a classroom is located are shaped by a multitude of factors, including education policy, curriculum, pedagogy, or, say, the role of the headteacher and the staff situation in a school, or the report of the last school inspection. All these factors can play a role in mediating teacher agency – in fact, they were all mentioned by the teachers in the study.

Finally, the life-course dimension, a dimension which emphasises the need 'to include both the contextual *and* the temporal dimension in the analysis [...], an understanding of changes and differences in agentic orientations against the background of biography and lifecourse' (Biesta & Tedder, 2007: 138, emphasis in original), is added to the subject-centred sociocultural perspective on professional agency. This dimension goes beyond momentary activities, placing them in the context of a time continuum. The concept of life-course agency considers the identity commitments of the subject and how they influence decisions when exerting agency (Eteläpelto *et al.*, 2013: 58).

Eteläpelto *et al.* define 'professional agency as exercised when professional subjects and/or communities influence, make choices, and take stances on their work and professional identities' (2013: 61).

> [T]o investigate professional agency in working life contexts we need to understand how agency is practiced, and how it is resourced, constrained, and bounded by contextual factors, including power relations and discourses, and further by the material conditions and cultures of social interaction in work communities. (Eteläpelto *et al.*, 2013: 61)

I consider the following aspects of this framework as particularly important for the enquiry on teacher agency in multilingual pedagogies and have incorporated them into the framework utilised for research design and analysis (Figure 1.4). Agency is exercised for specific purposes within particular sociocultural and material circumstances, while also being constrained and resourced by those conditions. It is closely entangled with professional identities, while (work) experiences, knowledge and competencies function as developmental affordances and resources for agency. Agency is especially crucial for developing one's work and work communities, taking creative initiatives, engaging in professional learning and renegotiating identities in changing work practices (Eteläpelto et al., 2013: 62).

The intervention framework for collaborative empowerment (Cummins, 2000) can be usefully related to this perspective on professional agency. The description of teachers' roles (definitions) as influenced by educational structures and as influencing educators' interactions with students, which in turn reflect various orientations existing in schools towards a linguistically diverse society, indicates a space where teachers may or may not practise their agency. Thus, drawing on the agency framework proposed by Eteläpelto et al. (2013) allows for an exploration of teacher agency in relation to multilingual pedagogies, as facilitated and conditioned by the sociocultural circumstances of the school and by professional subjectivities. The school context includes material circumstances, artefacts, power relations, work cultures, discourses and subject positions. Professional subjectivities involve professional identities (such as commitments, ideals, motivations, interests, goals), professional knowledge and competencies as well as work history and experience (Eteläpelto et al., 2013: 61). Furthermore, it is relevant for the present enquiry that teachers can be positioned differently concerning the linguistically diverse society. Therefore, their professional agency must be understood as (potentially) influenced by subjectivities outside of the profession, i.e. their life history, educational experiences and positions in relation to society's lines of difference such as class, gender, ethnicity or others.

1.2.2 The ecological approach to teacher agency

The ecological approach to teacher agency understands agency as an emergent phenomenon that is relational, as teachers operate by means of the social and material environment of the school, and also temporal – it is anchored in previous experiences, oriented to a future and located in the contingencies of the here and now (Priestley et al., 2015). In addition to its differentiation between macro, meso and micro levels in relation to the curriculum and its explicit conceptualisation of teacher agency, the ecological approach involves other useful conceptual features for exploring teacher agency in multilingual pedagogies. These features include the temporal dimension, consideration of the pedagogical repertoire and an appreciation of small decisions or choices. I address these features sequentially.

The ecological approach to teacher agency has its roots in pragmatism. It draws substantially on Emirbayer and Mische's (1998) analytical differentiation between three dimensions of agency: (1) the iterational dimension, where actors selectively reactivate past patterns of thought or action and include them as routines, thus providing stability and sustaining identities and institutions over time; (2) the projective dimension, which includes 'the imaginative generation by actors of possible future trajectories of action, in which received structures of thought and action may be creatively reconfigured in relation to actors' hopes, fears, and desires for the future' (Emirbayer & Mische, 1998: 971); and (3) the practical evaluative dimension, which involves the person's capacity to make practical and normative judgements and choices between alternative potential trajectories of action, responding to emerging dilemmas, demands or ambiguities of current situations. Against this background, teacher agency is not merely a capacity possessed by an individual teacher. Instead, it is an achievement situated in the respective educational context resulting from the interplay within the triad of all three dimensions.

The iterational dimension consists of the life histories of educators and their professional histories (including teacher education and accumulated experiences in the profession). Elements contributing to teacher agency include personal capacity (skills and knowledge), beliefs (both professional and personal) and values (Priestley *et al.*, 2015: 31). While these elements are all rooted in previous experiences, the iterational dimension also involves teachers' ability to choose from various pedagogical repertoires. That is, educators' habits and routines sustain their identities, interactions and institutional settings over time. However, their overall professional habitus also includes choices and options to manoeuvre between, framing how educators might actively and flexibly react to difficulties and opportunities in their work (Priestley *et al.*, 2015: 130).

Within the projective dimension of teacher agency, Priestley *et al.* describe a variety of motivations and aspirations that can lead to agentic actions. These factors might, for example, relate to pupils' development and well-being, often with long-term perspectives, and might be firmly anchored in educators' values and beliefs. Other motivations, however, might be more instrumental, such as upholding the 'normal' workings of the classroom. Such manifestations of agency predominantly originate from educators' prior experiences (for example, a negative school inspection resulting in teachers who want to avoid any risks) or from beliefs and motivations (for example, about the character of a particular school subject or wanting to do what is best for the pupils). These factors can shape a teacher's aspirations and, thus, the projective dimension of their agency in the short or the long term (Priestley *et al.*, 2015: 32).

The practical evaluative dimension concerns the day-to-day workings of the classroom and school and how educators navigate these contexts for their actions. It is within this dimension that agency is achieved and shaped by the environments, making it particularly relevant to teacher agency. The term 'practical evaluative' draws attention to what is possible and feasible in the respective context (the practical) and the teacher's evaluation of the initial 'issues' and the potential courses of action (Priestley *et al.*, 2015: 33–34). The ecological approach distinguishes between cultural, structural and material aspects: cultural aspects relate to 'ways of speaking and thinking, of values, beliefs, and aspirations, and encompass both inner and outer dialogue' (Priestley *et al.*, 2015: 30). The notion of outer dialogue and the description that teacher education contributes only a small part to the formation of a teacher's professional experiences – alongside daily experiences, the dialogue with colleagues, and the school culture as other influences (Priestley *et al.*, 2015: 31) – parallel the subject-centred sociocultural concept, which understands ideals and values as part of a teacher's professional identity. Both approaches emphasise the mediated character of teachers' values and beliefs. In fact, beliefs and values, how they are articulated and their relation to the discourses provided by education policy or school cultures are inevitably contested terrains that can either enhance or hinder teacher agency (Priestley *et al.*, 2015: 83). The second category, structural aspects, pertain to social structures such as relationships and different roles within the school as a workplace, including aspects like power or trust that can influence the achievement of agency. Finally, material aspects refer to various resources and physical aspects of the environment (Priestley *et al.*, 2015: 30).

The ecological approach to teacher agency offers the following definition:

> Rather than saying that agency is about the *potential to take action* – which is part of the definition but not the whole – we would say that teachers achieve agency when they are able to choose between different options in any given situation and are able to judge which option is the most desirable in the light of the wider purposes of the practice in and through which they act. *Agency is restricted* if those options are limited. *Agency is not present* if there are no options for action or if the teacher simply follows routinized patterns of habitual behaviour with no consideration of alternatives. (Priestley *et al.*, 2015: 141, emphases added)

Two features of teacher agency are implicitly thematised here that have some relevance for the exploration of such agency in multilingual pedagogies. Teachers' capacity to act is enhanced if they have a wider repertoire of possibilities to draw from (Priestley *et al.*, 2015: 31). The importance of a pedagogical repertoire, or a repertoire of teaching/learning approaches, has been highlighted in English primary school pedagogy in general, and in relation to dialogic teaching in particular. Indeed, the interest in a pedagogical repertoire or repertoire-based teaching (Alexander *et al.*, 1992) emerged as a critique of stipulated methods and oversimplifications prevalent in educational debates and policies, which often framed education and pedagogy in terms of dichotomies such as 'teacher-centred/child-centred' or 'transmission/discovery' (Alexander, 2008: 72–91, 2018: 563–564).

The other aspect is relevant for an enquiry into teacher agency in relation to society's broader power relations. Emirbayer and Mische (1998: 1002–1003) provide two explanations for the variable character of the interplay between structure and agency, and it is useful to relate them to society's linguistic power relations. Actors can shift between their agentic orientations, i.e. they can reconstruct – through processes of dialogue and interaction – the internal configuration of the triad of iteration, projectivity and practical evaluation. In doing so, 'they may increase or decrease their capacity for invention, choice, and transformative impact in relation to the situational contexts within which they act' (Emirbayer & Mische, 1998: 1003). As for Cummins's framework, which conceptualises educational structures and teachers' role definitions as determinants of the interaction patterns between educators, students and communities, it could be suggested that shifts within a teacher's agentic orientations react, at the school level, to society's linguistic power relations. However, it is also possible not to react, and actors may feel creative and deliberative, even if they merely reproduce the given context. People always act simultaneously in various temporal-relational contexts, allowing for a high degree of personal agency, being future oriented and problem solvers in the workplace while unhesitatingly reproducing broader schemas and patterns that help maintain the status quo and societal contexts, even if those might be perceived as problematic from a broader perspective (Emirbayer & Mische, 1998: 1008–1009). These considerations are conceptually significant for teacher agency in multilingual pedagogies because they point to the relevance of exploring the small aspects and tensions around teachers' work in this domain. Such an orientation towards small aspects is particularly relevant in a pedagogical field that is not acknowledged and officially legitimised by the school curriculum, and in which the aforementioned shifts, which can enhance or reduce a teacher's capacity to transform, might therefore be all the more important.

1.3 The Framework for (Researching) Teacher Agency in Multilingual Pedagogies

To understand teacher agency in multilingual pedagogies, a framework to guide data collection and data analysis has been developed. This framework provides a conceptual basis for exploring what constitutes, hinders and facilitates such agency. It brings together considerations around multilingual pedagogies as mapped out previously and aspects

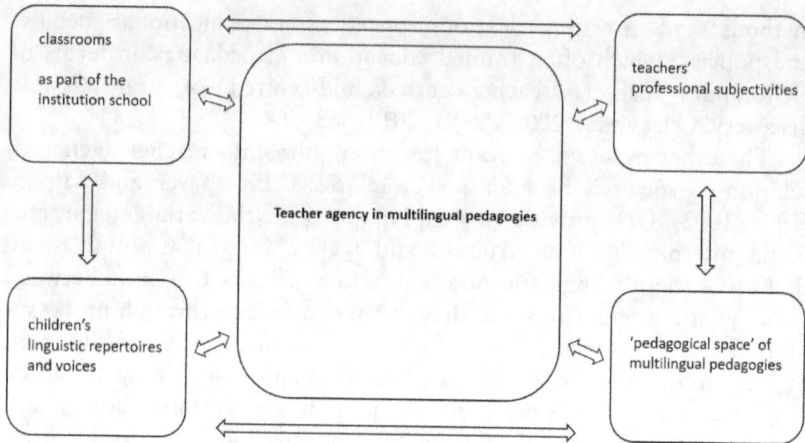

Figure 1.4 Interrelated elements that can contribute to teacher agency in multilingual pedagogies

identified in the two models of professional and teacher agency described above. The framework includes four elements that potentially contribute to teacher agency in multilingual pedagogies in the mainstream school (Figure 1.4):

(1) the classroom and the classroom as part of the institution of school;
(2) teachers' professional subjectivities;
(3) children's linguistic repertoires and voices;
(4) the 'pedagogical space' of multilingual pedagogies.

This framework facilitated the exploration of teacher agency and multilingual pedagogies as two simultaneously emerging phenomena under current conditions in the mainstream school (as described in the next chapters). It supports a nuanced understanding of how the four elements are interrelated and how they can contribute, as contextual factors, to the achievement of teacher agency in such pedagogies. Through the back-and-forth of an ethnographic enquiry, the framework provided pathways to identify features that are constitutive of teacher agency. As the analysis progresses, the blank space at the centre of the figure will be filled, while features hindering or (potentially) facilitating teacher agency will be thematised in the process.

- The classroom serves as the micro-level context for teacher agency – a place of teaching and other pedagogical actions, of everyday routines and interactions between the teacher and their pupils. It is the immediate sociocultural context where educators make decisions and where they practise, achieve and experience their general agency.

To achieve agency in a specific pedagogical domain – in this case, multilingual pedagogies – it is necessary to build on this general agency. Additionally, although not always explicitly conceptualised in debates about teacher agency, the classroom is always simultaneously a workplace context. In numerous ways, the classroom is also part of the school as an institution, including both the specific school and the broader educational system. Consequently, it is entangled with linguistic and other societal power relations.

- The teachers' professional subjectivities include their professional history (in particular teacher education), experiences and facets of professional identity (current commitments and motivations, goals and values, but also future-oriented perspectives) and professional knowledge (competencies and experiences). Biographical experiences regarding multilingualism or language learning also belong to this element. Teachers are positioned differently in relation to society's lines of difference, which might impact their experiences or reflexivity regarding teacher agency in multilingual pedagogies.
- Children's linguistic repertoires and voices form another element of the framework, acknowledging and highlighting the necessity to approach multilingual pedagogies in the superdiverse primary school from a speaker-centred perspective. Pedagogical approaches need to be responsive to the children's linguistic repertoires, and thus this element links to what has been described in Section 1.1 as the inclusion of the plurilingual speaker in approaches of translanguaging and multilingual pedagogies. It further connects to the considerations around the school as a place for multilingual pedagogies – as a place of children's lived language experiences, where their linguistic repertoires and the language ideologies of school and society come into contact, and where a pupil may or may not negotiate about the significance that this repertoire can have in school.
- The fourth element is the 'pedagogical space' of multilingual pedagogies: a reservoir of approaches that acknowledge, include, use, engage and promote children's plurilingual repertoires. It also involves knowledge about these approaches and practices and their underlying sociolinguistic and pedagogical concepts and rationales. This element will be addressed in more detail at the end of Chapter 5 in a stopover section with some conceptual inferences for multilingual pedagogies in response to the constellations encountered in the classrooms.

Teacher agency in multilingual pedagogies – practised when teachers make choices, take stances and practise approaches in the field – can be conceptualised as linked to these four contextual factors. Thus, the arrows represent links between these elements and teacher agency and the relationships between the respective elements. Conceptually, an important part of the enquiry has been to gain insights into whether the four elements and their connections involve aspects that can resource and support teacher agency in multilingual pedagogies and to understand which aspects constrain the achievement of such agency. Practically, the framework can allow schools, teachers and teacher educators to flexibly reflect on what the constellation around each element might look like in a given setting or classroom and what steps could advance and transform the status quo.

2 Researching Teacher Agency: The Study

This chapter reflects on the terminology used in this study before introducing the schools and teachers who opened their classroom doors. It then turns to the methodology and research design, data collection and data analysis. Additionally, it addresses (language) education policy in England as the broader context for researching teacher agency in multilingual pedagogies.

2.1 Terminology

Before turning to the classrooms, it is important to briefly consider how the terms 'bilingual', 'emergent bilingual', 'plurilingualism' and 'multilingualism' will be used in this book, along with the approach to notions of named languages and superdiversity that will be adopted.

A bilingual is understood as someone who uses two languages in their everyday life (Grosjean, 1989: 4), whereas an emergent bilingual is someone who is 'at the initial points of the continuum of bilingualism' (García, 2014: 5). The notions of multilingualism and plurilingualism are used in relation to society, the institution of school and the individual. Plurilingualism, in particular, highlights the dynamic and integrated relationships among the elements of the linguistic repertoire within an individual speaker (Cummins, 2017: 111). Thus, while I used the terms 'bilingual' and 'multilingual children' in the teacher interviews for reasons of intelligibility, terms including plurilingual children, plurilingual voices, plurilingual speakers, plurilingual literacy skills and plurilingual experiences are used in the following chapters to foreground the dynamic relationships among elements in a linguistic repertoire. This usage highlights the common interest shared by the perspectives of plurilingualism and translanguaging. Specifically, plurilinguals have a unique, integrated repertoire of semiotic resources that they employ and combine in creative and strategic ways in accordance with the context and other speakers in a given interaction (Vallejo & Dooly, 2020: 7). Finally, the term 'multilingual' is primarily used here in relation to pedagogies, while more generally, '[m]ultilingual classrooms can be defined as classrooms where children are speakers of a multiplicity of languages other than the language(s) of instruction' (Hélot et al., 2018b: 5).

An important terminological issue relevant to the present study concerns named languages and the labelling practices involved. The children featured in the following chapters will demonstrate how traditional notions such as 'first' and 'second language' have ceased to be meaningful, not only from the point of view of these children but also as an adequate description of their linguistic repertoires. These pupils are children of the multilingual turn, and to explore classrooms like those in this study, it is vital to consider a wide range of linguistic constellations on their part. For some of them, the description of 'first' and 'second language' may apply; for others, it does not accurately reflect their experience and language use at home; yet other children may speak one language with one parent and another with the other. For this reason, too, the study draws on the notion of the linguistic repertoire from a perspective that takes the speaker's perception as a starting point and eschews objectifications or fixed categories such as 'first' or 'second language' (Busch, 2017a: 56). When exploring the status quo of schools' responses to multilingualism and teacher agency in multilingual pedagogies, the central question is not whether named languages 'exist', but rather through which routines dominant language ideologies are brought into existence in school and which meanings are assigned to different languages. I agree with Li Wei's (2018: 27) assertion that the concept of translanguaging 'does not deny the existence of named languages, but stresses that languages are historically, politically, and ideologically defined entities'. Plurilingual speakers are aware of the existence of these entities as part of their own linguistic socialisation and find ways to resolve discrepancies and ambiguities when they occur (Li, 2018: 19). Mainstream primary schools in England play a crucial role in secondary language socialisation, and the power differential between teachers and pupils often leaves little room for navigation (e.g. Gundarina & Simpson, 2022; Kenner & Ruby, 2012). However, problematising named languages is, indeed, highly relevant, as it draws attention to the labelling and othering processes that are interwoven with dominant discourses around the imagined monolingual nation and their rejection of multilingualism, on which racist discourses draw and which they reinforce. As Li argues, '[b]y deliberately breaking the artificial and ideological divides between indigenous versus immigrant, majority versus minority, and target versus mother tongue languages, Translanguaging empowers both the learner and the teacher, transforms the power relations [...]' (2018: 15). While languages are named as 'English', 'Lithuanian' or 'Bengali' in the following chapters – as they were in the teacher interviews and the participatory activities with children – they are understood as elements of children's repertoires and are not further categorised as 'first', 'second', 'immigrant' or 'minority' languages.

Superdiversity is a concept whose transfer to the field of sociolinguistics (e.g. Arnaut *et al.*, 2016) has been welcomed, while it has also faced criticism for its ahistoricity, neglect of multilingual experiences in the Global South (especially Indigenous languages) and its focus on the (Western) urban context (e.g. Badwan, 2021b: Ch. 8; May, 2022b). These critical debates highlight the need to reflect on the positionality implicit in the notions employed in research on multilingualism and education. As flagged in the introduction, the present study is situated in a specific geopolitical place with distinct societal power relations. Within this European space, it further exists within the context of educational systems where the ideology and generation of the national language are inextricably intertwined with the imagination of a homogenous nation-state (Hobsbawm, 1992). The trope of monolingualism is still an integral part of the politics of belonging (Yuval-Davis, 2006), reinforced during times witnessing a rise of right-wing populism and far-right parties across many parts of the continent (Fekete, 2019). Within this complex positionality, I use 'superdiversity' as a critical term in relation to classrooms and children's 'superdiverse voices'.

To explain how 'superdiverse' is used in this study, I include an extract from participatory activities with children in Hira's Year 3 class.

'then I learnt Italy from school'

Probal and Abdul, who arrived about a year and a half ago at Victoria Primary, and Sana, longer settled, spoke about their language repertoires:

177	Probal:	When I was two years old, I knew, first knew Bangla
178		but when I went to school – I didn't want to go to school, then I had to,
179		then I learnt Italy from school and my friends helped me
183		[...] in Year 2, I came here [...]
186		Yeah and when I came here then
187	Sana:	I helped him
188	Probal:	Yeah, she was the one who talked to me and I couldn't understand, so she
189		taught me. [...]
192	Sana:	I was saying the word in English and then he didn't understand, so I told him
193		in Bang – in Bengali. I wanted to.

(Activities 1, Victoria Primary Y3, 29 June 2017)

Probal says that he speaks Bengali with his parents at home and on the mobile with his grandparents, who live in Bangladesh. In a

---

> dialogue between Abdul and Probal, it emerges that they sometimes speak Italian among themselves and with another boy who arrived in the class one year later (Activities 1, Victoria Primary Y3, 29 June 2017: Lines 226–233). 'Then, when we were in Year 3, Mahik came. I talked with him in Italian, also, I talked with him more in Bangla' (Activities 1, Y3, 29 June 2017: Lines 233–234). Contrary to Line 179, where Probal uses the country's name for the Italian language, he says 'in Italian' here, using again the Bengali name 'Bangla' for the Bengali language. Lines 177–193 illustrate that the children have clear recollections of when they first entered new linguistic environments – as did children in other activity groups. Importantly, they also highlight how the school's language statistics fail to accommodate the children's linguistic repertoires; the statistics only list Bengali as those pupils' 'first language'.

Writing about superdiversity in the context of translanguaging pedagogy, Conteh (2018, 474) points to a relatively high degree of normalcy with which adults and children live linguistic diversity in their everyday lives and within their 'superdiverse' neighbourhoods. The term was coined in migration studies to emphasise three interrelated aspects: a descriptive aspect portraying the change in demographic configurations stemming from global migration movements since the early 1990s; a methodological aspect overcoming the narrow, and often essentialising, focus on 'ethnicity'; and a practical and policy-oriented aspect identifying consequences for new provisions of public services (Meissner & Vertovec, 2015; Vertovec, 2007). For many primary schools in Europe, all those aspects – including, importantly, the normalcy of linguistic diversity – have some significance. On the one hand, features such as duration of residence, class, parents' education, legal status and others may all frame the conditions of pupils' lives. On the other hand, linguistic superdiversity also includes the complex linguistic repertoires that may reflect recent migratory trajectories of some pupils' families – as is the case with Probal and Abdul in the extract above – but may also be present in others who belong to longer-settled communities, which comprise different generations with their shifting experiences of languages (Martin-Jones *et al.*, 2012: 7). This would refer to Sana and the three children's teacher, Hira. All this is not necessarily a new phenomenon. Indeed, an 11-year-old child's description, 'I speak English at school, Gujarati on my way home to my friends. I read books at Mosque in Urdu, and I learn passages from the Koran in Arabic… My mum speaks Marathi' (Houlton, 1985: 1) resembles the ways in which the children talked about their experiences in the participatory activities. Chapter 5, under the heading of 'superdiverse voices', addresses three dimensions of diversity within the range of meanings that speaking a language can have for children. Starting with speakers' perspectives and their linguistic repertoire, my approach attempts to include such superdiversity as a relevant feature of primary school classrooms to which multilingual pedagogies must respond.

2.2 The Schools and the Teachers

The study was conducted in three maintained inner-city primary schools in London and the East of England, which I will refer to here as Castle Primary, Victoria Primary and Bird Primary. The three schools had a high percentage of children who have as a 'first language' – the phrasing follows here the terminology used in the schools' statistical systems – a language other than English.

Castle Primary is a three-form entry school located in an inner London borough traditionally associated with a very diverse population. The children in the school speak approximately 40 languages apart from English, and while there is not one predominant language group, many of its pupils speak Polish, Lithuanian and Romanian. About a third of the children are eligible for pupil premium, the supplementary funding scheme in the English education system that is intended to raise the attainment of disadvantaged children, which can roughly serve as a proxy for the socioeconomic situation of the children's families. Castle Primary had been classified as 'requires improvement' in the previous school inspection, and a new senior management team had been appointed since then. Victoria Primary is a large four-form entry school in East London. The language count on the school's statistical system lists 45 different languages as pupils' 'first language'. Around a quarter of the children speak Urdu and almost a quarter Bengali, while 17% of the pupils are listed with English as their 'first language'. Approximately a quarter of the pupils at Victoria Primary are eligible for a pupil premium. The third school in the study, Bird Primary, is located in the east of England. It is a two-form entry school where approximately 80% of the children are listed as having 'English as an additional language'. These children speak approximately 50 languages, but there is not one single large language group represented in the school. The count of pupils' home languages shows for the most commonly spoken languages that about a tenth of the children speak Polish, a tenth speak Urdu and 4% are listed with Akan/Twi-Fante. The number of children at Bird Primary eligible for pupil premium is low, according to the school inspection report. However, the headteacher pointed out that this description would not adequately capture the economic situation of many families.

These three schools had been open to participation, when about a dozen of primary schools in linguistically very diverse neighbourhoods were contacted via email in preparation of the enquiry. I had briefly known Castle Primary and Victoria Primary a few years earlier while working in the role of a supply teacher. However, I had not known any of the teachers or children involved in the study, and there had not been any previous contact to Bird Primary. In initial meetings with the headteachers, we agreed that they would ask their staff, except in Years 1 and 6, whether they would like to volunteer in the research. Thus, the final sample of teachers was random, but their Year 3, 4 and 5 classes can be seen as broadly located in the middle of the primary phase.

The teachers had varying lengths of teaching experience and held a variety of positions. At Castle Primary, Ellie was a class teacher in Year 4. She had the role of Year 4 group leader and was on a school management course at the time. Ellie herself had attended a small primary school in the north of England and explained that she 'always wanted to be a teacher' (Interview, 8 February 2017: Line 95). Now she was in her ninth year of teaching; after an induction year in the north, she had worked for seven years in a large primary school in the same borough where she teaches now, having joined Castle Primary at the start of the school year.

Mike was a class teacher in Year 5. He was also in his ninth year of teaching and had taken on the role of assistant head, with responsibility for teaching and learning. He said about his own education, 'I experienced every type of school, which at the time was a bit unsettling but probably made me who I am' (Interview, 30 January 2017: Lines 146–147), mentioning a small school, a boarding school and a university in the US. Mike had worked at a large newspaper for a year and for some months as an English teacher in South America and a poor neighbourhood in India. He was very busy in his assistant head role and often had another teacher covering his class in the afternoon.

At Victoria Primary, Hira was a class teacher in Year 3, a role she had already taken on the year before, which had been her induction year. She had attended primary and secondary school in London, remembering 'my primary school being very vibrant' (Interview, 27 June 2017: Line 23), and also studied for her Postgraduate Certificate in Education in London. Hira was the subject leader for music.

At Bird Primary, Heather was a class teacher in Year 3, Lower Key Stage 2 leader and lead for well-being, covering the domains of personal, social, health and economic education (PSHE) and learning behaviour. Heather started working at the school during the last placement for her BA Ed. and was now in her fifth year of teaching. Regarding her time as a student, she said, 'I had an amazing experience in primary and secondary school' (Interview, 12 January 2018: Lines 104–105).

Finally, Kelly was the other Year 3 class teacher at Bird Primary. After a career as a childminder, she had been trained at the school via a school-led initial teacher training scheme and was now in her second year of teaching. Talking about her own learning, Kelly explained that she is 'still really into learning things because I did my degree when I was very old' (Interview, 7 December 2017: Lines 145–146). At her school, Kelly shared the computing lead with another colleague.

While the three schools had, on the whole, diverse staff, all the headteachers, excluding one deputy head, were white, and of the five teachers in the study, only Hira had a Black, Asian and minority ethnic background. The selection of participants happened randomly; however, this group reflects statistics that indicate that 85.1% of all teachers in state-funded schools in England identified as White British in 2021 (DfE, 2023a). The pupils of the five classes are not introduced here, as this is, in my view, best done in the respective episodes from the classrooms and extracts from the participatory activities. Similarly, and as mentioned before, the teachers started describing their own language experiences when talking about the plurilingual children in their classes. This link will be thematised further in Chapter 6, and therefore the educators' linguistic repertoires are not described here.

2.3 Methodology and Research Design

The choice of ethnography as a methodology was justified by the necessity to explore the domain of multilingual pedagogies at the same time as the phenomenon of teacher agency. The study is located within the realm of ethnographic research in educational settings (Gordon *et al.*, 2001) and has adopted an ethnographic perspective (Green & Bloome, 1997: 183). In other words, while neither offering a comprehensive ethnography nor simply using some tools commonly associated with fieldwork, it takes a focused approach to examine particular aspects of the everyday practices of teachers and pupils in the sociocultural institution of primary school.

Participant observations were conducted in five classrooms, where I took fieldnotes during a total of 335 lessons. I spent 20 days, or one day per week spread over one school term, in a Year 4 and a Year 5 class at Castle Primary; two days per week in a Year 3 class at Victoria Primary over half a term, and one day per week over two terms in each of two Year 3 classes at Bird Primary. Additional fieldnotes were taken in assemblies, playgrounds, a small number of MFL lessons, conversations with EAL coordinators and two visits to complementary schools. With each class teacher, I conducted two semi-structured interviews that lasted, on average, 50 minutes each. Two participatory activities with a small group of children from each class were conducted and audio-recorded, lasting 45 minutes each: in Castle and Victoria Primary, six children from each class took part, and in Bird Primary, two groups of five children from each class participated; altogether, 38 children participated. Furthermore, I took photographs of the linguistic schoolscapes and accessed the schools' Teaching and Learning policies, English as an Additional Language policies and Modern Foreign Language policies. In each class, the components followed a similar chronology: after some weeks of observations, which continued throughout the research in the respective class, the first teacher interview took place. This was followed, in two successive weeks, by the two sessions of participatory activities, before conducting the second interview. Thus, each research component was linked to the previous one. The first interview addressed issues of the teacher's professional identity, general practices in the classroom, their role in the school and the plurilingual children. The second interview took place after the participatory activities and focused mainly on activities or possible activities around multilingual pedagogies.

2.3.1 Ethical considerations

The research followed the procedures for ethical approval of Goldsmiths, University of London, and the Ethical Guidelines of the British Educational Research Association (BERA, 2018 [2011]) were consulted. Access to the classrooms was negotiated via the headteachers, who then asked their staff for volunteers before asking the children and their parents for their consent for the participatory activities. Qualitative research carries the risk of impinging upon privacy, given its commitment to shedding light on people's perspectives, attitudes and feelings in some depth (Hammersley & Traianou, 2012: 106). Open questions were, therefore, used to offer teachers sufficient room to navigate the boundary between professional and private, with carefully worded questions that did not require the teachers to position themselves in line with pre-established categories. Furthermore, in the context of researching children's multilingualism, privacy boundaries can be swiftly crossed, and vulnerability can surface because 'speaking a language' is frequently interwoven with experiences of belonging and emotional bonds. This dilemma is potentially exacerbated by the unavoidable power differential between a researcher and a child whose language repertoire is being thematised, i.e. between an adult who asks questions that inevitably intrude on the child's private sphere, and the child who may feel that they must answer and cannot choose to decline. In the participatory activities, however, the power differential was not entirely suspended, although the children had more options to decide what they wanted to share and how they wanted to interact with each other.

I had deliberately chosen not to consult the schools' statistical system for the pupils' 'first languages' since, rather than predefining 'multilingualism' in a certain way, the overall research perspective intended to explore pupils' plurilingualism through participant observations and participatory activities. Usually, I did not address 'languages' in the brief aside chats with the pupils because, firstly, they were on task with their learning, and secondly, I was cautious not to exoticise multilingualism by foregrounding it in an artificial way or out of context. Exceptions were made during the initial days within a class to gain some basic understanding of the children's linguistic repertoires.

2.4 Data Collection and Analysis

The dynamic and dialectical epistemology of ethnographic work requires the inclusion of data's history as a significant feature of the research process. Thus, the following sections describe the processes of data collection and data analysis and also include a reflection on my positionality as a researcher.

2.4.1 Participant observations

The fieldnotes were oriented in three ways: first, towards classroom communication, interactions, teaching/learning approaches and the general atmosphere and dynamics of the classroom; second, towards the status quo of multilingual pedagogies: What is being done? What influence does the teacher exert? What choices does the teacher make? Third, my fieldnotes covered aspects of the school as a workplace, including, for example, interactions with year group colleagues. My conversations with the teachers were short and usually related to issues around children's responses to lesson activities, etc.

During the participant observations, I sometimes initiated a short conversation with pupils about their work or they asked for help. One teacher occasionally asked me to work with children who needed more support. In these interactions, I rarely addressed issues around multilingualism and only in an offhand way, ensuring that I was not intrusive. In the research process, the place for addressing language repertoires and experiences in school more directly with the children was the participatory activities. An exception to this was the first days in a class, when in brief, informal chats, I asked the pupils whether they spoke another language in addition to English. I did this because I wanted to hear from the children themselves how they described their language repertoires instead of drawing on school statistics or the teacher.

The fieldnotes were coded along the three broad orientations that guided the observations: (1) classroom communication/interaction, teaching/learning approaches, classroom atmosphere/dynamics; (2) instances of multilingualism; and (3) workplace-related (inter)actions. Afterwards, the resulting codes were brought together under the umbrella categories of 'teaching/learning routines' and 'voices being heard' to identify regularities and patterns that facilitated a description of the respective classroom as the context to which the teacher's agency relates and in which it is achieved. Moreover, in an iterative process, I took my perceptions from the participant observations into the interviews with the teachers, sharing impressions from the classroom when appropriate in the dialogical flow of the interview. In the course of the analysis, when the interview data was included at a later stage, themes could be identified that were significant for the respective teacher's general agency. Themes were understood as conceptualised within reflexive thematic analysis as proposed by Braun and Clarke (2006): '[a] theme captures something important about the data in relation to the research question, and represents some level of *patterned* response or meaning within the data set' (2006: 82, emphasis in original) and their further clarification that themes are '*patterns* of meanings (e.g. concepts, ideas, experience, sense making) that are underpinned and unified by a central idea' (Braun & Clarke, 2022: 229, emphasis in original). The teachers' general agency in the context of their classroom as a prerequisite for achieving agency in a specific pedagogical domain like multilingual pedagogies is the focus of Chapter 3.

I then focused on instances in the fieldnotes where multilingualism had become audible or relevant. These small numbers of specific situations were considered critical incidents within the 'large pattern' of the prevalence of monolingualism in the classroom, and their analysis required a distinctive approach. I used the lens of stancetaking, as developed in an interactional sociolinguistic perspective (Jaffe, 2009a) and further employed in the context of metapragmatic stancetaking (Spitzmüller, 2022) for this more detailed analysis. 'Stancetaking' refers to the possibility for a speaker to take up a position regarding the form or content of their utterance and acknowledges that this positionality is built into the act of communication (Jaffe, 2009b: 3). The stancetaker has been defined as someone who is 'simultaneously evaluating objects, positioning subjects (self and others), and aligning with other subjects, with respect to any salient dimension of the sociocultural field' (Du Bois, 2007: 163). As an analytical lens, stancetaking belongs to epistemological and ontological perspectives, where scholars in education, educational linguistics and sociolinguistics work with notions of 'ideology' and 'discourse' and refer for processes of 'subjectification' to Althusser's (1984) understanding of ideology, Foucault's discourse (e.g. 1971) and Butler's subjectivation (e.g. Davies, 2006). The use of stancetaking in this study aligns with the central concerns with language ideologies and discourses on language use, which translate into one's sense of self as a speaker (Busch, 2017a: 52), as mentioned in Chapter 1. Stancetaking can play a complex role in naturalising ideologies because it actuates them indirectly, while certain acts of stancetaking might also have denaturalising effects due to their performative character (Jaffe, 2009b: 22). In Chapter 5, the stancetaking lens is especially employed to zoom in on the classroom's monolingual norm.

Other fieldnotes regarding multilingualism were annotated more descriptively and linked to categories, such as the situations in which children spoke a language other than English or descriptions children gave when talking about their linguistic repertoires when I asked them on the first two days of the participant observations. Those notes were also used to choose the focus groups for the participatory activities. Finally, the fieldnotes regarding the workplace were coded and provided the background for the teacher interviews. Chapter 6 specifically focuses on the school as the five teachers' workplace.

2.4.2 Semi-structured interviews

The interview questions addressed two central thematic areas: teacher agency and children's multilingualism. Overall, these two themes were kept separate in the first interview, in which the main set of questions focused on professional identities and the workplace. The questions were worded openly and colloquially, for example, 'Tell me about what is important to you in your work, your teaching and your classroom practices?' The second set of questions addressed multilingualism, for example, 'Many of the children you teach are bi- or multilingual. What does this mean for you?' In the second interview, the thematic areas of teacher agency and children's multilingualism merged. Usually, the first interview was followed up by a question such as 'Are there areas of classroom practices where you feel you really bring your own ideas, your own identity as the teacher you are?' Later, as per the teacher Ellie in the interview extract quoted at the beginning of Chapter 1, the teachers were then asked, for example, when they would acknowledge the fact that a child speaks more than one language or when they would include or use those languages in the classroom. Finally, the interview moved on to the question of whether they liked to include the children's languages and, if so, which ideas they had for such inclusion. For the analysis, the interviews were taken through the six steps of reflective thematic analysis (Braun & Clarke, 2006, 2022).

2.4.3 Participatory activities

The purpose of the two participatory activities was twofold: to listen to how individual children describe their linguistic repertoires and their experiences as plurilingual speakers and to examine how children's repertoires and voices might be understood as one of the four elements that potentially contribute to teacher agency in multilingual pedagogies. The children were chosen somewhat randomly, even though I tried to bring together in each group children who had earlier mentioned various aspects of being bi- or multilingual, for example, (not) having literacy skills in their 'other' language(s) or having previously been schooled in another country. The aim was also to have a balanced 'presence' of different languages and a gender balance. Children with monolingual English family socialisation were not included, nor were pupils who were emergent bilinguals and still in a phase where their English skills would prevent them from participating equally in group talk. The first session was a language portrait activity, and the second was a focus group interview that included a mind map activity. In the language portrait activity, the children were asked to colour a silhouette (ÖSZ, 2010: 48): 'One colour for one language, a language you speak, a language that is important for you'. As a multimodal method, the language portrait has been widely employed in educational settings within a language awareness perspective (Busch, 2018: 2) and more elaborately in biographically oriented and speaker-centred research on multilingualism (Busch, 2017a, 2022; Purkarthofer & Flubacher, 2022). In this study, however, I did not ask the pupils explicitly to consider issues of representation, such as which colour to use for a certain language, to quantify its use or how to place colour/language in a specific section of the figure. After the colouring, the children were asked to present their drawings and to explain which language they had included, how they had learnt it and where and with whom they spoke it. They were also encouraged to ask each other questions.

The second participatory activity arose from talking with the children about their language experiences and followed the research paradigm of listening to them as expert voices for their plurilingual experiences (e.g. Busch, 2022; Ibrahim, 2019). Thus, the questions focused on children's experiences as plurilingual speakers in and out of school, for example, 'Do you speak this language in school?'; 'Do you use your language for learning at home?'; and 'Would you like to do more with your languages in school?' The children were then asked to use another copy of the language portrait silhouette as a mind map template and to write what they would like to do (or think they could do) with their languages in school. The question acknowledged the children as experts in their plurilingual repertoires without expecting them to be 'experts of multilingual pedagogies'. Finally, during the group interview, the children explained some of their ideas. The setting could increase the confidence of individual children and allowed them to decide at least some parts of the agenda (Greig et al., 2013: 238). The children had considerable leeway to interact during their work on the silhouettes and their presentations, and the setting ensured that the underlying understanding of the normalcy of multilingualism on their part was not disrupted by any supposition on my part about the meaning a child assigns to speaking a particular language. Therefore, while some children mentioned their biographical trajectories and their parents' migration, I avoided questions that ran the risk of coercing a child into a certain affiliation.

For the analysis of the language portrait activity, it was interesting to look at what the children said and also how they talked about their plurilingualism since both aspects could shed light on their language experiences. During the activity, the children mentioned many language practices, and the analysis aimed at identifying patterns and overarching aspects across all seven activity groups. The audio recordings and mind maps from the second participatory activities were analysed from a similar perspective. Children's answers to some questions, for example, whether they used their languages in lessons, were included in the reporting of language practices, as described above. The analysis of other answers, for example, to the question of whether their parents would support them with multilingual homework tasks, was guided by the interest to identify aspects of their experiences as plurilingual speakers that might be relevant for multilingual activities in their respective classrooms and could be linked conceptually to the development of multilingual pedagogies in general. Finally, for the analysis of the mind map as the last part of these activities, their ideas and suggestions were sorted into four groups. The children's ideas are addressed in Chapter 7.

2.4.4 Photographs and documents

Photographs were taken of the linguistic schoolscapes, and I accessed the school policies that were potentially relevant to languages, namely Teaching and Learning policies, EAL policies and MFL policies. When analysing the elements of the linguistic schoolscapes, I considered the purpose of the particular item, how it used a language other than English and what its origin or source was, for example, whether it had been made by pupils or had been downloaded from an online publisher. The policies were analysed in terms of how they mentioned and thematised multilingualism. The schoolscapes are addressed in Section 4.4, which thematises the symbolic acknowledgement of multilingualism.

2.4.5 A reflection on the researcher's positionality

The active role of the researcher is a vital part of both ethnographic work (Blommaert, 2018) and reflexive thematic analysis (Braun & Clarke, 2022), with both approaches being central to the present study. Norman Denzin (2017: 12) reminds us that, more generally, 'the qualitative researcher is not an objective, politically neutral observer who stands outside and above the study of the social world. Rather, the researcher is historically and locally situated within the very processes being studied'. Indeed, it is neither possible nor desirable to arrive at the research interest of teacher agency in multilingual pedagogies without having certain positions regarding both foci. In this sense, bringing the theoretical concepts outlined in Chapter 1 together is guided by my pedagogical and political positioning that teachers' agency and children's multilingualism matter. That is, my point of departure was the interest to bring these two 'things that matter' together and to explore them within superdiverse primary schools as a context with which I am familiar from my experience as a teacher who has worked in Berlin, Duisburg (a traditional rust belt city in Germany) and London. At the same time, however, the considerably vague phrasing in the assertion that teacher agency and children's multilingualism 'matter' reflects ignorance as a necessary point of departure for ethnographic work (Blommaert, 2018: 7).

I drew in different ways on the ethnographic toolkit – on the intersectionality of positionalities, which researchers use strategically to gain access to and understand a field (Reyes, 2020: 225). I foregrounded a teacher positionality to gain access to schools. Within the classrooms, my identity was as a combination of a notetaking researcher and, sometimes, a helpful additional adult. In the interviews, I adopted a researcher identity, asking questions from an interview guide while also responding dialogically, drawing on small observations from the classroom. In doing so, I implicitly (and very rarely also explicitly) referred to my own understanding of being a teacher, having experienced two different educational systems. Ultimately, it is not possible to know how teachers and children perceived my social characteristics – teacher, male, middle class, EU-white, German accent, mid-fifties – or which of them they found relevant. In the interviews, I 'bracketed' my presuppositions (Brinkmann & Kvale, 2015: 33–34) differently for the two thematic areas of teacher agency and multilingualism. Due to the overall constellation encountered, questions around teacher agency referred to aspects of a teacher's work that were usually observable as practices, while questions regarding multilingual pedagogies referred to an area that did not normally become observable in the official classroom. Thus, it became necessary to bracket my theoretical presuppositions to derive an understanding of the status quo from the logic of the classroom and the perspectives of teachers. The sequencing of the two interviews, however, allowed for a progression towards addressing the possibilities of multilingual pedagogies. Finally, in the participatory activities, my identity as a plurilingual speaker was relevant, albeit in a matter-of-course way.

2.5 Education Policy in England

Before the next chapter zooms in on the five classrooms as the micro-level context for teacher agency, it is essential to mention a few features of (language) education policy in England. Since the 1988 Education Reform Act, the English educational system has been characterised by continuous reforms and a general orientation towards performativity as the dominant approach to regulation. Stephen Ball (2003: 216) describes performativity as 'a technology, a culture and a mode of regulation that employs judgements, comparisons and displays as means of incentive, control, attrition and change'. As part of the 'New Public Management' within neoliberal reconstructions of the public sector, such mechanisms combined elements of de-regulation with processes of re-regulation and centralisation (Ball, 2003: 217). The fundamental transformation brought about through the National Curriculum reinforced the tendency 'in English educational discourse [...] to make pedagogy subsidiary to curriculum' (Alexander, 2008: 47). From the perspective of a primary school teacher, a variety of features come together here, most prominently the centralised curriculum, the centralised national curriculum assessments (SATs) and school inspections through the Office for Standards in Education, Children's Services and Skills (Ofsted), a non-ministerial department of the government. Furthermore, considering that the classroom serves as a sociocultural context for teaching and a workplace, it is important that the workload of English primary school teachers was the highest of all countries participating in the OECD's five-yearly large-scale survey except one (Long & Daneshi, 2022a; OECD, 2019).

Since 2010, successive governments have accelerated the process of academisation, whereby schools are taken out of or encouraged to opt out of the responsibility of Local Authorities and are, instead, run by charitable and social enterprise organisations of different sizes (academy 'chains' or Multi-Academy Trusts; for an overview see Thompson *et al.*, 2021). In 2023, 44.2% of all primary school children attended academies or free schools (DfE, 2024). The Department of Education has the capacity to convert schools into 'Academies' if successive Ofsted inspections graded them as 'requires improvement' and if assessed as having failed to improve. Such developments have reduced further the influence of Local Educational Authorities (Ball, 2018).

While from the perspective of the sociology of education, the principles of autonomy and control regarding the teacher's work in state education (Gewirtz & Cribb, 2009: 154–181) will necessarily always be in tension with each other, education policy in England strongly regulates both ends of the teaching process. The input regulation through the curriculum is centralised, and although the National Curriculum (DfE, 2013: 6) technically allows for teaching content beyond its specifications, the forceful output regulation with its combination of accountability procedures and school inspections, *de facto* severely restricts such possibilities. '[T]he neoliberal reconstruction of the professional role has thus impacted radically on the possibilities for agency' (Priestley *et al.*, 2015: 126).

Statistics related to languages and ethnicity have been problematised on linguistic, ideological and pragmatic grounds (e.g. Bonnett & Carrington, 2000; Busch, 2016; Vertovec, 2007). However, a few statistical figures can help to set out the context for multilingualism and education. In England, the number of pupils aged 5 to 16, whom schools recorded as speaking English as an additional language, constantly increased from 7.6% in 1997 to 16.2% in 2013, while the percentages of those children and young people varied considerably between approximately 6% in the South West and North East to 43% in Outer London and 56% in Inner London (Strand et al., 2015: 5). In the academic year 2023/24, 22.8% of pupils in English primary schools and 18.6% in secondary schools were recorded as speaking English as an additional language (DfE, 2024).

Education policy's overall position towards community languages was decisively shaped by the Swann report (DES, 1985), which suggested delegating the provision for community languages to the responsibility of the minority communities themselves instead of taking place in mainstream schools (Anderson & Macleroy, 2015: 244). This approach has guided education policy ever since, resulting in 'a general failure of mainstream education in the UK to recognise and value the linguistic and cultural capital that children bring and to draw on it as a learning resource' (Anderson, 2016: 18). Research has emphasised the significant role that complementary schools play in language and literacy learning, in addition to children's and young people's negotiations around identities and affiliations (e.g. Lytra & Martin, 2010). It is estimated that there exist between 3000 and 5000 of these schools in the UK (Borthwick, 2018: 186). However, they are often made invisible and remain disconnected from the mainstream education system (British Academy, 2019: 5). Their often difficult financial circumstances are exacerbated by the fact that both education policy and the general policy of austerity since 2010 under the Coalition and Conservative governments have curtailed the capacity of Local Education Authorities to support educational settings (Rampton et al., 2020: 12).

The same educational reforms that have restructured the state school system since the early 1990s by establishing market-like mechanisms (Ball, 2013a: 138–147) had a considerable impact on teaching English as an additional language. As the management of the schools' budget was moved to the individual school, this included the financial arrangements for EAL provision, and most EAL support teams, which had previously been part of Local Authorities, were disbanded (Rampton et al., 2020: 9). Since the late 1980s, EAL support has been integrated into the mainstream classroom. This 'mainstreaming' was primarily a response to the anti-discriminatory critique of separate provisions for pupils new to English. Yet, the wider organisational reconfiguration of schools and the fact that the curriculum does not include any specifications for EAL (Leung, 2016: 162–164) results in a situation that is simultaneously characterised by 'the lack of adequate initial and in-service teacher education, the lack of EAL-sensitive curriculum and assessment provision, and the lack of recognition of the importance of nurturing pupils' own languages in the school curriculum' (Leung, 2019: 18). In addition, routes of initial teacher education have diversified in the last decade, and in the academic year 2023/24, 56% of postgraduate trainee teachers entered the profession via school-led programmes (DfE, 2023b).

For the overall development of language education in England (for a summary Rampton *et al.*, 2020) as a point of reference for multilingual pedagogies within the primary school, it is helpful to draw attention to two paradoxical constellations: The negligence of EAL provision and EAL mainstreaming can be seen as an implicit endorsement for the English-medium school without efforts to develop alternative curricular arrangements in which children's home languages might play a role (Leung, 2016: 166). The other paradox is English as the elephant in the room, that is, 'the paradox of multilingualism and monolingualism [...] in that a great variety of ethnic minority languages (e.g. Bengali, Punjabi, Urdu, Polish) are spoken but many English speakers show little competence in other languages' (Lanvers, 2011: 63). In 2020/21 about 46% of pupils sat a General Certificate of Secondary Education (GCSE) in a modern foreign language. This situation results from an ongoing decline since 1997/98, when 86% had sat these exams (Long & Daneshi, 2022b), but may also reflect ambivalence about multilingualism and language learning in the wake of the Brexit referendum in 2016. Thus, the failure to build on existent provisions of language learning 'and to develop the UK's existing, and very extensive, competence in hundreds of languages already in use in the country, might be attributed to policy makers' ignorance of the importance of joined up thinking where languages were concerned' (Copland & McPake, 2022: 126). Implied here is a group that is often strangely absent in dominant debates about the 'language crisis' – the many plurilingual speakers of different ages. However, it might be suggested that the dominant political and economy-oriented debate begins to include the lived multilingualism of bilingual children, as in the words of the All-Party Parliamentary Group (2019: 2) on Modern Languages: 'GCSE and A Level figures are historically low. Exam entries in "languages with smaller cohorts" – some of the most strategically important for the future – are minuscule, despite 2 million bilingual children in our schools'. While GCSE and A level assessment is currently available in circa 15 languages (Rampton *et al.*, 2020: 12), and although the requirement for mainstream primary and lower secondary schools to choose only one of seven languages for teaching was removed in 2013, *de facto*, it is mainly European languages that schools teach as Modern Foreign Languages at these levels (Anderson & Macleroy, 2015: 247). Against this background, scholars emphasise the necessity to conceptualise pedagogical approaches that respond dynamically to local conditions and the languages pupils learn at home while promoting at the same time plurilingual language skills for all students (Anderson & Macleroy, 2015: 243).

3 Classrooms in Real Schools: Contexts for Teacher Agency

This chapter starts with the classroom as the first contextual factor of the framework for teacher agency in multilingual pedagogies. Inviting the reader to enter five classrooms, the chapter zooms in on their atmosphere, their affordances for children's voices and some of the many small decisions a teacher takes in language education and when running the classroom. The chapter thematises such choices, the working consensus a teacher has established and other key features of teachers' general agency. This approach allows for an exploration of such general agency as a precondition for understanding teacher agency in multilingual pedagogies and, in addition, helps to trace potential links between primary school pedagogy and multilingual pedagogies.

3.1 Ellie's Classroom: Small Choices and the Working Consensus

124 Ellie is on playground duty, walking slowly around on the spa-
cious Key Stage 2 playground that
125 surrounds the single-storey buildings. Some girls are practising a
dance; three boys are using
126 the wall as a goal. Older children chat in pairs or small groups,
while some younger ones are busy with
127 counting-out games. It all looks very relaxed, given that there are
approximately 350 Key Stage 2
128 pupils out there, and the large size of the playground seems to
contribute to this peaceful
129 atmosphere. On a separate pitch, children play football. Ellie is
approached by several children,
130 talking with them [...]
131 When the bell rings, the children line up, more or less everyone
stops talking,
132 before Ellie's class and another Year 4 move to their classrooms,
teachers talking to each

133   other in front of the lines and the pupils of the two classes mixing on the way. [...]
135   The children hang up their coats. It is lively in the corner with the pegs, but while the children make
136   their way to the carpet, the chatting dies down.
137   Ellie briefly explains the handwriting and 'next step' for English. [...]
139   Everyone goes back to the table and starts to complete the tasks. [...]
140   Some children go to the teacher to ask about the 'next step' task; she is moving from table to table.
141   'Okay, two more minutes'.
142   Ellie asks the children to return to the carpet.
                    (Fieldnotes Y4, Castle Primary, 10 January 2017)

This and the following vignettes from a literacy lesson capture well some of the features that are typical of Ellie's Year 4 classroom. The smooth, swift transition the children make from playtime and chatting while hanging up their coats to sitting on the carpet (Lines 135–136) signals the importance of 'the carpet' as a space for teaching and learning in her classroom (Line 137). The transition usually happens effortlessly without any interference from the teacher and seems to work symbolically, akin to a rapid recap of what has been called the 'working consensus', which is established in the interaction between teachers and pupils, usually at the start of a school year, by mutually negotiating 'interdependent ways of coping in classrooms' (Pollard, 1985: 158). Smaller routines – like the handwriting task and the work on the 'next step' (Lines 137 and 139), where pupils complete a short task that the teacher has set in their books as feedback or to extend previous learning – reduce the need for lengthy explanations and support the daily teaching–learning interaction by providing structure. The teacher sends the children off to the handwriting and 'next step' (Line 139) and asks them back about 10 minutes later, after the completion of those tasks (Line 142). It is indicative of the atmosphere that both movements occur almost without delay before the actual lesson begins:

144   All children on the carpet, one boy keeps talking.
145   Ellie is asking him for a reason, explaining clearly that 'This is a waste of time... Think about it'.
146   She introduces the children to today's task: Diary entry for Bill (from: Anne Fine, *Bill's New Frock*)
147   With IWB, the teacher explains the task, followed by a quick recap of the features of a diary entry.
148   Ewan explains features; three other children had their hands up.

149   Children are asked to take notes on their small whiteboards from three video clips. [...]

152   Ellie asks the children to share their notes; many children put their hands up. They read from the
153   whiteboards and Ellie comments: 'Good idea', 'I like that'.
154   On the flipchart, she writes down children's ideas for suitable words and phrases as ideas
155   for the diary entry, sometimes repeating and/or recasting phrases.
156   She talks expressively when picking up examples, with facial expression and some small gestures.
157   Then the children move to their tables and start writing in their literacy books.
158   Ellie goes around, looking at children's work and answering questions.

(Fieldnotes Y4, Castle Primary, 10 January 2017)

The calm and clear way in which Ellie responds to the boy who continues to talk (Lines 144–145) can be interpreted as a mixture of genuine and rhetorical questioning, an implicit reminder of the rules and a firm statement regarding her expectations. This is characteristic of her approach to running the classroom. When the children sit as a whole group on the carpet, the teacher expects them to listen and pay full attention. However, this is balanced against other lesson parts, where there is more room for children's voices and where the pupils are allowed to communicate (see below).

In Lines 146–154, Ellie introduces the lesson. Its main teaching is broadly conducted within what has been called 'interactive whole-class teaching' as endorsed by the National Literacy and Numeracy Strategies (DfEE, 1998, 1999), which remains influential in English primary schools even after those initiatives officially ceased in 2011 (DfE, 2011). The interpretation of *interactivity* in this approach has been contested both as a concept and in practice (e.g. Black, 2007; Smith *et al.*, 2004), not least because of the inherent contradiction between, on the one hand, a learner-centred, socioculturally oriented focus of interactive teaching with its emphasis on dialogue and teacher–pupil collaboration and, on the other, the objective-led pedagogical orientation of standard-based education as the dominant paradigm in education policy (Black, 2007: 279). The teaching and learning routines in this episode are characteristic of Ellie's classroom in several respects: (1) The introduction is short and, in this case, builds on the children's familiarity both with the story of *Bill's New Frock* as the ongoing literacy sequence throughout the week, and with the text genre of a diary, which is very accessible for children in Year 4 due to its usage of informal language (Line 146). (2) The teacher uses the interactive whiteboard to visualise the theme, learning objective and success criteria (Line 147). (3) Ewan, who explains the features of a diary (Line 148), is one of several pupils who regularly put up their hands when the teacher directs questions at the whole class. While the pace and flow of the whole-class teaching benefits from the small group of very articulate pupils, it also results in an overall constellation in which the voices of other children are significantly less audible because they participate much less frequently or with shorter utterances in classroom talk. (4) Work with small whiteboards and in other lessons with Think-Pair-Share phases can be seen as a response to this situation, as it actively includes all children in the task (Lines 149 and 152). (5) The use of the carpet as a spatial and communicative device is important in this Year 4 classroom. For the teacher, the setting means having the children's attention from a close range and monitoring interaction and learning processes:

42   […] I think, personally, I like where they all – not many people
43   keep them on the carpet and do sort of the main teaching with them there.
44   But I think that works. You have all of their attention; you can easily see what
45   they are doing. When they have got whiteboards, you can, you know, you are
46   looking at them, 'Right, yeah, you are doing this…'.
               (Interview, 24 March 2017)

While Ellie is the 'central voice' in the carpet setting, the power differential between her and the pupils is simultaneously reduced – at least symbolically and for a period. The classroom talk takes a more dialogical form than in the prototypical traditional initiation-response-feedback (I-R-F) version (Sinclair & Coulthard, 1975), or, for example, if the teacher displayed a written text as a model for the children's writing, as is often the practice in literacy lessons within primary schools. Although talk and knowledge construction is initiated and structured by Ellie, they are also co-constructed between teacher and children, in addition to between children. The teacher chooses a setting in which hers is the central voice, but where the children can experience teaching and learning as an interactional process in which their voices are listened to and in which they have some time to write and voice their ideas. Thus, the setting allows for a bidirectional flow of knowledge when the educator writes down children's ideas of words and phrases, which, in turn, they can use afterwards for writing their own texts (Lines 152–156). Furthermore, even though Ellie simply asks the pupils to share their ideas from the whiteboards, the setting supports a somewhat more dialogical character of the talk because it takes place in a space that is more intimate than the whole classroom. Thus, many children 'claim to read' and contribute from their notes (Line 152); they 'claim to speak' while, and in all probability also because, the arrangement gives them time to prepare what they want to say. In other lessons on the carpet, communication is sometimes even more casual or informal, as Ellie lets the children give short answers spontaneously without them having to put up their hands. (6) In this extract from a literacy lesson, the teacher utilises the multimodal possibilities of the video clips to elicit ideas and notes (Line 149). Yet, it is also at this point that another, pedagogically very relevant characteristic is discernible, which points – albeit by way of omission – to the perspective of *voices being heard*. The diary genre lends itself to including pupils' experiences, for example, when the task might ask them to write an entry concerning their own personal experiences or narratives instead of those of the fiction book's main character, but that is not the case in this lesson.

In terms of the sociocultural framework as described in Chapter 1, the episode shows how particular teaching resources and artefacts can be understood, first, as supporting the teacher's voice by providing written text on the interactive whiteboard (Line 147), second, as encouraging pupils to make their voices heard by using small whiteboards (Lines 149 and 152), and, on a different plane, as bringing the characters' voices from the book into the classroom via the video clips (Line 149). Together with the concept of 'interactive whole class teaching' as a secondary artefact, these resources mediate Ellie's teaching routines while she chooses to combine the resources in a specific way.

Two aspects emerge from this classroom that are relevant to teacher agency: 'small' choices on the part of the teacher and the working consensus. The lesson described here shows that a conceptualisation of a teacher's general agency needs to include a consideration of the *small choices* made within the daily routines of the classroom. In fact, Ellie had mentioned her use of the carpet setting as an example of these choices when asked,

34	TQ:	[...] are there areas of
35		classroom practices where you feel you really bring your own ideas,
36		[...] you make your own choices, you bring your own identity as
37		the teacher you are?
38	Ellie:	Hm, I think with all the lessons, whereas it's planned by one person – but we
39		all deliver it in different ways. And actually, you can go into each of the three
40		classrooms and you would see a completely different lesson. And we all have

41   the same flip chart, we all have the same plan, but the way we deliver it is
42   quite different [...]

(Interview, 24 March 2017)

Although she and her two colleagues in the Year 4 group collaborate closely in planning and reflecting on their lessons, which holds great significance for Ellie (see Chapter 6), there are many opportunities and necessities for small decisions, either consciously taken when teaching or built into the classroom routines. Thus, the teacher describes in Lines 39–42 an ownership over her teaching and the choices she makes within the respective frame set by the lesson plan and the slides prepared for the interactive whiteboard.

In Lines 157–158, the pupils start writing the diary entry in their books. In terms of time, this is the lesson's main section, and it is in those main parts of lessons, when the children work at their tables, that the 'working consensus' surfaces:

194   The atmosphere is comfortable and relaxed, i.e. children are allowed to communicate with
195   each other while working on the tasks; each time, they are allowed a short while to settle in before
196   starting a new task [...]

(Fieldnotes Y4, Castle Primary, 10 January 2017)

164   My impression is that Ellie trusts the children and expects them to be responsible for
165   their own work. This is my impression; Ellie says that yes, the children work
166   independently (that was what I was saying to her) but some children are really slow.

(Fieldnotes Y4, Castle Primary, 17 January 2017)

These arrangements can be seen as resulting from a 'working consensus' (Pollard, 1985) between teacher and children, which provides stability and calm. In these longer working phases with comparatively little intervention from the educator, the children have the opportunity to find and negotiate both work patterns and relationships with other children (Bourne, 2001: 105). In this regard, Ellie's classroom consists of two components that complement each other. While she is the 'central voice' during the phase of whole-class teaching, the arrangement changes when pupils work at the tables, and their voices can be heard while they talk to each other (Lines 194–195). As the teacher put it,

67   I don't enforce silence either because actually
68   if you listen to them, they are talking about the work in most cases, so I think
69   that that helps, because then you sort of you can dig it out of their
70   conversation a bit: 'Oh you talked about this, why are you not trying to write it
71   down?'

(Interview, 8 February 2017)

Apart from situations when she is working with a small group of children or discussions in science lessons, Ellie's depiction in Lines 69–71 comes closest to what has been described, particularly in the context of teaching and learning English as an additional language, as micro level and interactional scaffolding. In this approach, the teacher integrates content and language learning, using a range of strategies, e.g. 'talk about talk' or recasting pupil-initiated meanings in a register more appropriate to the respective genre (e.g. Gibbons, 2006: 125–142). Ellie's practice in Lines 149–156 and her reasoning above are instructive for teacher agency, as they show the kind of interplay in which teacher and learner agencies connect. The teacher increases her agency to teach by facilitating learner agency – in this case, the co-construction of knowledge when preparing the writing and accepting children's talk while they work on their texts – because she can respond more flexibly to the pupils' utterances and the writing process.

The working consensus emerges as part of the teacher's professional identity and knowledge, but also in relation to the context of the school.

75   TQ: ... do you think the kind of
76   atmosphere you are creating in your class [...] is it a sort of general atmosphere
77   you find in this school? [...]
79   Ellie: Hm, I think it depends on which class you are going into, to be honest. Some
80   teachers are incredibly strict: 'No, don't speak, you just go on with it...' But I
81   had it always like that. If you are talking about your work and are getting on,
82   you know, that's that's fine. And if people are talking about what they had for
83   dinner or what they did during the weekend, they do need to go and turn
84   their cards. But they respond quite well to that, and usually if they turned it,

85   they are usually getting on. I think it's what I have always done; it is just as
86   long as you are getting on, then you can have a chat and actually sharing is
87   better than struggling on your own. Yeah.

(Interview, 8 February 2017)

Marking her personal evaluation with the phrases 'to be honest' (Line 79) and 'But I had it always like that' (Lines 80–81), Ellie distances herself from 'some teachers [who] are incredibly strict' and who, *de facto*, – 'don't speak, you just go on with it' (Line 80) – silence children into being 'writing pupils'. Ellie asserts here her ownership of the working consensus she has established with the children, linking it to her professional experience and identity by stating, 'But I had it always like that' (Lines 80–81), and providing a reiteration, 'I think it's what I have always done' (Line 85), before concluding with a kind of pedagogical maxim about learning: 'actually sharing is better than struggling on your own' (Lines 86–87). In this interview passage, the working consensus emerges as a vital area of the teacher's general agency. Given that consensus is a precondition of teaching, this might almost appear a truism. Yet, a conceptual consideration of this linkage is also relevant for teacher agency in multilingual pedagogies in that those pedagogies need to be contextualised within the general pedagogy presently practised in the classroom. In pragmatic terms, it could be said that teacher agency in the specific domain of multilingual pedagogies can only be achieved when it is anchored in and can build on the educator's general agency exerted in the classroom. However, the working consensus also reflects the pedagogical stances of the teacher and their perspectives on teaching, and it can therefore help to shed light on possible transitions from a teacher's general agency to an agency in the field of multilingual pedagogies. Given that 'a positive relationship, or working consensus, will not just appear' (Pollard *et al.*, 2008: 149), but is the result of a process that is largely initiated by the teacher and mutually negotiated by teacher and pupils (Pollard *et al.*, 2008: 149), and because there is a range of organisational and interactional routines to choose from, the working consensus constitutes a key area where teachers exert 'influence, make choices and take stances on their work and professional identities' (Eteläpelto *et al.*, 2013: 61).

When describing Ellie's classroom, it is important to state that the working consensus outlined above is not without tension. That is, on the one hand, 'through negotiating the working consensus, the children recognize the greater power of the teacher' (Pollard *et al.*, 2008: 149). On the other hand, even though a consensus has been established, from the teacher's point of view, this needs to be renegotiated sometimes and with certain children. Thus, in Lines 83–84, 'they do need to go and turn their cards', Ellie refers to a behaviour monitoring chart that every class in her school has in place, and which is a common practice in many primary schools in England. About three or four times per day, the teacher asks a child to 'turn the card' to a 'yellow warning'. Her pedagogical approach, however, and the working consensus that the teacher has established provide a learning environment where the children have the opportunity – to a certain extent – to take and experience responsibility for their learning. Her classroom illustrates how the teaching/learning routines, which she organises, can partially be seen as a manifestation of her general teacher agency, while reciprocally, this environment contributes to her teaching and the productive and relaxed atmosphere in her classroom.

3.2 Mike's Classroom: Personal Involvement in Writing

94   After the break, children are coming in from the playground.
95   Mike counts down to ensure that everyone is focusing. He explains organisational details about an
96   upcoming trip [...].
97   'If you don't behave, you won't be coming on the trip'.

(Fieldnotes Y5, Castle Primary, 23 January 2017)

At the start of many lessons in Mike's classroom, the pace signals some urgency. The counting down and quick use of a boundary, or even a sanction marker (Lines 95 and 97), are characteristic in this respect. 'I have done quite a few years with supporting NQTs [newly qualified teachers], and I think that a lot of people – they do think that behaviour isn't hugely important' (Interview, 30 January 2017: Lines 27–29); '[the children] know it is all because I want them to do well, every single one of them. And I think that is what people – teachers sometimes get wrong, is the fact that they don't have that sense of compassion along with the strict rules' (Interview, 30 January 2017: Lines 126–129). The way Mike describes his working consensus by including a comparison with other teachers resembles Ellie's description, even though the two working agreements differ considerably. The following lesson part illustrates a related feature that is typical of the way Mike runs his classroom:

98   The teacher displays the learning objective: 'to write a grieving paragraph'
99   about a character in a longer story they had read the previous week.
100 The children are asked to write about how the disappearance of one character affects the story's
101 main character, Johnny. Several children start writing, while most wait.

102   Mike gives examples of emotional language, linking it to the frightening setting of an abandoned
103   warehouse. He talks in a very engaged way, adding expression by acting out some movements a bit
104   and by facial expressions.
105   '...to evoke this in the reader' ... He explains that each description will get a 'tear ranking' out of five.
106   Mike reads a text from the IWB as modelling, clarifying some of its words and phrases.
107   [...] he explains the success criteria.

(Fieldnotes Y5, Castle Primary, 23 January 2017)

The overall pattern of the lesson's main teaching follows the interactive whole-class teaching, as described previously for the other classroom. However, the interactive components are designed differently, resulting in another form of relationship between the teacher's and the children's voices. Mike begins to give examples in a notably engaging way (Lines 102–103) before displaying his longer model text (Line 106), in which he draws on some of the ideas used in those examples. In his words, 'We try in Year 5 to model every time and not just model the right thing but model how we think of putting stuff together' (Interview, 30 January 2017: Lines 330–331). Mike's teacher's voice is a more central point of reference than Ellie's, both in terms of presence and 'physical' audibility in a classroom that is much smaller and in which the group tables cover the whole room except a tiny reading corner and regarding the teaching arrangement itself. This arrangement *begins* by providing the pupils with examples and a model text (Lines 102 and 106). A co-construction of knowledge and a dialogical principle is less evident than in the literacy lesson reported from the Year 4 classroom, but Mike's teaching setting creates a particular atmosphere:

111   The atmosphere is somewhere between a literacy lesson and a writing workshop. The teacher
112   keeps asking three or four more questions about the main character's experiences and emotions;
113   eight or nine children put their hands up.
114   More children seem to start writing on their small whiteboards.
115   All write now, while Mike carries on asking stimulating, guiding questions
116   without children answering, 'Why has the mission become more challenging without Toule?' [...]

118   After approximately ten minutes, Mike asks children to read out sentences from their whiteboards.

128   The teacher gives feedback, praising and encouraging. He is very lively and energetic.

129   As an aside to me, 'You can't teach that by adjectives etc., you can only spread it' […].

134   Mike explains with another aside, 'That is the hardest bit now, to be quiet, not to be intrusive'.

(Fieldnotes Y5, 23 January 2017).

Significantly, there is some flexibility in the transition between the teacher's instructions and his use of the modelling text (Line 106), on the one hand, and the children's commencement of writing, on the other hand. Different children seem to decide for themselves at which point they begin with their writing; some respond right away with first notes (Line 101), while others join in later (Line 114) before eventually all children are working on their paragraphs (Line 115). As in Ellie's lesson, there is a bidirectional flow of ideas, where the teacher asks questions to stimulate ideas (Lines 111–112 and 115–116), and the number of pupils who put their hands up each time is relatively high, with almost one-third responding (Line 113). However, the children's ideas are presented *after* the model text and are not written down by the teacher; in this sense, they have a different function for the writing process than in the other classroom, where the teacher wrote down the contributions of the children in the main teaching phase.

The overall character of this literacy lesson seems to result from this flexibility of transitions between the lesson phases and, foremost, from the lively, encouraging feedback Mike gives the children (Line 128). During the lesson, there was no situation in which he addressed behaviour, mirroring the intensive and very focused writing atmosphere in the classroom. The teacher was involved here with his own writing skills by presenting the model text and the story about Johnny and Toule, which was his own work. Therefore, his two comments (Lines 129 and 134) must be seen in the context of this investment, highlighting his positioning along a 'teacher–writer/writer–teacher' continuum (Cremin & Baker, 2010). Mike offers clear views on teaching writing – his aside in Line 129 on the status of grammar teaching being an expression of this. To understand teacher agency here, it is helpful to include the teacher's professional interest and personal involvement in writing. The active atmosphere evoked around the children's writing by organising a (partially) workshop-like setting, which he maintains by praising the pupils' ideas and encouraging their voices throughout, is an important component of Mike's general teacher agency. This agency is mediated by classroom routines, which are influenced by the teacher's choices regarding this writing setting. In addition, his second self-ironical aside (Line 134) indicates an awareness that to be successful, this setting depends on a certain balance between his voice as teacher–writer and the children's voices.

3.3 Hira's Classroom: The Everyday Task of Multitasking

9   Monday morning, the children line up loosely, in front of the three-storey Victorian building that
10 stands in the middle of a huge playground. Most parents leave the playground; others just
11 retreat to chat with other parents [...].

14 The classes start moving in single files, children chatting, teachers ensuring that everyone is
15 moving, while latecomers hasten towards the queues. The teachers navigate their classes
16 into the different doors and up the narrow staircases [...].

18 Hira gives the children time to settle in for the early morning work [...].
19 'There shouldn't be such noise'. She tells the children to sit next to someone
20 they have not sat next to before.
21 Then, she counts down and takes the register [...], while the children answer multiplication problems.

(Fieldnotes Y3, Victoria Primary, 12 June 2017)

Arguably, the small institutional routine of the register is as much a factor of practicality – for attendance and in case of a need to evacuate the building – as it is symbolic. On the one hand, it brings the child's name and voice together by acknowledging their presence when their name is called out, and a mutual greeting between teacher and child takes place. Hira mentions this aspect of daily recognition, greeting and voice in relation to children who are new to the English language: 'You know, I ask them "How do you say hello?" and things and then when taking the register, they get familiar – little things that matter to them. It puts a smile on their face' (Interview, 27 June 2017: Lines 414–416). On the other hand, the fact that the register is taken in such a way that greetings overlap with the expectation that the children are already working on a task (Line 21) points to the working consensus and positions the children as pupils, that is, as members of a group that comes together for the purpose of learning in school. Yet, simultaneously, the teacher's Monday morning routine of letting children choose where they sit during the week acknowledges the social aspect of children's relationships as a salient feature of the classroom. The pedagogical tenet that each child needs to find their voice within the group of children for their learning to succeed is palpable here and symbolically addressed in such moments. In a sense, the variety of voices children answer with when their name is being called can be understood as a literal reminder of *voices being heard*.

In this vignette, the children work on the multiplication of two- and three-digit numbers by a one-digit number:

41 The maths task is differentiated for four different groups [...]
44 The teacher sits next to the flipchart and works with the Pebbles group. Daniel comes over from
45 his table with a worksheet, stands next to Hira and asks for clarification.
46 She appears to speak with him and works at the same time with the Pebbles group.
47 Daniel returns and Hira continues with the small group on the carpet.
48 After a while, she calls out, 'I should not hear the voices of anyone except the investigation
49 table'. She tells a boy off, '... or you go next door'.

(Fieldnotes Y3, Victoria Primary, 12 June 2017)

As in Ellie's classroom, Hira uses the carpet space for whole-class teaching or work with a small group of children. However, the length and interactive character of these phases vary considerably. The carpet phase is often short, and its main focus is on explaining directly and modelling rather than on co-constructing meaning with a more interactive approach. Small whiteboards are not used, but in some lessons, the carpet phase includes interactive elements, such as Think-Pair-Share. This extract contains an aspect that is very significant for Hira's classroom and therefore for her general teacher agency: while she is scaffolding the Pebbles group of seven children through the grid method for multiplication, she simultaneously explains something to Daniel, who left his table to ask her something (Lines 44–46). Moreover, when she is working with one group, she also supervises the other children and thereby controls the working consensus, about which she reminds all children here (Line 48) before addressing one boy explicitly (Line 49). This might be described through Kounin's (1970) classical concepts of 'with-it-ness' (the teacher's awareness of what is happening in the entire classroom) and 'overlapping' (the ability to attend to two or more issues simultaneously), which have been compared more recently with 'multitasking' (Pollard *et al.*, 2008: 311). It could be seen as comparatively trivial to absorb such ordinary aspects of the profession into the concept of the teacher's general agency. However, in line with the fact that the existence of different needs is a condition of many primary school classes, this extract points to 'multitasking' as a more fundamental feature, highly relevant in this classroom.

'[S]ometimes I feel I would need to rip myself in half', explains Hira to characterise situations when she has to respond to the different needs of children in her classroom all at once (see Chapter 1, p. 24). This points to issues pertaining to the broader institutional context. Thus, the teacher mentions that besides a child who is on the autistic spectrum and has a learning support assistant (LSA) on a one-to-one basis, other children need additional support. For example, Wakil has been statemented and shares an LSA with another pupil, but this LSA has been assigned to the child in another class.

252 I don't want him [Wakil] to
253 get there where for one hour he doesn't do nothing, so I am taking the
254 decision, you know, where I, I need to work with the boy, or someone works
255 with him, but he has consistency [...]
256 he likes to
257 be familiar with the people, he either works with me or Marian [LSA].

(Interview, 27 June 2017)

The teacher also refers to another boy, Salim: 'I really, really try and it upsets me that he can't access as much as I want him to and he really doesn't and I feel sad that he is not seen [...] straight away. It is so difficult to get children seen, you know, if something is wrong with them' (Interview, 27 June 2017: Lines 240–244). The number of LSA hours allocated to her class has been reduced since the previous year, and she shares an LSA with another class instead of having one post assigned solely to her class, as had been the case previously. Overall, the situation mirrors the increasing financial pressure local authorities face in England in providing support for pupils with special educational needs and disabilities.

Yet, two aspects are relevant when considering Hira's general teacher agency as it emerges in the classroom. First, she stresses her agency in 'so I am taking the decision' (Lines 253–254) and expresses her emotional involvement in 'it upsets me...' and 'I feel sad that...' (Lines 241–242). Second, an understanding of a teacher's general agency needs to include the small choices within teaching routines, as argued in Ellie's context, *and* the small decisions that are required to ensure the everyday management and smooth running of the classroom for all children. On the whole, Hira's Year 3 classroom underlines the relationship between the classroom and general teacher agency, as conceptualised within the sociocultural perspective. While the classroom is a space where the educator practises and experiences her teacher agency, it is at the same time the proximate context that *mediates* such agency. This is important for further exploration of teacher agency in multilingual pedagogies because it allows for conceptual consideration of the classroom's complexity as a mediational means for teacher agency. In other words, the conditions of the respective classroom – the material resources, the number of staff, the class size and many other circumstances – can *facilitate* professional choices and stances but also *restrict* them. Foremost, the classroom – understood as part of broader sociocultural conditions – frames and configures a teacher's priorities. Consequently, 'the possibilities for formulating certain problems, let alone the possibilities for following certain paths of action, are shaped by the mediational means employed' (Wertsch *et al.*, 1993: 342).

3.4 Heather's and Kelly's Classrooms: EAL Responsive Routines and Teaching of Text Genres

10   [Monday morning], the Year 3s go the short distance to their classrooms on the ground floor.
11   The children come in very calmly and Kelly greets them. The room is very small
12   but everyone seems to be used to it; children go straight to their tables [...]
16   They start their handwriting task, while the teacher is taking the register [...]
21   They start to work on a spellings worksheet for the new week.
22   Kelly asks, 'Where do you put a prefix, at the front or at the end?'
23   Six children put their hands up to answer.
24   Then, they talk about the meaning of the prefix 'dis'. [...]
27   With all ten words, it is done in a similar order: the teacher reads the word, a child
28   explains, the teacher repeats or recasts the explanation and gives another example
29   of the word used in a sentence. [...]
34   Then all the children start on the worksheet. [...]

(Fieldnotes Y3/1, Bird Primary, 20 November 2017)

The activity sheet for spelling (Line 21) is designed through closely cooperation by the Year 3 teachers Kelly and Heather for an entire week (in contrast to the commercial schemes or animation video schemes frequently used in primary schools in England). It encourages the learning of word meanings that the children might not be familiar with.

The procedure in Lines 27–29 – modelling pronunciation by the teacher, explanation by a child followed by the teacher's repetition or a recast with more clarity and, finally, an additional explanation by contextualising the word in another sentence – provides the pupils with the opportunity to hear the respective word several times and in various contexts.

644	TQ:	[...] I understood that you have also – one of the intentions you also have
645		apart from the spellings is to enhance their vocabulary at this point [...]
649	Kelly:	Yeah I think because I want them to learn because the other thing is, if they
650		understand more words, they can access a more complex text and then
651		everything gets more interesting, you know, they need that and I think, if we
652		just stick to learning simple, simple, sample, sample by rote, you know all those
653		words, like if you go in some classes elsewhere, then you restrict them, they
654		don't learn about meaning [...]
655		but then if they expand their vocabulary, their
656		writing is amazing.

(Interview, 7 December 2017)

The teacher seems to explicitly claim her agency regarding this integrated approach to teaching spelling, grammar and vocabulary with 'I want them to learn…' (Line 649) and, as with Ellie and Mike before, she uses a contrasting juxtaposition to underline her own position: 'like if you go in some classes elsewhere, you restrict them, they don't learn about meaning' (Lines 653–654) while linking her and her colleague's approach to children's learning in literacy more generally (Lines 650 and 656). The element of discussing meanings in an interactive way whereby they are jointly constructed between children and the teacher is also characteristic of the guided reading sessions, the daily 20–30 minutes set aside for explicitly teaching the various competencies needed for reading comprehension. The following extract is representative of the teaching of writing in Kelly's and Heather's classrooms:

| 73 | Kelly displays the learning objective on the IWB: 'Can I understand the features of an |
| 74 | instruction text?' and explains that they would look at instruction texts again today. |

75	She points to the poster on the wall that lists features of instruction texts. [...]
78	The teacher gives the children three minutes to talk with their partner about what
79	they remember about instructions.
80	All children seem to be very motivated and start straightaway to talk with their partner.
81	Children are asked to write an equipment list for cleaning an animal of their choice
82	and a bullet point list of steps for the instructions. They would write the text tomorrow.
83	'If you cleaned a sabre-toothed tiger, what precautions would you take?'
84	Children start to write.
85	In the first three or four minutes some children are talking about their ideas,
86	almost everyone seems to have an idea. [...]
89	Kelly is going around ensuring that all the children understood the task and are working.

(Fieldnotes Y3/1, Bird Primary, 27 November 2017)

The learning objective is worded in an accessible way, and with the first-person pronoun (Line 73), it seems to be aimed at voicing the learning objective from the children's position. Like at the beginning of Ellie's lesson (p. 55, Lines 146–147), the teacher directs pupils' attention to the *features* of the text. However, while Ellie's literacy unit was based on a book, the unit to which this lesson belongs focuses on 'instruction texts', and the emphasis is on teaching and learning language-related, structural and thematic features of this genre. Thus, the lesson excerpt is situated within a genre approach to teaching writing, following the requirements that were part of the National Literacy Strategy (DfEE, 1998). Even though the New National Curriculum for English primary schools in 2014 shifted the emphasis from genre/text type to 'writing for purpose and audience', the genre approach continues to underpin medium- and long-term planning in schools to ensure that pupils can access a wide range of texts and learn the features of different genres to use them in their writing (NLT, 2017).

The introductory reading text for the unit was '*How to wash an elephant*', and teachers and children worked on questions like 'What is the purpose?' and 'How does the text tell you what to do?' to find features of instructions. To recap the features, Kelly uses two routines that the two teachers frequently employ. She points, although only as a gesture here, to the mini poster (Line 75), a device used for recording key vocabulary taken from the classroom talk while teaching, sometimes drawing visual organisers – a teaching strategy opposed to, say, putting up prefabricated posters, as is often the case in classrooms. Furthermore, short group talk is used, even though it is not shared here with the whole class afterwards, as it is common practice in Think-Pair-Share activities (Lines 78–80). Arguably, Kelly signals her trust that the children learn from each other in such a situation. The task in this lesson (Lines 81–82) is part of a typical sequence, which consists of reading and working with a model text, writing in response to it, some modelling by the teacher, detailed planning of their text (sometimes including text mapping), writing their text and editing it. In this lesson, Kelly gives an example by way of illustration to emphasise that children can be imaginative in their instruction text (Line 83), yet does not provide any further details. Moreover, how pupils start writing here (Lines 85–86) is characteristic of the two teachers' working consensus: pupils have a short time in which to settle into a new task or are encouraged to share ideas with a partner. Yet, after a few minutes, they are expected to start working quietly in two very small classrooms whose size literally does not provide teachers and children with much space in phases of individual work to negotiate the established quiet working consensus.

90   The atmosphere can be described as: all children working purposefully;
91   this is more or less so –
92   that is, some also talk a bit once in a while. It is all done in a very relaxed manner,
93   in a sort of self-controlling, but also somehow naturally flowing way.
              (Fieldnotes Y3/1, Bird Primary, 20 November 2017)

While the relevance of teaching genres is widely acknowledged, its concrete practice has also been critiqued for following somewhat rigid and formulaic methods where pupils are taught a set of conventions (e.g. Cremin & Myhill, 2012; Myhill, 2001), neglecting the fact that pupils should not merely reproduce written genres but 'use them to make sense of their life experiences and their literacy experiences. In this way, writing is an act of social meaning-making: learning to make meaning in texts is about learning to make meaning in contexts' (Cremin & Myhill, 2012: 12). This assertion points to an issue of fundamental pedagogical relevance for the perspective of voice in teaching writing. Furthermore, for the exploration of teacher agency in multilingual pedagogies, it is important to note that the question of whether and how schools can strive to create links to the experiences children make out of school and at home is not an aspect that emerges 'only' regarding the language and literacy experiences of plurilingual children. Similar to the consideration put forward regarding the writing of the diary entry in Ellie's lesson, Heather addresses the current conditions of teaching writing in the English primary school. Her evaluation follows an interview passage, where she spoke of a learning support assistant telling her about the time when education policy allowed teachers more flexibility:

963   But I
964   find now we are so rigid in how we have to teach it [the writing] and then it's [the own text] at the very
965   end [of a unit]. Now we have modelled this, we have shown you how to do it, now
966   choose your own animal or whatever it would be [...]
968   we are not as, like, fluent with it and we sort
969   of keep control more because we have to prove this and show that.

(Interview, 16 March 2018)

This serves as an unequivocal reminder that questions of teacher agency in language and literacy teaching in a given classroom, and whose voice and experience become audible in the given timeframes, are inescapably embedded in broader contexts of education policy and societal power relations.

It is instructive to ask how the teaching routines identified here as characteristic of Heather's and Kelly's classrooms might relate to their general teacher agency. The approach of teaching language and literacy based on text genres is one in which teaching writing and EAL teaching approaches informed by systemic functional linguistics (e.g. Gibbons, 2002; Martin & Rose, 2008) overlap. Kelly's and Heather's use of the genre approach and EAL responsive elements as *integral parts* of other routines appear to contribute to their confidence when speaking of pupils who have recently arrived with little or no prior knowledge of English.

499   we – personally for me, I feel never nervous, I had so many times when
500   [headteacher] said, 'Oh, you have a new child starting tomorrow, no
501   English' and I just say, 'Ah, I've done it before'. They learn so quickly, as well.
502   You just have to – It's just being dedicated and finding the time. This is why
503   having an LSA in the classroom is so important as well. Because then you have
504   two of you. One of you can really push that [...]

513 […] whether the children have EAL, speak another language – then yeah . .
514 yeah and I think like just the way we teach sort of covers everyone really.
515 I always say, like assume they don't know and then you always – everyone is
516 going up to understand […]

(Interview, 16 March 2018)

The teacher articulates clearly her own professional experience in 'personally for me…' (Line 499), 'Ah, I have done it before' (Line 501) and 'It's just being dedicated and finding time' (Line 502), but also points out the institutional context as a precondition for this professional confidence: 'This is why having an LSA in the classroom is so important as well' (Lines 502–503). She describes the inclusive perspective of the teaching routines (Line 514) and explicitly states a maxim she acts upon in her teaching: 'I always say, like …' (Line 515). Regarding Mike's classroom, I argued that his personal involvement concerning writing is a component of his general teacher agency. For Hira's classroom, the small decisions taken to manage the everyday running of a classroom for all pupils are an important element of her agency. Regarding Heather and Kelly, an additional aspect emerges: the teaching routines described here can be understood as part of such agency, where the educators make choices and take stances on their professional work. However, what distinguishes Heather's and Kelly's agency from Mike's agency is the area to which it pertains. That is, for Mike, the area of *teaching writing* can be seen as a point of reference. In contrast, for Heather and Kelly, it is, on the one hand, more explicitly the *teaching of writing to bilingual children* as mirrored in the genre approach with a more general orientation and, on the other hand, with a more specific focus on bilingual children in what has been portrayed here as 'EAL responsive approaches' to the teaching of spelling and reading. Their routines are both *a result* of the teachers' choices and *a factor that enhances* their agency in terms of teaching the children in their classrooms. The approaches have evolved within the prominent status EAL teaching has in their school and are, in this sense, supported by the school's context and a manifestation of the teachers' collective agency. Indeed, Kelly acknowledged this linkage:

865 […] But if
866 you go to another school, it [as a pupil, to have EAL] can be a hindrance. They wouldn't – When I was –
867 being in other schools […] I was covering a
868 Year 3 for a day […]. And there was a boy in

869   there and the teacher said to me 'Oh, just to let you know, he doesn't do
870   maths [...]
872   because he doesn't speak English', and I was like, 'He can do maths though!'

(Interview, 7 December 2017)

Kelly pointed out how much the situation irritated her, while twice slipping in comments on her own school: 'Here it's different from other schools. Other schools *(mimicking, whispering)* '"Oh, my God, we got some – and they don't – and they don't speak English"' (Interview, 7 December 2017: Lines 898–900) and 'So it depends, where you are. Here it's an asset, elsewhere it's being seen as – you know, [the boy is seen as] a tool' (Lines 914–915). As previously mentioned, she uses the contrast to another school to emphasise her professional investment in the teaching routines, placing this agency explicitly in the context of her school. Thus, the extracts from these two classrooms help to understand the specific way in which *teaching routines*, *English as an additional language teaching* within its 'mainstreaming' paradigm (Costley, 2014; Leung, 2016), and *teachers' general agency* can be seen as interconnecting. For the further exploration of teacher agency in multilingual pedagogies, it is helpful to note not only this nexus but also the ambiguity that is notably involved here. That is, the overall precarious status of EAL teaching in the English education system (see Section 2.5) can lead to a situation where routines around the teaching of EAL may develop as an area in which teachers achieve and exert agency. In this domain, they need to make choices regarding teaching and organisational routines, and such decisions become all the more necessary given a general lack of conceptional, curricular and organisational clarity around this teaching and a scarcity of staff resources allocated. As Ellie described,

361   [...] some of them arrive speaking no English at all and
362   there is very little support for them. I mean [EAL coordinator] does her best to take them
363   to the phonics [lessons]. That's in the morning, but then after, in every other lesson they
364   are just in the classroom and there is no extra support. And sharing the TA [teaching assistant]
365   you know, having them once a week in the morning, it really means actually
366   you can't provide that much support. [...]

(Interview, 8 February 2017)

Teacher agency in regard to EAL teaching must be understood as precarious itself; that is, the way teachers' choices are framed by the classroom and the context school can either *facilitate* or *constrain* this agency. A comparable constellation emerged regarding Hira's general teacher agency that is both facilitated and restricted by the conditions and complexity of her classroom and the challenges it poses.

This chapter explored the classroom as a contextual factor for teachers' general agency, based on the assumption that such general agency is the prerequisite for agency in relation to a more specific pedagogical domain like multilingual pedagogies, while naturally a transition from one to the other cannot be taken for granted. The key features of teacher agency identified here – the small choices made in language teaching and in the running of an inclusive classroom, the establishing of a working consensus and the teaching of EAL-related approaches, in which teachers are involved with professional and/or personal investments – were discernible across all five classrooms, though sometimes less prominent or relevant in a specific situation or subject area. Thus, as features of teachers' general agency, they can provide points of orientation for exploring further what might constitute or contribute to teacher agency in multilingual pedagogies. At the same time, examining the status quo allows for contextualisation of teacher agency in multilingual pedagogies in relation to primary school pedagogy more generally. As became evident in the descriptions of the classrooms in this chapter, aspects like dialogue, the interplay and power differential between children's and teachers' voices or the affordances for pupils to bring their experiences into school are pedagogical principles and considerations that are both relevant to and contested in current primary school pedagogy (in England) more broadly.

As educators exercise their agency by influencing classroom routines, making particular choices and taking stances on their work and professional roles, the classroom in its entirety emerges as *constituting* a means that mediates teacher agency. Crucially for teacher agency in multilingual pedagogies, the exploration of classroom conditions revealed their profoundly ambiguous nature as simultaneously *facilitating* and *constraining* teacher agency.

4 Schools: Contexts for Multilingualism?

Tracing how teachers respond in their classrooms to students' multilingualism, this chapter explores the sociocultural context that schools provide on the institutional level for the achievement of teacher agency in multilingual pedagogies. Starting with the classroom – and the classroom as part of the institution of school – as the first element of the framework for teacher agency, the sections identify the prevalence of monolingualism, the dominance of an 'EAL discourse' and a symbolic acknowledgement of multilingualism as features that hinder the achievement of teacher agency in multilingual pedagogies. However, these features also involve some tensions and ambivalences, which – even though small – are relevant for understanding how such agency might be supported by making connections with other elements of the framework, i.e. the children's linguistic repertoires and voices, the educators' professional subjectivities and a 'pedagogical space' for multilingual pedagogies.

4.1 Multilingualism in the Classrooms

Across the five classrooms, monolingualism was dominant in the official classroom setting, while multilingualism was featured in 'unofficial' talk among children. That is, languages other than English as the language of instruction did not appear in teaching and learning activities initiated by educators: they were neither audible in the 'official' talk nor visible in written tasks or the resources provided. With the status of being the only exception, the following episode occurred in Hira's class in a unit about 'fairy tales' involving two children: Daniel, who had attended school in Romania and, about eight months earlier, had been entirely unfamiliar with English, and Sanba, who speaks Sinhalese at home and had arrived around the same time, having been schooled previously in Italy.

56 Daniel sits at his table and Hira gives him a reading booklet in Romanian downloaded from
57 the Twinkl resources. He reads the fairy tale 'Hansel and Gretel' in a Romanian version.

58 Daniel does not have anyone to listen to him but is reading for himself with expression.
59 It looks a bit like he is imagining someone listening. From his facial expression, it is obvious
60 that he is really enjoying it.
61 Afterwards, he goes out to work with the teaching assistant.
62 When coming back about ten minutes before the end of the lesson, he sequences the pictures
63 of the story.
64 I work with Sanba and Shahib. Sanba reads a simple [English] version of the story with a slow but
65 relatively reasonable and fluent pace. She reads with a very soft voice.

(Fieldnotes Y3, Victoria Primary, 20 June 2017)

There is no further information about Daniel's work with the learning support assistant on this day – she most likely read the same English version of 'Hansel and Gretel' with him as I did with Sanba and Shahib. Marian works regularly on phonics and reading with pupils new to English, mostly in an adjacent room. In this lesson, the teacher asked me to read and sequence the story with Sanba and Shahib. The contrast between Daniel, who visibly enjoys reading (Lines 58–60), and Sanba, while participating in reading practice and preparation for the sequencing task (Lines 64–65), is stark. Daniel brings his voice to the classroom, at least for himself, which allows for the experience of self-efficacy (Bandura, 1982) and a lively *reading voice* – the same voice in which he has acquired, performed and, importantly, experienced his reading skills before. This vignette illustrates what has been described in the first chapter as the inclusion of the bi/plurilingual speaker and their voice. It highlights the pedagogical necessity to consider the school as a place of language experience. In a translanguaging setting (preview in home language and reading the same text in English; e.g. Celic & Seltzer, 2013: 68), the child can experience his language as a resource (Ruiz, 1984/2017). Consequently, the affective and empowering elements of the reading experience are palpable here – not least because the Romanian text allows Daniel to read *independently*. The child's enjoyment and the audibility of his competent, expressive reading in the classroom show that for Daniel, at this point of being an emergent bilingual pupil, 'reading voice' and 'Romanian voice' are interrelated. This perspective, which recognises Daniel's voice as simultaneously a 'reading voice' and 'Romanian voice', highlights the importance of what was outlined in the first chapter as a requirement for multilingual pedagogies: the necessity to create learning arrangements where pupils can experience the paradigm of 'language as a resource' when *'doing something'* with their full linguistic repertoire in school. Thus, this episode from the Year 3 classroom is an instructive instance of how *voice being heard*, use of linguistic repertoire, and pleasure concur as part of a child's language and learning experience.

Given that the monolingualism of the official classroom talk and learning tasks was omnipresent throughout the classroom observations, the following interview extracts show how the teachers assess the current situation. Being a bilingual English and Bengali speaker, Hira was asked whether she would use Bengali with the seven Bengali-speaking children in her class.

532   I, hm, I don't know, I don't really use Bengali with other children – although

533   sometimes they speak to me in Bengali, they do speak to me in Bengali but

534   I think on a day-to-day basis, I don't think I do . hm . anything with language,

535   you know apart from that they learn French, we don't do anything with other

536   languages.

(Interview, 27 June 2017)

After Ellie explained, as quoted at the beginning of the first chapter, that children were not encouraged to use their other languages besides English, she described a one-off event:

219   [...] like with our culture week that is our big thing where they

220   come in, they talk about their own culture, they dress up in their traditional

221   clothes, speak the language, they teach their friend that sort of thing. But it's

222   not all the time. That is one dedicated week [...]

226   TQ: How did the children perceive it, did they enjoy it?

227   Ellie: Yeah, they do. They don't really get that much of a chance . to speak about their

228   home language within lessons. [...]

244   I mean they talk in their own language, I saw them, between them, but not very

245   often. I don't think we encourage the use of their home language.

(Interview, 24 March 2017)

Finally, Heather:

445 I talk with them about their lives and
446 the different languages they speak and the countries they visit and their
447 families. And I do ask 'Do you speak to your...?' like 'Can you communicate
448 with your nan?' [...]
452 But I never talk to them about how – like
453 learning the language. I never I never feel like I am interested – Like *(with emphasis)* I am
454 interested but maybe the children don't think I am interested because I never
455 say *(imitating)* 'How would I say that in Polish?' or 'How do you say that in
456 Urdu?' or something.

(Interview, 16 March 2018)

The teachers' evaluations confirm what could be inferred from the observations as a monolingual status quo in the classroom. However, another aspect that is instructive for questions around teacher agency also emerges: the educators hint at a kind of tension or friction that exists in their interactions with the children described here. In Hira's case, there is a tension between children who speak occasionally to her in Bengali, whereas she interacts with them as part of a school described as 'we don't do anything with other languages' (Lines 535–536). In Ellie's extract, there is friction between the one-off event of the school's 'culture week' and the usual routines, where 'they don't really get that much of a chance to speak about their home language within lessons' (Lines 227–228) and where the school does not 'encourage the use of their home language' (Line 245). Heather, finally, reflects on the tension between the fact that she talks with children about their languages but does not make their plurilingual voices heard in the classroom.

These tensions can be best understood as surfacing at the periphery of the official classroom; that is, they are neither part of the classroom routines nor do they belong entirely to the realm of language practices among pupils but are part of the interpersonal space within which educators and students interact, knowledge is developed and identities are negotiated (Cummins, 2000: 44). In this sense, teachers and children enact the phenomenon that has been described concisely as compartmentalisation of the use of their languages on the part of the children and institutional silence on the part of the official school (Kenner & Ruby, 2012: 2). The educators themselves did not use a term like 'tension' or 'friction', and this is relevant for understanding teacher agency in this context, as it points to the relatively small significance such tensions have for them in comparison to other aspects of their professional life. Yet, regarding the dominance of monolingualism in the classrooms and in relation to the institution of school as a location where linguistic repertoires encounter official language ideologies, it is not only important *that* teachers mention these tensions but also *how* they express them. In all three extracts, the teachers convey a short evaluative reflection on the use of the children's languages in school, and those reflections shift towards a more definite proposition: Hira reinforces, 'I think on a day-to-day basis, I don't think I do...' (Line 534), to 'apart from that they learn French we don't do anything...' (Lines 535–536), which broadens the references from the time aspect 'day-to-day basis' and her own classroom into a more general assessment about the whole school (throughout her interviews, Hira uses the pronoun 'we' to indicate whole school approaches). Ellie formulates her views rather hesitantly, with a long pause at the beginning, 'not particularly. . . . . I don't think we do encourage it that much in lessons' (Line 218). She then incorporates the perspective of the children, stating, 'they don't really get that much of a chance...' (Line 227), before concluding and reinforcing her assessment with the repetition, 'I don't think we encourage the use of their home language' (Line 245). Finally, in the last extract, the interpersonal character of the space in which teacher and children talk about languages, and in which plurilingual voices are potentially heard or not heard, is even more noticeable. Heather explicitly includes the perspective of the children: 'Like [...] I am interested but maybe the children don't think I am ...' (Lines 453–454). These teachers combine the description of the monolingual state of their teaching and the 'official' classroom with a reflective attitude that will be discussed further in Chapter 6. At this point, it is key that such reflections – and the implicit acknowledgement of tensions around the monolingual status quo – were articulated in relation to the educators' own experiences and interactions with their plurilingual pupils. Seen within the framework for teacher agency in multilingual pedagogies, these tensions concern the relationship between the elements 'classroom', 'children's linguistic repertoires and voices' and 'teachers' professional subjectivities'. The monolingual condition of the classroom renders its walls impermeable to children's plurilingual repertoires and voices, thus constraining the teacher's agency to implement multilingual pedagogies. However, at the periphery of the official classroom, teachers experience friction that can lead to productive reflections, thus potentially facilitating teacher agency in multilingual pedagogies.

Another similarity across the five classrooms is *multilingualism in the 'unofficial' talk among children*. The distinction between 'official'/'unofficial' talk and spatial aspects of language use has been addressed in studies on plurilingual children in primary schools (Bourne, 2001; Fashanu *et al.*, 2020; Kenner & Ruby, 2012) and in the concept of 'safe houses'. Canagarajah (2004: 121) understands 'safe houses' as spaces (and domains of time) that are comparatively free from surveillance by teachers, such as asides between pupils, passing of notes, small group and peer activities and sites like the playground. Examples of such spaces could also be found in the five classrooms: in the reading corner, Sonia and Adriana talking in Romanian; sitting on the carpet, Adriana scribbling a note to her friend in Romanian on a small whiteboard; on the playground, Adriana and Bianca talking for a while in a space with some privacy; or, in the corridor, Destiny speaking with her younger sister in Twi. In the participatory activities, the children talked about using their languages other than English 'off-task' and also for learning purposes, and their perspectives on their language repertoires will be reported in Chapter 5. For the development of multilingual pedagogies and an exploration of teacher agency, the distinction between official and unofficial talk and the related aspect of space is relevant for two reasons. It makes it possible to consider what kind of talk or use of texts – including different languages – is planned and provided for by the teacher in the official classroom. Additionally, it facilitates an analysis of the classroom simultaneously as *one* space and as differentiated, consisting of *various* places where language repertoires and ideologies come into contact differently, and where their meanings might be negotiated in diverse ways.

4.2 Multilingualism in the Schools

The focus now moves beyond the individual classroom to consider the three schools – Castle Primary (Mike/Ellie), Victoria Primary (Hira) and Bird Primary (Kelly/Heather) – as the classrooms' institutional contexts, in which the teachers' responses to the multilingualism of their students are embedded, thus covering a further aspect of the framework developed for understanding teacher agency in this study. As outlined in the first chapter, the individual classroom and the school are both understood here, overall, as the *micro level*, where teacher agency in multilingual pedagogies is enacted. The role of the *meso-level* actor can be taken up by any institution that provides guidance for such pedagogies, or alternatively, it might be assigned to a knowledgeable actor in a school. In the English educational system, such an arrangement, in which the school becomes a meso-level actor, must be seen as the result of an education policy that, for decades, has weakened and dismantled the role and influence of Local Educational Authorities (Ball, 2013a: 87–89, see Section 2.5) Therefore, it also points to the societal conditions around mono- and multilingualism that are understood as the *macro level* in this exploration of teacher agency.

Similarities in the responses of the three schools to the children's multilingualism relate to the following areas: (1) multilingualism in the school environment; (2) provision and procedures for English as additional language learners; (3) multilingual resources and artefacts; (4) contacts with complementary schools; and (5) modern foreign language teaching.

(1) All three schools mentioned the diversity of their communities at the beginning of the introductory texts on their home pages. At Castle Primary and Bird Primary, this was underscored by figures provided about languages: children speak about 40 and 50 languages, respectively, across the schools. Correspondingly, multilingualism was prominently visualised on signs beside the entrances, which showed the word 'Welcome' together with translations in about a dozen languages and different scripts. In Victoria Primary, a similarly designed poster was placed in the reception area. In addition, in the reception area of Bird Primary, handwritten signs in various languages were displayed, with photographs of those staff members who spoke the respective language(s).

In the corridors and halls of the three schools, multilingualism was visible in four types of displays. First, displays and mini posters referred to the *'Welcome' theme* and had been downloaded from online publishers. Second, displays showcased children's *work from modern foreign language learning* (children's letters from an exchange with a class in France at Castle Primary, and texts in response to a picture book and concrete poetry texts at Bird Primary), and these displays had been designed with great care. Another kind of display belonged to the approach of *'Language of the Month'* (LoM) or 'Language of the Term', showing words and greetings of the respective language, sometimes together with a map, a flag or other illustrations. 'Language of the Month' originates from Newbury Park Primary School in London, which developed free accessible resources, including an activity booklet (Debono, n.d.), word cards and video clips in which children introduce greetings, simple questions and numbers in many languages. How the teachers in this study handled the 'Language of the Month' resources will be addressed in more detail in the last section of the chapter. Furthermore, mini posters with a simplified version of British Sign Language (BSL) could be found in two schools: at Castle Primary, a 'sign of the week' was used in assemblies and put up in the classroom, and at Bird Primary, a template with greetings in BSL was supplemented by the current 'Language of the Term'. Finally, multilingualism was visible in *topic-related displays* that showcased artwork and texts by children and included labels with keywords in different languages. There was one example of such a display at Castle Primary in accordance with its school policy. Similarly, at Bird Primary, topic displays in a Reception class and a Year 1 class had been annotated by the teachers with the languages they spoke, Arabic and Gujarati, respectively, in line with the school's EAL policy that mentioned the inclusion of children's languages on displays.

(2) In all three schools, the role of the EAL coordinator was taken up by teachers who taught young children. At Castle Primary, the coordinator was a part-time teacher in Year 1, who also taught French in Key Stage 2; in Victoria Primary, the EAL coordinator was a teacher and phase leader in Early Years; and at Bird Primary, the EAL coordinator was a Year 1 class teacher and Key Stage 1 lead. At school admission, the parents are usually asked about a child's 'first language'. This language is recorded in the statistical system, with only one option to fill in. The procedures for children who arrived with no or little English were organised similarly in all three schools. They were assessed using the five-point scale for EAL proficiency (DfE, 2017), which was an official requirement when the study's fieldwork took place. These children were taught in class, with only the teaching of English phonics organised separately. At Castle Primary, the EAL coordinator worked with a group of 12 children every morning for 20 to 25 minutes on phonics and grammar. Three children from Ellie's class took part in these lessons, but the teacher explained that she only had a learning support assistant one morning per week, without other additional support. In Victoria Primary, an LSA worked with children in groups of two, from different classes across a year group, on phonics and reading. In Mike's class and Kelly's and Heather's classes at Bird Primary, there were no emergent bilingual children at an early stage of learning English. However, in their school, the phonics lessons for pupils new to English were also taught separately.

The five educators' descriptions of how English as an additional language and multilingualism had been addressed in their initial teacher education appeared to mirror the precarious situation described in the first chapter. Mike had attended a Teaching English as a Foreign Language course before working in South America. He also mentioned an in-service training session run by the EAL coordinator in school but had not attended any other training specifically addressing multilingualism (Interview, 30 January 2017: Lines 477–483). Similarly, Ellie remembered that multilingualism did not feature in her training (Interview, 8 February 2017: Lines 604–606). Hira's teacher training did include multilingualism, but her description suggests that it had been addressed in a very limited way: 'We did look at it in teacher training having all the different needs, and obviously the bilingual learners are not the only needs' (Interview, 27 June 2017: Lines 431–432). In her school, an EAL training organisation had run an INSET session at the start of the school year. The situation, however, was different for the two teachers at Bird Primary, as their school provided EAL in-service training for other schools. Thus, Bird Primary operates as a meso-level actor regarding the EAL domain, and the EAL responsive approaches described in the previous chapter can be seen as part of this meso-level expertise. Other approaches that fall into the category of EAL responsiveness were the text-mapping method and differently shaped signs that symbolise the various parts of a sentence, which were used often in Key Stage 1, sometimes in Year 3 and also in MFL lessons. The context of Bird Primary may be understood as the school explicitly communicating an ethos of multilingualism. In this sense, the staff members' *'I speak ...'* signs in the reception area were meant both symbolically as a reflection of this ethos and practically for parents who need to communicate with someone who speaks their language. Moreover, the school drew on these linguistic resources when a child new to English had an informal chat with a staff member who spoke their language to get a general understanding of their language and communication skills.

(3) During the observations, the children and teachers in the five classrooms did not use multilingual materials, except in the episode described at the start of the chapter and in the modern foreign language lessons. As none of the schools had a library room, they used bookshelves in the corridors instead, and those, in addition to the bookshelves in the classrooms, contained only books in English. There were apparently only a few resources in languages other than English. They were either intended for younger children (e.g. at Bird Primary, a Reception class teacher mentioned a trolley for the Early Years/Year 1, from which parents could borrow books, including bilingual editions, on Fridays), or they were meant only for new arrivals with no or very little English (Interview Heather, 12 January 2018: Lines 459–463). In Ellie's class, no dictionaries were used for the emergent bilinguals, a fact that Hira also mentioned, linking it to the issue of time pressure. When asked whether she would use dictionaries for these children, she replied, 'I haven't. Sometimes it depends [...] but I need to use it more, the dictionary' – *You would like...?* – 'I would like to use it more because sometimes you get so engrossed in – to get something in their books that it's "Okay, let's do it...", then you forget about [the dictionary]' (Interview, 27 June 2017: Lines 469–475). The teacher did, however, mention her usage of tablets to look up words or that the LSA would occasionally provide audio stories – but this was not part of the data from the observations. Overall, the situation around multilingual resources and artefacts appears inconsistent regarding resources for newly arrived children and emergent bilingual pupils. The usage of such resources may also depend on the respective theme, as with the fairy tale episode before. However, in line with the observations and the class teachers' descriptions of the monolingual status quo of their classrooms, it was evident that there was no regular or systematic provision of multilingual resources within the schools on an institutional

level and that such use was not developed into a regular practice or more independent learning routines on the part of the emergent bilingual children or the other plurilingual children.

(4) None of the three schools had contact with the complementary schools that some of their pupils attended. This fact clearly deserves research in its own right, but such an enquiry was beyond the scope of the present study on teacher agency. As part of the fieldwork, I visited two complementary schools mentioned by children (here and in the next paragraph, some languages are not named to allow for anonymisation). Although the notes from these short visits do not permit a suitable analysis, it appears useful to report here the view of one headteacher that points to the broader context of educational policy and linguistic power relations. When asked whether she considered it desirable to develop contacts with the primary school attended by a considerable number of her pupils, the headteacher explained that in lessons, her pupils recognised content from their learning in the primary school and mentioned that sometimes they 'could tell their teacher'. Yet, any interest on her part in such contacts had ceased when, some years before, she had enquired about the possibility of a GCSE but was officially informed that there were not a sufficient number of pupils to take it (Fieldnotes, 27 March 2017: Lines 34–39).

(5) Modern foreign language teaching was organised in different ways at the three schools. At Castle Primary, the pupils learnt Chinese in Key Stage 1, taught by a student on a governmental scheme from China; in Key Stage 2, the children learnt French. At Victoria Primary, the pupils started to learn French in Year 3, taught by specialist teachers from an agency organisation that also provided physical education and dance lessons at the school. At Bird Primary, French was taught from Year 3, while another modern foreign language was taught from Year 1 to Year 6. All the doors in the school were labelled in English and these two languages. Although I took fieldnotes in some MFL lessons, this did not, for various reasons, happen with sufficient consistency. In Year 5 at Castle Primary, French was currently not being taught due to a lack of staff. At Victoria Primary, it was not possible to obtain informed consent from the external specialist teacher. Due to these inconsistencies, the study focused on the agency of class teachers. As the few notes taken in MFL lessons had not shown the use of languages other than English and the modern foreign language taught, they have not been included in the data analysis.

In conclusion, the three schools constitute sociocultural contexts that acknowledge multilingualism in their environment and support the learning of newly arrived EAL learners by providing additional staff resources within the possibilities and limits of their current staffing situations. In Ellie's and Hira's classrooms, however, the schools did not, on the whole, provide bilingual resources to support emergent bilinguals.

Moreover, the schools offered neither a meso-level context that would provide guidance nor a micro-level context that would provide resources for teachers' activities within approaches of multilingual pedagogies that address *all* plurilingual pupils or, in fact, all children.

4.3 An EAL Discourse

From the outset, when contacting schools, the research process needed to handle the issue of terminology. To avoid jargon or channelling certain perspectives, I used phrasings such as: 'My study aims at exploring what the role and agency of teachers is, and how it develops in classrooms where many children bring with them more than one language' (email to Castle Primary, 6 December 2016), outlining in everyday language the perspective of the speaker and the linguistic repertoire to circumvent the usage of pre-established categories, such as the first or second language, and other labelling processes potentially involved. The phenomenon described in this section emerged when teachers replied to the question, 'Many of the children you teach are bilingual or multilingual. What does this mean to you?'; for example, in Mike's response:

291 Well, it is inspirational to start with. You know, when I am standing there and
292 there are – I mean it is one of my great regrets that – not learning another
293 language, I mean maybe one day I will but – Standing there in front of the
294 children where you know you have got seven, eight, nine different languages
295 represented in the classroom. It is pretty inspiring, isn't it, as an adult standing
296 there. Ahm, in terms of the provision we provide, I think it is about modelling
297 the right use of English, it is about ensuring that, if there are any patterns [...]
298 from – [...]

302 [...] so it is about picking up on those, making sure that
303 they get an immediate feedback, whether it is verbal or whether it's written,
304 and again that is very important,
305 but –, ahm, EAL learners, so we are constantly turning around and looking, are
306 they okay

(Interview, 30 January 2017)

The teacher answers with an evaluation (Line 291, 'it is inspirational'; Line 295, 'it's pretty inspiring'), in which he contrasts the children's language skills with his own language experience. In addressing this experience, Mike combines a physical description of the classroom (Lines 291–292, 'I am standing there and there are – '; Lines 293–294, 'Standing there in front of the children...') with a description of how he feels about his monolingualism. He mentions his language experience in other interview passages as well, and this will be discussed further in Chapter 6. For the analysis here, it is beneficial to note two aspects: first, the teacher chooses to refer to the children in a rather abstract way: 'You have got seven, eight, nine different languages represented in the classroom' (Lines 294–295). The children as plurilingual *speakers* are somehow omitted, a possibility that, arguably, had been offered in the question. Second, in Line 296, and chiming with this omission that almost seems to be marked by a hesitant 'Ahm', Mike shifts to speaking about teaching strategies, 'in terms of the provision...', before introducing the term 'EAL learners' together with the assertion that the children's learning needs are met (Lines 305–306). Afterwards, he describes teaching strategies such as modelling and think-alouds, which are integral parts of his lesson routines (Interview, 30 January 2017: Lines 326–339). One may argue that this emphasis on the educator's apparent omission is overstated. Nevertheless, it needs to be seen in conjunction with his response when asked whether he knows which languages the children speak:

355   I should do . *[smiles]* I should do . no . . but I can find that out that . . I mean I
356   know we have got R. – three or four, I would say, speak Lithuanian. I
357   would say, we got maybe four Polish . children, ahm, a couple of Roman –,

(Interview Mike, 30 January 2017)

Mike appears to be aware that he 'should' know about the languages the pupils speak. However, he does not specify where this expectation originates by referring, for example, to school procedures, pedagogical purposes or beliefs. In this way, the children who speak English and other languages are not seen as plurilingual speakers but chiefly or exclusively as EAL learners.

While Mike referred to *all* multilingual children in his class, as this had been offered implicitly by the question, his colleague Ellie responded differently to 'Many of the children you teach are bilingual or multilingual. What does this mean to you?':

361   Challenges, definitely, ahm, some of them arrive speaking no English at all and

362   there is very little support for them. I mean [EAL coordinator] does her best to take them
363   to the phonics. That's in the morning, but then after, in every other lesson, they
364   are just in the classroom and there is no extra support. And sharing the TA,
365   you know, having them once a week in the morning, it really means actually
366   you can't provide that much support. So it is challenging [...]

(Interview, 8 February 2017)

The teacher describes what she sees as an unsatisfactory teaching/learning situation for herself and the three children, who are at an early stage of learning English. In other words, when asked what her pupils' bi- or multilingualism mean to her, Ellie also does not address multilingualism among the 'many children' in her class. Instead, she focuses on what is currently most pressing for her.

Similarly, Hira also refers to children who arrived with no previous knowledge of English in her answer:

334		They have another language, they are from another culture, so obviously, they
335		are not familiar with the school, they are not familiar with the language, you
336		know, sometimes it is an alien place to be so that – *[laughs]* I was, I was
337		probably an EAL child, when I was in school, I was an EAL child. But it's quite,
338		hm, scary. [...] it is not that you are not smart enough; it is
339		just not getting the language [...]
343		[...] sometimes you know you think
344		of EAL – they are not smart, they don't have it all. But it's not that. It is about
345		just the language, making sure that they understand the thing, or they can use
346		their words, their language so that they can understand [...]
350	TQ:	So you were
351		using your Bangla with him? [referring to a child the teacher had mentioned before]
352	Hira:	Sometimes, if he didn't understand, I did with him. [...]

(Interview, 27 June 2017)

Hira picks up the phrasing of 'bilingual and multilingual' pupils by referring to children without prior knowledge of English. She changes from a third-person perspective (Lines 334–335, 'They have another language...') to a first-person angle and includes her own experience in this shift: 'I was probably an EAL child, when I was in school, I was an EAL child' (Lines 336–337). In doing so, she seems to identify with this language experience (Line 336, 'sometimes it is an alien place to be' and Lines 337–338, 'but it is quite, hm scary'). However, by laughing and using an adverb of probability, she expresses a certain ambivalence towards using the term 'EAL child'. In lines 338–339 and 343–345, the teacher articulates the risk that the children's learning potential may be misjudged before returning to her perspective as a teacher who supports their learning, saying that 'they can use their words, their language' (Lines 345–346) and mentioning her practice to sometimes speak Bengali with a child who has just started to learn English (Line 352).

For understanding both teacher agency in the context of English as an additional language teaching and how plurilingual children are thematised by educators, it is instructive to look at how Heather and Kelly responded to the questions which included the term 'bilingual or multilingual children': the question, quoted before, asking what it would mean for them to teach bi- and multilingual children, and how, in their view, these children would experience school? Heather replied, 'I think it's fascinating for me and it has taught me so much [...] learning how to teach EAL through visual – I use my hands so much now I am like –, you know, text-mapping, things like that – even if I would go into a school with only English children, I would do it that way' (Interview, 12 January 2018: Lines 369–375). Similarly to Hira, Heather described the experiences of children new to English as 'probably quite terrifying at first' (Interview, 12 January 2018: Line 487) and remembered two boys from Syria some years earlier: 'They had no English whatsoever and they were absolutely terrified – but they were also terrified because of what they had experienced and they had been rushed across' (Interview, 12 January 2018: Lines 495–498). She recounts how one of them told her, before moving to another town, 'I was so scared, I knew nothing and I couldn't explain anything. But I always remember that you were smil – you used to smile at us and you said we were brilliant to my dad' (Interview, 12 January 2018: Lines 502–505). In line with her interview passage in Chapter 3, Heather implicitly indicates her professional investment in teaching emergent bilingual pupils here.

Regarding multilingual children's experience of school, Kelly explains:

845   I think here it is more usual to be multilingual, everyone is different, everyone
846   speaks another language, everyone apart from me. So they don't think

847   anything else, it's just part of who they are. And I don't think, there is –
848   it doesn't make you a second-class citizen in any way. [...]
859   [...] I think in this school [...]
860   it's really cool and it's just being part of this school. I think the children that
861   only, 'only' speak English probably feel a bit left out. But you know the whole
862   thing is, our academic language is English.

(Interview, 7 December 2017)

Kelly refers to her own linguistic repertoire (Line 846) and thematises multilingual children's experience of normalcy in the school while emphasising it as a particular feature of her school (Lines 845 and 860) before she asserts the exclusiveness of English as an academic language (Lines 861–862). An omission similar to that found in Mike's account, quoted above, occurs when the pupils' multilingualism is acknowledged, even explicitly, as 'it's just part of who they are' (Line 847), whereby they are not thematised as *speakers in the classroom*.

Across all interviews, it proved challenging to talk about multilingualism in the classroom among those children who were not at an early stage of learning English as an additional language. Either the teachers omitted them as plurilingual *speakers* or focused in their answers on those children who had arrived relatively recently without prior knowledge of the English language. It is helpful to understand this phenomenon as an 'EAL discourse'. Butcher *et al.* (2007: 485) use the term 'EAL discourse' in their study of policies concerning initial teacher training and bilingualism. Although not explicating the notion itself further, they see the dominance of 'EAL' in teacher education terminology as reiterating 'a deficit view of bilingualism, equating it to or confusing it with EAL support' (Butcher *et al.*, 2007: 486). The term EAL discourse also proves productive in analysing what occurred throughout the interviews: an omission of the linguistic repertoire of multilingual children and a restriction of their multilingualism to EAL learning aspects. It has been asserted that a discourse constructs its object in a certain way, thus limiting other ways in which the topic could be constructed (Hall, 1992: 291) and that '[t]he knowledge which a discourse produces constitutes a kind of power, exercised over those who are "known"' (Hall, 1992: 294–295). This notion of discourse effectively describes the phenomenon illustrated by the extracts above, where plurilingual pupils are constructed as children whose plurilingual repertoire can be neglected in school or limited to aspects of learning English as an additional language. The official classroom 'knows' about these children, and it is necessary to ask how the EAL discourse would need to be shifted within primary school pedagogy to develop multilingual pedagogies further in those classrooms – a process in which terminology, 'knowing about', pedagogical practices and resources for these practices cohere.

'EAL discourse' provides a useful analytical lens within an enquiry of teacher agency when, as above, employed with a view to the power/knowledge nexus explored by Foucault (e.g. 1971), where power is seen as having both an oppressive *and* a productive side. The *repressive* element of the EAL discourse is how it overlooks the linguistic repertoires of plurilingual children. However, in exploring teacher agency, it is equally relevant to consider how *productive* the discourse is and how it interrelates with other discourses in education. Thus, it must be asked what the EAL discourse accomplishes from the teachers' point of view and how their responses are linked to the materiality of the discourse, in other words, its institutional manifestations in the form of practices and organisational procedures (see also Ball, 2013b: 21). The EAL discourse is productive in the sense that it generates categorisations and statistics, which provide the basis for the allocation of additional funding and facilitate other procedures described previously in Section 4.2, such as the assessment of newly arrived pupils or particular teaching practices, with a net effect of strengthening the discourse.

Two aspects of teacher agency are significant in this regard: EAL-related practices and procedures enable teachers and schools to respond to the needs of children and allocate some resources. At the same time, and as argued in Chapter 3, educators need to exercise agency in the provision of EAL teaching, not least because the provision is often precarious and contested. Furthermore, the provision for children at various stages of learning English and mastering more text genres as they progress through their schooling is closely interwoven with discourses of *social justice* in education. In the extracts quoted here, all the teachers mentioned, in various ways, aspects implicitly linked to equality: 'EAL learners, so we are constantly turning around and looking, are they okay?' (Interview Mike, 30 January 2017: Lines 305–306); Ellie's evaluation 'that there is no extra support' (Interview, 8 February 2017: Line 364); Hira's description of the risk that pupils new to English may have their learning potential misjudged (Interview, 27 June 2017: Lines 338–344); Kelly's statement 'it doesn't make you a second-class citizen in any way.' (Interview, 7 December 2017: Line 848); and finally Heather's recollection of teaching two pupils who had fled a war. The five teachers foregrounded their confidence in teaching children new to English, including EAL responsive approaches or, more generally, using scaffolding/modelling strategies in teaching reading and writing (Mike, Heather and Kelly). They also emphasised the difficulties in supporting those pupils who arrived with no previous knowledge of English (Ellie and Hira). It is extremely relevant for the exploration of teacher agency in multilingual pedagogies and for an understanding of these educators' professional stance that in all interviews, 'English as an additional language' is *not* seen as a deficit on the part of the children or their families but understood as normalcy in school and as a routine part of the professional task of a teacher.

The following extract, however, indicates the limitations of this stance when Kelly responds to the question about whether she was aware of which languages apart from English her pupils speak:

671 Yeah, yes, I mean, we know when they came to school, and we treat – then
672 we teach them all as an EAL child. So the idea is that they need to learn a good
673 model of English and still keep their heritage language going. Not saying, 'You
674 mustn't speak that'. So I wouldn't say that it doesn't matter that – what
675 language they speak. But the approach will always be the same [...]
676 [...] So, like, I wouldn't do anything different for a child whose
677 home language is French than for a child whose home language is Polish.

(Interview, 7 December 2017)

The EAL discourse allows the teacher to articulate her pedagogical position within a social justice perspective. Chiming with her explicit statement about multilingualism, which 'doesn't make you a second-class citizen in any way' (p. 90, Line 848), Kelly dismisses an overly discriminatory practice (Lines 673–674). She appears to be able to disregard the contradiction emerging from the fact that the normalcy of children's multilingualism is acknowledged – as before in 'it's just part of who they are' (Line 847) – while the monolingual norm is simultaneously affirmed with 'I wouldn't do anything different for a child ...' (Lines 676–677). Yet, her wording 'So I wouldn't say that it doesn't matter that – what language they speak. But...' (Lines 674–675) almost marks a kind of gap, where this very contradiction becomes palpable – not unlike the small 'gap' in Mike's 'It is pretty inspiring, isn't it, as an adult standing there. Ahm, in terms of provision...' (p. 86, Lines 295–296). In this way, the teacher can advocate the normalcy of multilingualism on the part of the children, along with their participation in monolingual learning. The normalisation of multilingualism is divided or halved in a stance that assigns multilingual normalcy to the children. Conversely, the monolingual ideology and pedagogy of the institution of school can remain largely unaffected.

Correspondingly, the EAL discourse could be found in the school policies of all three schools, where multilingualism was mentioned either only under the heading of EAL provision for new arrivals or within sections on monitoring procedures of the learning environment and displays. Ultimately, the discourse must be seen as an expression of the dominant orientation towards subtractive bilingualism in second language teaching. Its omission of children's plurilingual repertoires and its reduction of pupils' multilingualism to EAL learning aspects result from and reproduce the dominant monolingual lens through which pupils' bilingualism has traditionally been seen. The inherent logic of the monolingual lens is that once a child starts to be seen as more or less successful following the lessons, their bilingualism fades into the background. Therefore, the three instances mentioned in the extracts above – Mike's 'disclosure' that he does not know which languages the pupils in his class speak and his reference to the statistics stored in the office (Line 355), Kelly's assertion that 'the whole thing is, our academic language is English' (Lines 861–862) and Hira's description of how she used their shared language, Bengali, with a newly arrived child 'Sometimes, if he didn't understand…' (Line 352) – are effects of such an EAL discourse, although at first glance and considered separately, they seem to be located on very different planes.

The 'EAL discourse' is also a *hindrance* for teacher agency in multilingual pedagogies in that it *preforms* how the linguistic repertoires of the children and language ideologies – and, as Brigitta Busch (2017a: 52) phrases it, 'discourses on language and language use' – come into contact with each other in school. This discourse not only regulates that contact with children's multilingualism; seeing it more comprehensively, as the notion of discourse would suggest, also involves the teachers and their agency. Various institutional aspects, such as the fact that their training had addressed – if at all – only EAL teaching approaches, and the lack of meso-level elements for multilingual pedagogies, such as teacher guidance and provisions of teaching/learning resources, influence or impact their choices and actions.

In the enquiry, the 'EAL discourse' emerged from the interviews as a category in agreement with the status quo of classrooms and school policies, and, as such, it clearly constitutes a hindrance to teacher agency in pedagogies that evolve around plurilingual children. And yet, looking at the 'EAL discourse' – grounded in the current workings of how pupils' repertoires and the logic of a monolingual lens are brought into contact in schools – is also useful when asking what might *facilitate* teacher agency. Indeed, by including the aspect of 'power' and following Stuart Hall's assertion that a discourse 'limits the other ways in which the topic can be constructed' (1992: 291), it becomes possible to ask what may support a teacher in going beyond current dominant knowledge about plurilingual children and in 'knowing differently' concerning their current classroom. The EAL discourse considerably reduces the space for achieving teacher agency in multilingual pedagogies. It constitutes the status quo against which teachers speak about children's multilingualism, as illustrated in this chapter. As described in Section 4.1, the teachers hinted at a tension or contradiction that can exist in their interaction with their pupils, although they did not use such explicit terms. I have argued that this might be because they occur at the periphery of the official classroom and because such tensions have little significance for educators compared to other aspects of their professional life. Drawing on the perspective of the EAL discourse, such 'small spaces' of tensions or frictions – and, importantly, reflections that teachers articulate around them – might be seen as opportunities for 'knowing differently' about plurilingual children in the classroom.

4.4 A Symbolic Acknowledgement of Multilingualism

The EAL discourse did not render multilingualism entirely invisible within the three schools. On the contrary, multilingualism featured in their linguistic schoolscapes, and the following examples – a book box, the use of the 'Language of the Month' ('LoM') resources and the aspect of representation of multilingualism in the school environment – point to a symbolic acknowledgement of multilingualism as a shared feature encountered in those classrooms, halls and corridors.

At the beginning of a new term, the EAL coordinator at Castle Primary hands out a box with books tailored to each class and a mini poster titled 'Welcome to Year…'/'In our class we speak…', listing the languages as recorded in the school's statistical system (Figure 4.1).

Figure 4.1 A4 poster in Mike's class

The books are from an EAL resources pool, corresponding to a checklist in the school's Teaching and Learning Policy that mentions dual-language books. In Mike's class, half of the assortment comprised picture books, including three bilingual ones, some non-fiction books on countries and narratives or traditional stories set in other countries. These books were arranged on the windowsill beneath the mini poster, whereas in Ellie's class, the box remained unpacked until the end of the term. However, neither pupils nor teachers mentioned these books when discussing the use (or non-use) of different languages in the classroom.

All three schools used the 'Language of the Month' approach. In Bird Primary, it was explicitly stated in the EAL policy as part of valuing the languages a child speaks. The 'LoM' displays, with word cards including a transliteration into Latin script and a translation, were found at different places and in various sizes. In Ellie's class, the doors of a cupboard were used for the word cards (Figure 4.2), whereas there was no

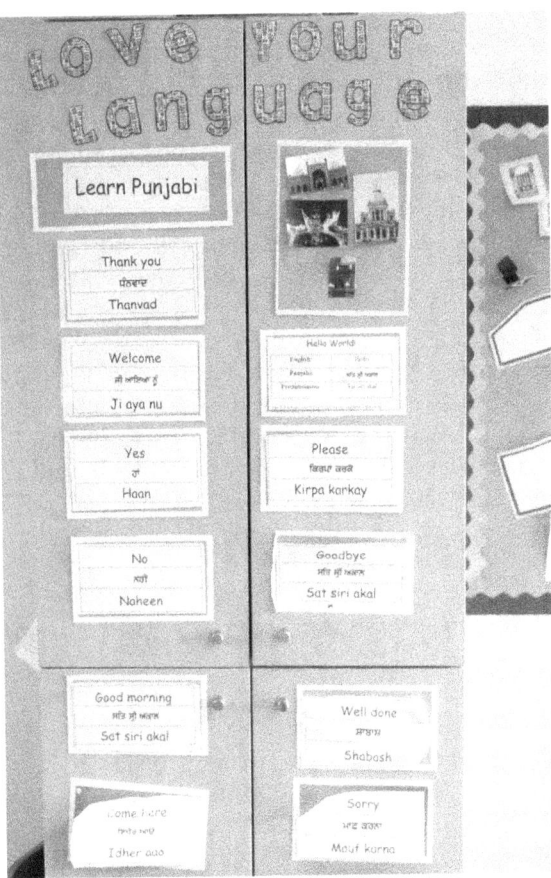

Figure 4.2 LoM display in Ellie's class

designated area for this in Mike's classroom. In Hira's Year 3 classroom, there was a large display with the current 'LoM', and similar A4 posters with two other languages. Kelly and Heather used their classroom doors for the mini posters. When asked how, in his opinion, multilingual children would experience school, Mike answered, 'I think actually, it is celebrated here, you know, we got "Language of the Month" and you know we are a hugely diverse school' (Interview, 30 January 2017: Lines 414–415). When asked what the 'LoM' approach entailed, he explained,

431   It is a display that goes up in the classroom. I haven't actually seen it
432   recently, so it might be a question for [name of EAL coordinator]. I know […] she is in Year 1
433   quite a lot. So maybe that's not been done that much this year. But last year
434   'Language of the Month' was mentioned in assemblies […]

(Interview, 30 January 2017)

Mike describes 'Language of the Month' as a practice in assemblies and not for the classroom (Lines 433–434). However, it is not only Mike who appears to express uncertainty. Ellie also described her ambivalence about the approach: 'We get the "Language of the Month" and how do you say these words? – we don't know' (Interview, 24 March 2017: Lines 496–497). It turned out that the teacher was not aware of the video clip resources (Interview, 24 March 2017: Lines 498–510), and both her and Mike's excerpts point to some gaps in the communication among the teachers involved or the EAL coordinator's workload, as mentioned by Mike (Lines 432–433).

Ellie's ambivalence was shared by Heather in Bird Primary, who explained that she also does not use the resources for teaching basic words in the given language: 'We have "Language of the Term" which you probably haven't [seen] because I am terrible – But it's on the door' (Interview, 16 March 2018: Lines 306–307). Asked for the reason, she refers to her own experience:

321   I don't know […] But you know
322   one thing when I was at school, I hated learning languages because I got told
323   that my French accent was really bad and it put me off. And I get really
324   scared that I am pronouncing things wrong […]

(Interview, 16 March 2018)

In these three classrooms, the 'Language of the Month' resources were not used, although for different reasons (the other two teachers did not mention 'LoM'). Mike appears not to be aware of the approach as a pedagogical practice for the classroom; Ellie was not aware of the existence of video clips and the possibility of making languages audible; and Heather, whose school used different 'Language of the Term' material without audio resources, did not have the confidence to use it (Lines 323–324). However, the teachers' descriptions indicate a more general and conceptual issue, and Mike's explanation, 'It is a display that goes up in the classroom' (Line 431) and Heather's 'But it's on the door' (Line 307) epitomise the symbolic take on multilingualism that prevails in the schools. In other words, the multilingual 'Welcome' signs, the unused boxes with books and the 'LoM' resources, which remain merely a display, are elements of a *symbolic* acknowledgement of the children's multilingualism that does not correspond to practice in the classroom. Thus, Mike's and Heather's formulations capture literally how 'symbolic multilingualism' provides a place for the children's languages on the sidelines of the official classroom because, contrary to other displays, which usually showcase children's work, displays around 'symbolic multilingualism' are *not* the outcome of classroom activities.

As with the EAL discourse, it is useful for an exploration of teacher agency to ask what symbolic multilingualism might accomplish on the part of the teachers. Following the suggestion that visibility is a prerequisite for recognising multilingualism first 'as a fact, then as a value and, finally, as a possible added value' (Gajo, 2014: 116), symbolic multilingualism fulfils the function of making the languages 'visible'. It allows Mike to state that 'it [multilingualism] is actually celebrated here, you know we got "Language of the Month"…' (Lines 414–415) while simultaneously concealing the fact that these languages do not have a 'value' for activities and learning in the official classroom. If, therefore, symbolic multilingualism succeeds in making the monolingual status quo less visible and cushioning possible pedagogical tensions by giving educators the impression that some use is made of their pupils' languages, this must be seen as a hindrance to the achievement of teacher agency in multilingual pedagogies.

The phenomenon of symbolic multilingualism is closely related to how multilingualism is represented in classrooms and school corridors. Talking about the experiences of newly arrived pupils, Hira explains:

408 […] we are always
409 being told, you know, try to make it a bit – you know, the classroom a bit more
410 familiar, put their flag up, you know, 'Hello' and – like on my door I have 'Hello' […]
413 in different languages; 'Hello', have little words, you know, that remind
414 them of their country […]

(Interview, 27 June 2017)

Figure 4.3 Door of Hira's Year 3 classroom

The teacher refers to a way of representing multilingualism that was present in all three schools: the words 'Hello' and 'Welcome' were written on small national flags or, as Hira describes here, on flags in the shape of speech bubbles placed on doors or in entrance areas (Figures 4.3 and 4.4). This aligns with findings from other linguistic schoolscapes (e.g. Laihonen & Szabó, 2017) and reflects the dominant language ideology, which associates 'languages' with nation states, imagining them as monolingual. Hira describes this type of representation of languages in the context of welcoming new pupils. In terms of the exploration of teacher agency in multilingual pedagogies, two aspects are important. First, concerning the school as a context for multilingualism, it is a highly contradictory gesture that aims to include plurilingual children while simultaneously excluding them through the chosen type of representation (Quehl, 2022). Representing multilingualism through national flags might be well-intentioned. However, as used on Hira's classroom door and throughout the schools, it is pedagogically

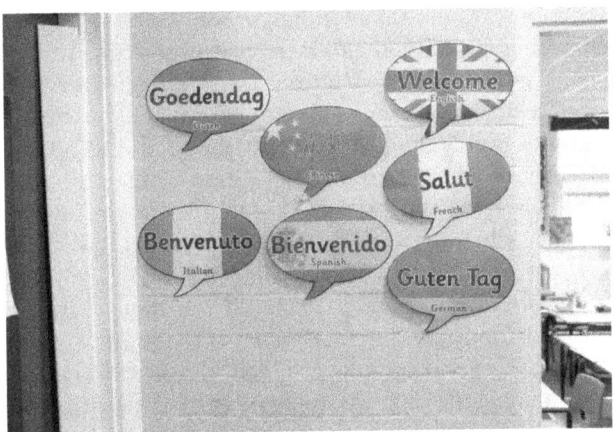

Figure 4.4 Display next to Kelly's classroom

problematic due to its risk of othering processes in the thematisation of multilingualism. This aspect will be addressed further in the next chapter. Indeed, it does not consider the many pupils who live their plurilingual normalcy without linking it to nation-states – in other words, '[f]rom the bilingual child's perspective, the language they have belongs to them and not to the nation or the state' (García & Lin, 2016: 10). Second, it is pertinent regarding teacher agency that these flags and 'Welcome' signs are printouts that have been downloaded from online publishers, drawing attention to the question of accessible resources and the amount of time that educators have at their disposal.

While symbolic multilingualism must be understood as a hindrance to the achievement of teacher agency in multilingual pedagogies, the examples in this section might nevertheless be used to move beyond the status quo and to ask how they could be developed further in ways that would facilitate agency. That is, what kind of reading resources could the box contain, how could the 'Language of the Month' resources be used in more interactive ways that connect with the pupils' and educators' language experiences, and how could teachers and children represent multilingualism in ways that reflect those experiences? Finally – and contrary to buttressing the status quo by pretending that 'something' is done with multilingualism – the very existence of the symbolic acknowledgement of multilingualism might be seen as conveying a particular, yet minor, ambivalence in schools towards their monolingualism – not unlike those frictions that teachers described in Section 4.1.

This chapter addressed the ways in which schools and educators respond to their pupils' multilingualism. The official classrooms were characterised by a prevalence of monolingualism while the teachers also described frictions around the monolingual status quo, yet below a level where they would perceive them as relevant tensions. It is significant for the achievement of teacher agency in multilingual pedagogies that the reflections offered by teachers were formulated in relation to the interactions with their pupils. Turning to the school as an institutional context for such an agency, I found that none of the schools took on a meso-level role by providing bilingual resources in the two classrooms with emergent bilinguals or offering guidance and resources for multilingual activities that address all plurilingual pupils. Drawing on the definition that agency is achieved when teachers can choose between different options, restricted when the options are limited, and absent when there are no options available (Priestley *et al.*, 2015: 141), it is possible to conclude that the teachers were *hindered* from achieving agency in multilingual pedagogies because the sociocultural context school did not provide conceptual and material resources that would allow them to choose between different options. Furthermore, two other hindrances have been identified: the 'EAL discourse' and 'symbolic multilingualism'. Both features belong to the institutional level of the school and convey its ambivalence vis-à-vis multilingualism. The 'EAL discourse' allows teachers to respond to the needs of emergent bilinguals as English learners and to teach them as a regular part of differentiation. However, this discourse was identified as a *hindrance* to teacher agency in multilingual pedagogies because of its restrictive view of the plurilingual child as either an 'EAL learner' or a quasi-monolingual pupil. With a similarly paradoxical effect on teacher agency, 'symbolic multilingualism' superficially acknowledges the children's multilingualism while rendering the monolingual status quo less visible, thus turning the acknowledgement *de facto* into a *hindrance* for achieving teacher agency in multilingual pedagogies.

5 Between the Monolingual Norm and Superdiverse Voices

This chapter explores the conditions of monolingualism and multilingualism in the five primary school classrooms in more detail. The findings presented in its first part allow for an understanding of what has been described in the previous chapter as the prevalence of monolingualism in the official talk and the use of texts in the classroom. In the second part, findings from the participatory activities with the children offer insights into the linguistic repertoires and language experiences of pupils. Following the framework for teacher agency in multilingual pedagogies, this chapter asks how the relationships between the monolingual norm and teacher agency, and between teacher agency and the children's linguistic repertoires and voices, can be understood. Finally, I discuss what the findings of this chapter mean conceptually for multilingual pedagogies in the primary school. The 'pedagogical space' of such pedagogies – proposed as the fourth element of the framework – is simultaneously a response to the children's superdiverse voices and a precondition for the achievement of teacher agency.

5.1 The New Monolingual Norm

The vast majority of fieldnotes taken in the five classrooms illustrate the schools' monolingual practices in the official classroom – a monolingual norm in English primary schools that has been thematised for more than two decades. Bourne (2001) describes how children learn quickly to navigate the classroom's 'monolingual habitus' (Gogolin, 1997), using their other languages only for informal talk. Kenner and Ruby (2012) use the term 'institutional silence' to portray a school environment where pupils learn to compartmentalise their linguistic repertoire contrary to their plurilingual practices at home, and Welply (2017) also views English monolingualism as implicitly expected in school rather than overtly formulated. Others, though, report school policies that explicitly prohibit the use of 'home languages' (Gundarina & Simpson, 2022; Pearce, 2012). As critical incidents, the following episodes can offer windows into how such a monolingual norm is shaped and negotiated, and how its nature can be understood. Such insights are instrumental for studying the school as a place of language experience, where linguistic repertoires and language ideologies come into contact, and where, in the process, the actors negotiate the meanings they ascribe to those repertoires and ideologies in school. These processes are of sociolinguistic and pedagogical concern, and their analysis helps to shed light on how teacher agency is involved in the monolingual status quo and can be involved differently in further developments.

5.1.1 'I said you must speak English': A norm in the making

The first two vignettes from Ellie's Year 4 classroom involve two emergent bilingual pupils, Adriana and Sonia, who had been new to English when joining the class approximately four and a half months before these episodes occurred. They spoke Romanian and had attended primary school in Romania before coming to London. The maths lesson had started two minutes earlier when Adriana, Sonia and Khadija were still attending the EAL intervention group (where they usually work on phonics) and focused on two-step word problems.

84   [...] Adriana, Sonia and Khadija are back from the EAL group.
85   Sitting at one table [...]
88   Starting to work, taking the question for 'the next step' from the IWB.
89   Sonia asks me something about maths; I am giving an example on the small whiteboard,
90   then she asks, 'Can I translate?'
91   She explains the task/my explanation to Adriana in Romanian.

(Fieldnotes Y4, Castle Primary, 10 January 2017)

The lens of stancetaking, as described in Section 2.4, offers insights into how Sonia signals her *positionality* and navigates the *meanings* that the two languages, Romanian and English, have for her in the classroom. Alexandra Jaffe (2009c) maintains that in bilingual contexts, a speaker has language choice as a stance resource and that the significance of this choice is related 'to the specifics of the sociolinguistic context, including the political economy in which the two languages circulate as well as ideologies about language and its relationship to individual and collective identity' (Jaffe, 2009c: 119). Sonia's and Adriana's classroom cannot be seen as a bilingual context, nor does Sonia have a bilingual repertoire fully at her disposal. Nonetheless, it is in this specific learning environment that the two children must find their positions as emergent bilingual learners. In the extract, Sonia initiates the interaction and asks for an explanation, which is given in English and also visualised on a small whiteboard with mathematical symbols and numbers (Line 89). Sonia signals both her intention to pass the explanation on to Adriana and to use Romanian (Line 90, 'Can I translate?'). By marking this switch from one language to another, several aspects of stancetaking are discernible. I understand the 'use of different languages' as the stance-object in this interaction, following the description that the stancetaker simultaneously evaluates objects, positions subjects (i.e. self and others), and aligns with other subjects regarding any salient dimension of the sociocultural environment (Du Bois, 2007: 163), and the add-on that such significant dimensions are not only material but can include language itself (Jaffe, 2009b: 5). Thus, Sonia's positioning consists of an evaluation that the use of Romanian is important for her friend's learning and of an alignment with the participant observer in the sense that she expects me to approve of this use of Romanian. By asking for permission, she positions herself as a pupil who needs to request approval before using Romanian and simultaneously as a bilingual speaker who takes care of her friend's learning by using their shared Romanian language.

However, a second episode from the same maths lesson can shed light on the complexity of the processes involved in Sonia's positioning. It followed a few minutes after the first vignette and was written down immediately after it occurred.

122	TQ:	Why do you sit next to each other?
123	Sonia:	She wants me to help her. She said help me.
124	TQ:	Do you speak Romanian, when you are helping her?
125		(referring to the situation above)
126	S.:	I don't speak Romanian. I speak English.
127	TQ:	Why?
128	S.:	She doesn't speak English. I said you must speak English.
129	TQ:	Why?
130	S.:	(shrugs)

(Fieldnotes Y4, Castle Primary, 10 January 2017)

Here, the object of the stance is not simply the use of the two languages in the classroom, but more distinctly, such usage *and* learning itself. A note of caution is necessary: as a participant observer, I initiated the conversation because the two children had changed their seats (Line 122, 'Why do you sit next to each other?') and introduced the theme of languages (Line 124, 'Do you speak Romanian when you are helping her?'). The second question was linked to the first episode. Yet, this could have evoked what Harré and Van Langenhove (1991: 402–403) call a 'forced self-positioning', which might trigger more easily the bipolarity of 'speaking Romanian'/'speaking English'. Nevertheless, even with such a qualification, the utterances help understand the child's positioning. Sonia's evaluation of using Romanian and English in this situation differs considerably from the first extract, as she is distancing herself from the use of Romanian. Giving a direct answer to the question, 'Do you speak Romanian?' (Line 124), she explicitly evokes her subjectivity and states it with some confidence: 'I don't speak Romanian. I speak English' (Line 126). She then highlights her stance towards speaking Romanian by positioning the other girl as a non-English speaker: 'She doesn't speak English' (Line 128). Sonia emphasises her own position even further by talking not only about Adriana but about the talk with her by way of 'accountive positioning', i.e. as talk about talk (Harré & Van Langenhove, 1991: 397). In doing so, she presents herself as someone who both cares about Adriana's learning and, as such, is in a position to give her some advice about language use: 'I said you must speak English' (Line 128). While Sonia used Romanian previously to support Adriana's learning in maths, she now appears to address the use of Romanian and English on the more fundamental level of learning in general. In the intertwined meanings of 'learning English' and 'English for learning', this constitutes the typical situation of emergent bilingual learners in school.

The shift from *using Romanian for Adriana's learning* to *learning English/English for learning* is crucial for Sonia's ongoing positioning regarding language use in the classroom and, thus, for understanding the continuous shaping of the monolingual norm. The object of Sonia's stance, which she evaluates and in relation to which she positions herself, is not *'a language'* or even *'use of different languages'* as before, but *'languaging for learning'* – as in '[p]eople language for many purposes' (García, 2009: 31). While Sonia's self-positioning is still in line with her previous positioning as a bilingual speaker who supports her friend's learning, she is changing the stance-object of her positioning towards the general learning in the classroom. Taking a stance vis-à-vis this learning, the pupil modifies her alignments – seen as a continuous variable, not as a dichotomy between alignment versus disalignment (Du Bois, 2007: 162) – both with Adriana and the participant observer. The researcher can be seen, in the context of Year 4, as roughly representing the classroom's arrangements. In these alignments – and articulated in 'I speak English' (Line 126) and 'I said you must speak English' (Line 128) – Sonia's identification with the subject position of a *successful pupil* becomes apparent. However, that subject position and identity as a learner, which the child imagines for herself, is bound to a classroom context where all official learning – except the modern foreign language lessons – takes place in English.

> [I]nstitutional contexts like schools heavily specify certain roles (student, teacher) and their interactional and linguistic prerogatives and patterns. Teachers and students may conform or depart from these conventions

(taking up diverse stances), but these conventions constitute a fundamental framework for the speech production and interpretation of those individual acts of positioning. (Jaffe, 2009b: 13)

It was characteristic of the institutional context of Sonia's (i.e. Ellie's) classroom and the other four classrooms that the monolingual norm was neither based on the claim that English is the only language nor on an assertion that English is the only legitimate language. Instead, the norm can be best described as 'English is the only official language for learning'. Sonia's 'I speak English' (Line 126) appears to express her aspiration for mastery of English and the wish to take up the subject position of the *successful learner*. Yet, this position is offered only within the discourse of subtractive bilingualism based on a monoglossic orientation as the dominant practice of EAL pedagogy (García & Flores, 2012: 234). That is, by striving for mastery of English and – in Butler's (1997: 116–117) understanding of subjection – for mastery of the subject of the successful learner, the child is simultaneously subjected to the classroom's 'new' monolingual norm. I use the adjective 'new' here to describe the norm because of its dual meaning: On the one hand, the norm is new for Sonia and Adriana, as they are confronted with a profoundly new language experience. Indeed, a transition into a new school setting or/and a process of international migration are frequently described in language biographies as significant moments in the lived experience of language, when someone becomes self-conscious as a speaker because the new environment questions their hitherto naturalised and unchallenged way of speaking (Busch, 2012). On the other hand, 'new' arguably points to the particular language ideological constellation that is operative here. Sonia is not subjected to the position of a monolingual speaker in the classroom but rather that of a plurilingual speaker who does not use her entire linguistic repertoire for learning in school. That is, the norm is not enforced in what might be seen as an 'old-fashioned' way via school policy or sanctions, as reported, for example, by Pearce (2012) or Gundarina and Simpson (2022). Instead, it is produced through a pedagogical setting that does not offer, for emergent bilinguals, any alternative to becoming monolingual *learners* in the classroom. However, in conjunction with the merely symbolic acknowledgement of multilingualism, the norm is ultimately strengthened, as described in Section 4.4.

Sonia's stancetaking in her primary school classroom demonstrates how by 'making a claim about language (use[rs]), speakers position themselves as members of social groups but also as knowledgeable participants of discourses on language' (Flubacher & Purkarthofer, 2022: 7–8, all brackets in original). Thus, language ideologies and discourses on language use translate both into attitudes and how one perceives oneself and others as speakers (Busch, 2017a: 52), and this lens helps trace the monolingual norm as seen from the children's perspective and their language experience. An understanding that Sonia's positioning and subjectification refer to being a *speaker* and a *pupil* is equally important for considerations of primary school pedagogy because it highlights that the context for the child's language experience is the (official) classroom *in its entirety*. Since the monolingual norm is an integral part of this classroom, where she is required (and strives) to position herself as a *successful learner*, the plurilingual speaker who does not use her entire linguistic repertoire for learning is the only position made available to Sonia. In the terminology of school and education policy, Sonia and Adriana are at an early stage of EAL. However, this stage is also a critical phase for learning what has been termed 'institutional silence' (Kenner & Ruby, 2012: 2) regarding pupils' multilingualism on the part of the school. Here, children become accustomed to compartmentalising their use of languages into the 'official' English language for learning purposes and the 'private' language for chatting with friends or supporting comprehension discretely, as in the case of the first vignette.

5.1.2 Recharging the monolingual norm as part of the working consensus

While the previous two episodes provide insights into a monolingual norm in the making for two emergent bilinguals, the episode reported in Chapter 1 ('Miss said, she needs to write in English', p. 11) constitutes a situation in which the norm is being 'recharged' for the many other plurilingual students, who have had either a bilingual primary socialisation, or have already acquired far more English skills or used English throughout their schooling as the language of learning. Following the findings presented so far, I want to argue that how the monolingual norm is shaped is best understood as part of the working consensus 'which encapsulates the idea of teacher and children negotiating interdependent ways of coping in classrooms' (Pollard, 1985: 158). The norm comprises features of the working consensus, as mentioned in Chapter 3; that is, the consensus is initiated by teachers and the greater power lies with them, while it also needs to be mutually negotiated between teachers and pupils. It is beneficial to understand how the monolingual norm operates in the context of Pollard's (1985: 190–194) proposition that within the existing unequal power relations, pupils have a choice between strategies of compliance, negotiation and opposition, including their corresponding shades. The findings from Ellie's classroom are, in this regard, in line with Bourne's (2001: 105) junior school study, where direct opposition could not be observed. From this angle, the new monolingual norm mediates between society and the school's power relations regarding mono- and multilingualism on the one hand and plurilingual children on the other, in that it acknowledges the fact of many students' plurilingual repertoires while warranting that the norm of monolingualism in the official classroom is maintained and reproduced.

Importantly, when children's linguistic repertoires come in contact with the norm in the classroom – within the working consensus – and when, as a result, the meanings of repertoires and ideologies are negotiated, such encounters do not occur in isolation but are interwoven with various pedagogical processes. These processes belong to what I earlier called 'the classroom in its entirety' (p. 75), being the necessary contextualisation for Sonia's experience as a speaker *and* pupil. Teaching and learning arrangements form a significant part of those other processes. Here, English language learning plays a relevant role; for example, when Ellie supports Sonia and Adriana in their work, when the pupils have the opportunity to use their emerging English skills during small group work, or when the teacher ensures that the two girls can occasionally contribute with their very brief answers during whole-class work. All these situations are framed by, and reproduce, the monolingual norm because their affordances for learning are made exclusively in English and without the provision of bilingual resources, such as dictionaries and online tools or other resources in Romanian. Yet, from the perspective adopted in Chapter 3 concerning 'voices being heard' – as a lens that connects pedagogy and multilingual pedagogies – these processes also constitute opportunities for those pupils to make their voices heard as emergent English speakers and, by becoming legitimate speakers in the classroom, to envision themselves as successful learners. However, Adriana, Sonia and Khadija in Ellie's class, along with Daniel and Sanba in Hira's classroom – five children who arrived around the same time in their new schools – had achieved very different positions in terms of their audibility in English. As the extracts illustrate, Adriana was more dependent on using Romanian than Sonia, and the same is true for Daniel in comparison to Sanba. Thus, the children's current experiences of being heard in school and envisioning themselves as successful pupils appear to differ considerably from each other. Finally, it is necessary to point out two preconditions existing in Ellie's classroom that work in favour of the audibility of Adriana, Sonia and Bianca as Romanian speakers: the working consensus permits pupils to talk during phases of individual work and children who share the same language sometimes have the opportunity to sit next to each other. Children can experience themselves as legitimate speakers of a language other than English in the classroom's 'private' spaces only if these or similar conditions exist.

This section has focused, so far, on showing how the classroom's monolingual norm is shaped and what 'work' it accomplishes on the part of the children. Now, the emphasis will shift to the relationship between the norm and teacher agency. Whereas a monolingual norm seems to be, by definition, a factor that *hinders* teacher agency in multilingual pedagogies, the following extract from an interview with Ellie addresses a situation that can – as a critical incident – shed light on what the norm accomplishes on the part of the teacher. I had asked her whether she had paired Adriana with Bianca in the afternoon lessons.

539 No, not really. Originally, I had paired them because they both speak
540 Romanian. But we had a bit of a drama, where it got stuck in translation
541 between Sonia's mum, Adriana, Bianca – and everyone thought – everyone
542 said something different because – and then it was said in English, and then it
543 got very jumbled. So what we said was we wouldn't ask Bianca to translate to –
544 like I wouldn't say to her specifically, 'Can you tell her in Romanian?' So, we
545 made that decision and we wouldn't do that. But obviously, if she *[laughs]*
546 they speak to each other in Romanian or – But it's not that we would instigate
547 that sort of thing [...]
550 But . I think . . they are actually probably doing better
551 from not being translated to because I found within the first few weeks they
552 were very reliant on Bianca saying it for them [...]

(Interview, 8 February 2017)

The teacher refers to a situation in which Bianca had been asked to translate for her during a conflict between Sonia's mother and Adriana. Without an English/Romanian bilingual adult in school at her disposal, Ellie was faced with a situation that she could not solve or control with her own language resources, as a teacher would often do with similar arguments. Whereas the conflict itself had occurred outside the domain of school, it was brought into the classroom and experienced as 'a bit of a drama where it got stuck in translation' (Line 540). As a response, the teacher established a kind of rule: 'So what we said was we wouldn't ask Bianca to translate to – like I wouldn't say to her specifically, "Can you tell her in Romanian?" So we made the decision that we wouldn't do that [...]' (Lines 543–545). Ellie's shift in the pronominal use from 'I' to 'we' points to a more authoritative stance. It emphasises that this was a conscious decision that could change the way that the three girls had been using language until then, and may also hint at the fact that the decision was made with some coordination with colleagues in school who follow up on the settling-in process of new arrivals. The monolingual norm – 'English is the only official language for learning' – is evident here, as the intervention about language use refers to the *practice of translation*, and the teacher did not intend to police the use of Romanian as such. Indeed, in Lines 545–546, 'But obviously, if she – (laughs) they speak to each other in Romanian', the teacher recognises, both by the wording and paralinguistic emphasis, that the children draw on their whole linguistic repertoire as a matter of course. Importantly, Ellie's evaluation aligns with the working consensus in her classroom, where children are allowed to communicate during phases of individual work.

Noticeably, there exists a considerable mismatch between the situation that Ellie tried to resolve and her decision to stop the practice of translating. In fact, the teacher did not – as might have been possible – respond with a recommendation related to the outside domain. With her decision, she instead took the issue a step further into the field of classroom practices, and her response approached the conflict as if it had arisen from the children's language practices in the classroom itself. This mismatch can be usefully understood as an effect of the monolingual norm, i.e. the norm provides the lens through which the situation is seen and tackled. As the teacher's reaction problematises the practice of translation, the decision inevitably includes the usage of Romanian in the official classroom, which is controlled and whose significance for learning is devalued. In addition, Ellie does not distinguish, either in her description of the situation or in the rule she has introduced, between different *purposes* of translating, for example, for procedures of classroom organisation, learning English or subject content. This apparent *lack of clarity* is significant because it mirrors a missing clarity in the classroom regarding the use of Adriana's and Sonia's first language. The teacher described a complex situation, and a thorough analysis may need additional information, not least about Bianca, whose role differed from that of a language broker or interpreter (e.g. Dinneen, 2017) since she had not translated here for a member of her own family. Ellie recalled that in the situation, Bianca had offered to translate what the teacher assumed to be merely a question on the part of Sonia's mother and not an argument brought from outside into school (Interview Ellie, 8 February 2017, Lines 578–587). However, the description of the teacher is indicative of an understanding of the monolingual norm and teacher agency, chiming with a lack of strategies and resources officially in place for Adriana and Sonia to use Romanian in their learning.

Indeed, within the logic of the monolingual norm, it is not necessary to specify *different purposes* of first language use, and the mismatch of Ellie's decision to stop the practice of translating in her classroom highlights, therefore, the importance of the *strategical* use of any approach that draws on more than one language. Moreover, questions around the different purposes of first language use need to consider the time aspect, as Ellie mentions implicitly, 'But . I think they are actually probably doing better from not being translated to ...' (Lines 550–552). These lines need to be acknowledged as expressions of the educator's experience in her classroom under current pedagogical conditions. Yet, seen through a more critical lens, her evaluation, referring to the earliest times of Adriana's and Sonia's learning of English, also underlines this absence of pedagogical strategies and differentiation between various purposes of language use.

I wish to argue that what the monolingual norm accomplishes for teachers is precisely to *avoid* the question of what to do 'strategically' with the children's first languages (as in Adriana's and Sonia's case) or the non-English components of pupils' language repertoires (as in Bianca's case, see pp. 11–12) for learning. The norm is based on a clear distinction between 'English is the only official language for learning' and what might be phrased as 'other languages are unofficial and not for learning'. By consistently reproducing this dividing line, the norm contributes to how a classroom is defined and – following the understanding of the classroom as a context for teacher agency – what a teacher might perceive as the 'classroom' in the first place. The monolingual norm ensures that the teacher's general agency relates to a classroom where teaching/learning takes place in English and where teachers do not need to make decisions about, plan for or resource activities in languages other than English. However, as shown in Section 4.1, the situation is not without tensions and ambivalence because educators interact with plurilingual students. I have suggested viewing these tensions as occurring at the periphery of the official classroom. Within the sociocultural understanding of the classroom as a mediational means for teacher agency (see Section 1.2), the children – and their linguistic repertoires – are potential mediators or form part of the mediators of a teachers' agency, as it is relational and embedded in professional interactions. At the same time, the monolingual norm belongs to the category of secondary artefacts that play a role in sustaining and transmitting ways of pedagogical practices. To see the monolingual norm from this angle points to the contested field of multilingual pedagogies in mainstream schools, where teachers can make decisions and achieve agency while the possibilities to become aware of certain issues are meditated by the means available. In this regard, it is highly instructive that the teachers did not seem to perceive tensions and ambivalences as such, showing that compared to other elements of the classroom's complexities, they were of relatively little significance. Thus, the monolingual norm *reduces* the complexity of the classroom, as seen from the perspective of teachers with their general agency regarding the running of the classroom.

5.1.3 'I think they felt like they couldn't put it on there': Reflecting the invisible norm

The following example from Heather's and Kelly's classes indicates how the norm might work for those plurilingual pupils who have received most or all of their schooling in English as the language of instruction and includes Heather's reflection on a situation that belongs to the realm of homework projects. Over the half-term holidays, the children had been asked to create a 'River of Reading' on an A3 or larger sheet, a kind of creative flow diagram where they drew or glued and labelled anything they had read over the week (see Cliff Hodges, 2010). As always with homework projects, the children brought the posters into school in the following weeks and presented them before they were hung on the wall or pegged on a string across the classrooms. After half term, I spoke with children about their 'Rivers'. I asked Florin (Heather's class) and Kacper (Kelly's class) – who read at home in Romanian and Polish, respectively, as I knew from the focus group activity – separately whether they had done so during the holidays. The two children answered with 'yes'; however, upon being asked if they had included these readings in their posters, they both replied, 'I forgot' (Fieldnotes Y3/1, Bird Primary, 26 February 2018: Lines 64–65; Y 3/2, 1 March 2018: 48–49). I mentioned this observation to Heather:

796		Yeah. It's funny with Florin saying he forgot, and Kacper. I don't think they did forget,
797		I think they felt like they couldn't put it on there, I wonder. I mean we would
798		not – not that any of the teachers at this school would ever, ever say that
799		they couldn't put that as a – but I wonder whether they think that's not what
800		they mean, they mean something written in English. I don't know, not that
801		that has – would ever be said.
802	TQ:	*What do you mean...?*
803		I wonder whether Florin was telling the truth when he said that he forgot, and Kacper.
804		I wonder whether they actually . don't . wouldn't think that was that is what we are talking about
805		when we were saying 'River of Reading'. Even when we were giving it out, we said <u>anything, anything</u>

806		you read. But we didn't say it, 'in a different language'. And maybe if we had said that. I just got the
807		feeling that Florin didn't forget, and specially Kacper. I think they didn't forget that, […] didn't put it
808		on there on purpose.
809	TQ:	*So they have a feeling for what counts more, what counts less?*
810		Yeah . yeah which is really sad.

(Interview, 16 March 2018)

The theme of the extract is the monolingual norm, addressed via an omission in Florin's and Kacper's posters. While I had also mentioned Destiny, another child from her class who had included her reading in Twi on the 'River of Reading', Heather starts here to reflect upon the boys' non-inclusion of their reading experiences in Romanian and Polish, respectively. She empathises with their perspective (Line 797, 'I think they felt like they couldn't put it on there, I wonder') and then turns directly to an assertion that no one in school would advocate such an exclusion, pointing to the aspect of the school as an environment that explicitly recognises pupils' bilingualism and encourages parents to use 'home languages' with their children (Lines 797–798, 'I mean we would not – not that any of the teachers at this school would ever, ever say that'). This might be best understood as a reflection of a tension between pedagogical beliefs and the invisible monolingual norm in the school. In the following, 'but I wonder whether they think that's not what they mean …' (Lines 799–800), Heather continues along the same lines, trying to see the situation of a somewhat naturalised monolingualism from the perspective of bilingual children. In Line 806, 'But we didn't say it, "in a different language". And maybe if we had said that', the teacher emphasises the importance of making such an inclusion explicit and encouraging children like Florin and Kacpar to incorporate their reading in non-English languages.

The context of the 'River of Reading' activity seems to encourage the teacher's reflection precisely because the rationale for the task had been to bring children's out-of-school experiences with multiliteracy and reading into school. The apparent paradox that Florin and Kacpar still follow the dividing line of the monolingual norm enables Heather to thematise an existing tension. In doing so, her approach to reflexivity displays similar facets as when she was reflecting on the friction between the fact that she talks with children about their languages but does not make their plurilingual voices heard in her classroom (see p. 79). First, Heather attempts to see the situation from the children's perspective (Line 797, 'I think they felt like …'; Line 799, 'I wonder whether they think …'); second, her reflection follows an interaction or task she has initiated herself (or, as with the 'River of Reading', in cooperation with her colleague) and; third, she evokes an angle of what I would call a 'need for explicitness' on the part of the teacher to cross the dividing line between the official and unofficial languages in the classroom and to increase the audibility of the latter (Line 806, 'But we didn't say it, "in a different language" …').

If the monolingual norm, as described in this chapter, is seen as a *hindrance* to teacher agency in multilingual pedagogies, the teacher's reflexivity emerges at this point of the enquiry into what *constitutes* and *facilitates* teacher agency in multilingual pedagogies as a crucial and integral part of that agency. Located at the transition between the current state of affairs, framed by the monolingual norm, and future developments, teachers' reflexivity must be considered a constitutive factor for their agency in this pedagogical domain. In other words, teachers have to develop an acknowledgement of the monolingual norm and a reflective evaluation of how it works in their respective classrooms to achieve such an agency. In Chapter 7, the five teachers' perceptions and negotiations of the dividing line between the official English language and the children's plurilingual repertoires will be addressed further.

5.2 Superdiverse Voices

The participatory activities complemented the fieldwork in the classroom by giving the children a voice in the research process. They provided an opportunity for them to talk in ways of their choosing about their linguistic repertoires and experiences and to voice their ideas for activities linked to multilingual pedagogies. Although the main focus is here on the children's description of their repertoires and experiences, *how* they talked about them is also thematised. As the use of the language portrait with small groups of children was embedded in the study of teacher agency in multilingual pedagogies, the overall interest was in children's linguistic repertoires and voices as significant points of reference for multilingual pedagogies and as an element contributing to such agency. In the context of language biographical research, Brigitta Busch argues:

> Although biographic approaches rely on individual accounts, they are not primarily interested in the uniqueness of the particular life story as such but in what its apparent singularity can reveal about specific dimensions of language practices and ideologies that are neglected when taking an assumed 'average' speaker as representative of a certain group. (Busch, 2017a: 55)

Similarly, the following findings focus less on the uniqueness of the child's language experience – as important as it is. Instead, they address aspects of children's language practices and experiences of multilingualism that were not usually audible and observable in the classroom due to pedagogical conditions that neglect the plurilingual speaker, since it is assumed that the 'average' student is either 'monolingual', an 'EAL child' or a 'bilingual child, who is a monolingual student'.

5.2.1 A multiplicity of languages: Superdiversity in the classroom

Linguistically very diverse conditions emerged first regarding the *number of named languages* that the children in a single classroom have in their repertoires and second, in relation to the *diverse meanings* that the practices of those languages have for the children. The statistics showed 10 languages on average in each of the five classes; for example, the school's system had recorded and categorised the following languages for Ellie's Year 4: Akan/Twi-Fante, Bengali, Bulgarian, Chinese/Cantonese, English, Igbo, Lithuanian, Portuguese, Romanian and Telugu. The teachers mentioned in the interviews the number of languages the children in their class could speak: 'It would be very handy to speak a lot of Eastern European languages, I think' (Interview Ellie, 8 February 2017: Lines 372–373); 'It is very difficult to do a blanket focus on language when you have so many dispersed languages, and that is a challenge for teaching' (Interview Mike, 20 March 2017: Lines 293–295); 'there are so many different languages, it is hard to cater for them' (Interview Hira, 14 July 2017: Lines 37–38); and Heather, '… so many different languages […] We need time, like, spare time to discuss different languages and experience writing in different languages' (Interview, 16 March 2018: Lines 741–745). The teachers articulated a perception and sentiment of uncertainty, given the number of languages children in their classes have in their repertoires. While the number of different languages spoken by pupils has been evident since educational projects have responded to an increasing number of plurilingual pupils attending schools in England (e.g. Hawkins, 1984; Houlton, 1985), any exploration of teacher agency in multilingual pedagogies must also take note of a simple yet fundamental paradox that often characterises current debates around schools and multilingualism in European contexts. Teachers are asked to respond to the increased number of languages spoken by pupils in their classrooms, whereas the very same linguistic superdiversity is perceived as an obstacle to doing so.

However, the number of languages is also relevant concerning the linguistic repertoire of each child. In all five classrooms, some students had two or more languages apart from English in their repertoire due to their migration trajectories or those of their parents. Even though this group of pupils was relatively small, their presence is an important expression of the superdiverse condition for multilingual pedagogies and the different affiliations that children have to their languages. The following children exemplify such constellations: Emilija speaks Lithuanian and is registered with Lithuanian as her first language in the school's language statistics. Upon being asked, when talking about her language portrait, whether she is 'speaking a lot of Spanish because you coloured in quite a lot', she says, 'Yeah, I was born there' (Activities 1, Castle Primary Y4, 8 March 2017: Lines 112–113). Emilija explains that she learnt Spanish letters in Nursery and Reception in Spain. Afterwards, she stayed with her grandmother for one year in Lithuania before joining her mother in London during Year 1. She also describes how she likes reading in Spanish (Activities 1, Y4, 8 March 2017: Lines 121–122), and when asked, 'Do you have a favourite language or is this something you could not answer?', the child replies 'I would say yes because I like to speak in Spanish' (Line 291). Her teacher, Ellie, was aware of Emilija's linguistic trajectory. However, the Spanish-speaking LSA, who is assigned to the class for one day per week, was not aware that they share a language other than English.

Similarly, Khadija had a biographical connection to more than one language before coming to Britain. As the child of Bengali-speaking parents, she was born in Northern Italy, where she also went to school for three years. Khadija came to London circa six months before she responded to the question of whether she has a favourite language: 'The language that I most want to speak is Italian. Because I am born in Italy, I know Italy, I went to nursery in Italy and I went a bit to school in there, and Italy is my favourite country as well. But I like England as well' (Activities 1, Castle Primary Y4, 8 March 2017: Lines 274–276). Khadija speaks Bengali with her parents, participates actively in lessons in English, and is seen by her teacher as a keen learner. Writing about 'lava and rocks', she used the verb 'transform', providing an opportunity to ask Khadija whether her Italian helps her to find or to remember words in English, a question she answered with 'sometimes'. Moreover, she explained, 'I speak in English in school. [...] I speak Bengali always with my parents [...]' – *TQ: Do you use your Bengali with another child in school?* – 'In school? No' (Activities 2, Castle Primary Y4, 15 March 2017: Lines 34–38). The examples of Emilija and Khadija, along with the descriptions given by Probal and Abdul in Section 2.1 (pp. 39–40), illustrate how the language statistics of the schools do not accommodate the children's linguistic repertoires, as neither Emilija's Spanish nor the Italian of the three other pupils featured in that system.

5.2.2 The meanings of speaking a language: Superdiversity in the classroom

Khawla Badwan (2021b: 165–167) cautions against the use of the term 'superdiversity', warning that it risks perpetuating an 'us' versus 'them' dichotomy in enquiries into the languaging practices of 'certain groups', mirroring powerful divides in broader society, even though it has the stated intention to counter essentialist assumptions (Martin-Jones et al., 2012: 7). As a vignette in this section will show, children are aware of such a risk when identifying themselves as a plurilingual speaker. I want to argue, however, that the primary school under linguistically very diverse conditions can become a place where dichotomous distinctions fade in everyday routines and the professional stance of educators. Such a stance could be found, for example, in Kelly's assertion that 'here it is more usual to be multilingual, everyone is different [...] it doesn't make you a second-class citizen in any way' (Interview, 7 December 2017: Lines 845–848), and, arguably, in teachers' general position that sees 'English as an additional language' not as a deficit on the part of the children and their families. And yet, the intertwined phenomena of the monolingual norm, EAL discourse and symbolic multilingualism are all clear indications that primary school pedagogy has yet to find adequate responses to the linguistic diversification found in classrooms. Developing such responses requires teachers to gain insight into their students' linguistic repertoires to 'know differently' beyond the EAL discourse and to draw on this knowledge to achieve agency in multilingual pedagogies.

The participatory activities aligned with the ethnographic perspective that took the classroom as a point of departure, exploring how linguistic superdiversity presents itself when educators listen to children's voices. An analysis of the children's talk during the portrait activity in all seven groups allowed the identification of three dimensions of diversity within the range of meanings that speaking a language – or of having a language in the linguistic repertoire – can have for children: (1) the diversity of meanings which language practices have for children; (2) the diversity of contexts of interactions, and places to which these meanings are related; and (3) the diversity of literacy skills that children acquire in their languages. An extract from Amelija, a child in Mike's Year 5, illustrates what children included when talking about their portraits (Figure 5.1):

107	Amelija:	This is my picture. So the first one is blue because I did Russian because my mum speaks
108		Russian and my mum usually like tells me Russian stuff I like try to learn and I sometimes
109		watch Russian programmes like episodes of them. So I try to learn Russian so I can speak
110		Russian more, so yeah...
111		And the next one is Lithuania. I mean Russian is in our language 'Russia', and then the

Figure 5.1 Amelija's language portrait
Source: Österreichisches Sprachen-Kompetenz-Zentrum (ed.) (2010). Reprinted with permission.

112		yellow one is Lithuania because like I speak Lithuanian at home and like on Fridays I go to
113		Lithuanian school. So
114	TQ:	You go to [description of location] on Friday?
115	Amelija:	Yeah. And then in Lithuania, we say Lithuvia. And then the green one is Italy because my
116		mum's friend is Italy [...]
117		So she usually comes to us and she like speaks it. [...]
118		The other one is England, the red and that's
119		what I speak now and when I'm in school. And in Lithuania, we call it 'Anglia'.
[...]		*[They talk about which words they had learnt first as toddlers.]*
128	Mariana:	What is your favourite language?
129	Amelija:	Ahm probably . ahm Russian because . . it depends, because I like Russian,
130		because I like their language—hm it is cool. And how they speak, it's really

131	nice. And Lithuanian, I like it because I go to Lithuania and I see all like my
132	auntie and my grandpa . . yeah

(Activities 1, Castle Primary Y5, 9 March 2017)

Amelija starts her presentation with Russian, which she is learning from her mother, and also by watching programmes in Russian (Lines 107–109). Speaking and listening to Russian is described as a learning context with her mother at home. It is facilitated by the fact that Amelija's mother is from Lithuania, a country whose changing language policies in Soviet, post-Soviet and present times (Riegl & Vaško, 2007) are reflected in children's families. A broadly comparable situation regarding a further language, which features in the family and is of interest to a child, was described by children with South Asian family backgrounds. In addition to the languages Telugu, Bengali and Tamil, respectively, these children referred to Hindi as a language spoken by their mothers or, as in Khadija's case, as the language of the movies she watches with her.

In the presentation of the language portrait, Amelija refers to Lithuanian as the language she speaks at home and when visiting relatives in Lithuania (Lines 112 and 131–132). While she refers to these contexts in an uncomplicated way, for other children such language practices can appear more contentious and negotiated, and this will be thematised below. While speaking Lithuanian at home is unmarked, the emotional investment in speaking the language becomes more pronounced in 'And Lithuanian I like it because I go to Lithuania and I see all like my auntie and my grandpa . . yeah' (Lines 131–132). At the same time, speaking Lithuanian is linked to another context of interaction and place. The complementary school is another location where Amelija uses her Lithuanian (Lines 112–113), and it emerges in the dialogue between the children – triggered by my question, 'Is Amelija the only one who is attending the school on Friday?' – that this language practice in the complementary school is negotiated between the girl and her mother.

177	Anna:	I used to go on Wednesday [...] and I am not going anymore.
178	Amelija:	I don't like it as well but I have to
179	Anna:	yeah
180	TQ:	What does it mean, you have to…?
181	Amelija:	My mum says I have to but I really don't want to
182	Anna:	Because it's really hard.
183	TQ:	Oh no, I asked her. You can have a guess or [say] what you think, but I am asking Amelija…

184   Amelija: My mum thinks I don't speak really well Lithuanian. I know how to speak, but she says
185   I need to learn how to write and I don't want to.
                 (Activities 1, Castle Primary Y5, 9 March 2017)

A complementary school can be seen as both an interactional and a learning context, and this is related to how the classes are organised. It is important to note that Amelija's complementary school follows, as the headteacher explained, the official literacy curriculum of Lithuania. Thus, the girl emphasises that the homework is her reason for trying 'to persuade Mum' not to send her to these classes anymore, explaining that without the homework, she would like to attend (Fieldnotes, Castle Primary Y5, 13 March 2017: Lines 95–96).

Amelija associates the English language with learning in school when presenting her drawing (Lines 118–119). When asked whether she uses Lithuanian 'sometimes in a lesson or for learning', the child's response indicates that her use of the language in lessons can be best understood as part of 'friendship talk' (Lines 39–40).

35   Amelija: I don't really speak Lithuanian in my class like when we are learning, not like now
36   because we are speaking you know we are talking about the languages – but only
37   sometimes if someone of my friends speaks my language I would talk to them like…
38   TQ: …like?
39   Amelija: […] I talk to her in Lithuanian because if we
40   don't want other people to know like the answer or something, only then.
                (Activities 2, Castle Primary Y5, 13 March 2017)

Moreover, Italian features in Amelija's portrait as a language spoken by a friend of her mother when she visits. The child does not take part in this language practice herself but feels a connection to the language because of her mother's friendship (Lines 115–117). Other children referred to the language of a friend or a parent's friend in similar ways. Thus, such languages can become part of children's multilingual environment and are familiar enough to be included in the language portrait.

Amelija's example shows how children pointed to languages that they use in specific contexts of interactions and places and how the meanings of the respective language for the child were shaped by these contexts. Concepts such as 'language-in-use' and 'community-of-practice' feature prominently in debates around the multilingual turn (e.g. May, 2014; Meier, 2017). Here, however, my point is not to put forward categories as such but to show that the language portrait activity can help to shed light on the *diversity and the range of meanings* that languages can have for primary school pupils. That is, in relation to the Lithuanian language practices described by Amelija in this extract, the 10-year-old girl uses Lithuanian at home with the family and when visiting relatives in Lithuania. In school, where all learning takes place in English, except in modern foreign language lessons, she occasionally uses Lithuanian for informal brief exchanges within friendships, partially linked to the learning task. Finally, in the complementary school, she acquires and extends her literacy skills in Lithuanian.

In Sana's presentation, language use, interactional contexts and literacy skills are described differently (Figure 5.2)

73	Sana:	So I can speak English and when I was in Nursery I didn't know English, but I
74		knew what they were saying but I couldn't speak, and I didn't know how to
75		write English.
76		And then I speak Bengali [...]
77		So I really speak with my mum and dad and my brothers and
78		sisters in Bengali and sometimes English as well. And I speak French as well at
79		school and I am still learning it.
		[...]
94	TQ:	Sana, what about reading and writing? Can you read and write in Bengali?
95	Sana:	I . I can read in Arabic, but I can't read in Bengali, I can't write in Bengali but I
96		can write in Arabic.
97	Probal:	Because of the Quran.
98	TQ:	Where did you learn that?
99	Sana:	I go to mosque Thursday and Friday. So today, I am going to mosque.

(Activities 1, Victoria Primary Y3, 29 June 2017)

In understanding the range of meanings a language can have for children, the focus here will be on Sana's language practices of Bengali, and her account is extended by a miniature sketch of the range encountered in other pupils' descriptions. Regarding the home context, Sana says that she speaks with her parents and siblings 'in Bengali and <u>sometimes</u> English as well' (Lines 77–78). Other children also used

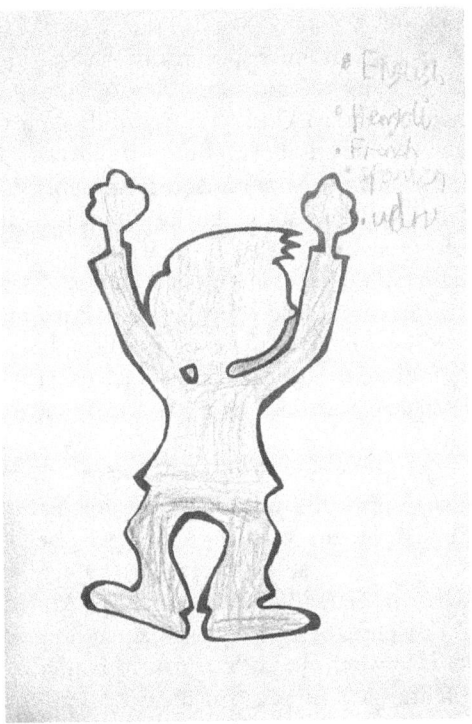

Figure 5.2 Sana's language portrait
Source: Österreichisches Sprachen-Kompetenz-Zentrum (ed.) (2010). Reprinted with permission.

various quantifiers to describe their use of a language at home. When I asked, 'You said that you learnt Urdu at your grandma's house. Are you speaking Urdu with your mum and dad as well?', Sana's friend Azayiz replied, 'Yeah, kind of...' – *TQ: and sisters and brothers...?* – 'Only a sister' – *TQ: What do you speak with her?* – 'English and sometimes Urdu' (Activities 1, Victoria Primary Y3, 29 June 2017: Lines 112–119). Khalid said that he speaks Italian and English 'all the time' at home (Activities 1, Bird Primary Y3, 22 January 2018: Line 212), and Anna explained that she speaks English with her brother but Lithuanian with her mother, sometimes mixing in English words (Activities 2, Castle Primary Y5, 13 March 2017: Line 12). The aspect of various 'ratios of ingredients' of a child's linguistic repertoire used at home with different family members is important for multilingual pedagogies because it might result in different meanings they give to a language depending on the language use and the experienced self-efficacy (Bandura, 1982), i.e. the experience and belief to act successfully by using the language.

Concerning the classroom and the context of friendships in school, Sana, along with other children, spoke about using Bengali. Many pupils said that they sometimes speak their language in the classroom and on the playground. The language use they described varied between talking to friends or using it more specifically for 'sharing secrets'. Given the diversity and the range of meanings children might attribute to the same named language, approaches within multilingual pedagogies need to respond to such diversity. Educators need to be aware that in the very same classroom, there can be simultaneously students who have recently arrived with a non-English-speaking background, for whom it is crucial to draw on the language they used for learning previously, and others with the same named language who assign a very different meaning to this language – for example, because they were born in Britain. Such a constellation could be found in three of the five classrooms: Adriana, Sonia and Bianca in the episodes in Section 1.1.1 (p. 11) and Section 5.1.1 (pp. 103–104), Probal in Section 2.1 (p. 39) and Sana, referred to above, are cases in point.

The third dimension of diversity featured when children were talking about their language portraits was a context for learning to read and write the non-English language. Being asked whether she can read or write in Bengali, Sana answers, 'I can read in Arabic, but I can't read in Bengali, I can't write in Bengali but I can write in Arabic' (Lines 95–96). She indicates a shift where the language spoken at home does not expand into literacy skills. However, the child learns to read and write Arabic in the framework of liturgical literacy practice (Rosowsky, 2016). The way Sana repeats the sentence, although in a different succession, seems to emphasise that shift while also expressing self-esteem with an awareness that she can only acquire *one* other script at her age. Sana's classmate Nadia described how she would read in church soon, and for her, this appeared to be an incentive to use and improve her reading skills in Polish, which she had acquired at home and used when reading stories to her sisters (Activities 1, Victoria Primary, Y3, 29 June 2017: Lines 164–175). As with spoken language, the superdiverse condition was evident when the children talked about reading and writing. However, only children like Amelija or Sana, who learnt literacy in complementary settings, mentioned this knowledge themselves without being prompted. For multilingual pedagogies, it is useful to consider the diversity of literacy skills that children have acquired as a dimension in its own right in relation to the *range of meanings* a language has for children. The students mentioned various arrangements for learning and using their literacy skills: learning through parents teaching them, grandparents bringing primers from India, learning when visiting a school on holiday in Ghana, borrowing books in Twi in a local library and learning in complementary schools and mosques. Children who had been to school in another country explained that they used the language for reading books and for searches on the internet for homework projects.

The diversity emerging from the children's talk around their language portrait drawings did not come unexpectedly. A primary school pedagogy that sets out to incorporate approaches of multilingual pedagogies cannot circumvent these insights. On the contrary, children's superdiverse voices, the complexity existing in classes due to the number of languages, and the various meanings children attribute to them need to be acknowledged and taken as starting points for multilingual pedagogies in the primary school under superdiverse conditions. Consequently, a teacher's knowledge about the three dimensions of diversity identified within the range of meanings that speaking a language can have for the children in their classroom can be seen as supportive towards the achievement of teacher agency. The dimensions are inevitably a vital part of the complexity that teachers (do not) perceive around multilingualism, even if they are not usually thematised within a status quo framed by the monolingual norm, EAL discourse and symbolic multilingualism. Yet, they may provide some orientation for strategical or practical choices, and listening to the children's 'superdiverse voices' does not only help to go beyond the mere perception of the 'number of languages' but crucially acknowledges children as plurilingual speakers.

5.2.3 'I speak it, but I am born in England': Claiming ownership over what being bilingual means

The following vignette involves Adriana, Sonia and Bianca. It shows how negotiations about the meanings of components of children's language repertoires and language ideologies take place almost inevitably, even though they may come to the fore more in situations where the status quo is being challenged by pupils who depend to a considerable extent on using a non-English language for their learning.

169		The EAL teacher is working with Sonia and Adriana.
170		The two girls run across two thirds of the classroom, over to the table where Bianca
171		and Emilija sit (and where I was just passing by).
172		[...]
173		Adriana asks Bianca something.
174	Bianca:	I don't know [turns around to the table]
175		How can I know that? [friendly, shrugging]
176	TQ:	What is it that she is asking?
177	Bianca:	'Bizarre'.
178		Apparently, the EAL teacher had sent them over to ask Bianca [...] for the
179		meaning of the word. Here the conversation continues:
180	TQ:	Do you speak Romanian?

181	Bianca:	I speak Romanian. I speak it, but I am born in England. I am from Oxfordshire,
182		from a nice little village.
183	Tanya:	I speak a bit of Russian. I am from [borough]. But now I am in [neighbourhood]
184		'Bizarre' unsolved.

(Fieldnotes Y4, Castle Primary, 10 January 2017)

Three notes to contextualise this episode: the presence of the EAL coordinator is an exception in this lesson, as she usually does not have a time slot assigned to the class; as in other lessons, no dictionary is used by either the teacher or the students; finally, the working consensus of Ellie's classroom allows Adriana and Sonia to move quickly to the other table without transgressing any classroom rules. The analysis focuses on Bianca through the stancetaking lens to understand how she addresses what has been previously called 'the meanings of speaking a language'.

The situation was initiated by the EAL teacher, who sent Sonia and Adriana to Bianca to ask for the meaning of 'bizarre', a word that came up in the text she was reading with them. Adriana and Bianca spoke in Romanian (Line 173), as they do in other informal situations in the classroom and on the playground; therefore, the usage of Romanian can be seen as unmarked. The situation has been prompted by the EAL teacher, and it could be argued that the rule described by the class teacher previously – that they would not explicitly ask Bianca to translate – is being broken here. However, in my understanding, this is not the case, since Sonia and Adriana have been sent to ask only for a single word. With 'I don't know' (Line 174), Bianca turns back to her table and repeats in English what, in all probability, she had said to Adriana in Romanian a moment ago. By switching back to English, she makes the situation accessible for others, and 'I don't know' and 'How can I know that?' (Lines 174–175) can be seen both as a comment to herself and as an offer for others to join in. Yet, Bianca does not simply state that she does not know the word 'bizarre' in Romanian. She also evokes 'bilingualism' or 'bilingual repertoire' as objects of a now extended conversation. One may only speculate about the reason for this step, but it is certainly significant that she makes her comment – 'How can I know that?' (Line 175) – in the form of a rhetorical question with a shrug immediately after the exchange with Adriana, i.e. in a situation where she had been asked to translate a word and where it was pointed out to her that a word was missing in her Romanian vocabulary. If 'bilingualism' is understood as the stance-object that Bianca puts forward, she can be seen to evaluate here what bilingualism means for her. Her experiences include switching languages naturally and becoming aware of missing words. She positions herself as a *bilingual speaker*, while the chosen form of a rhetorical question is indicative of how familiar she is with this position, including a routine of acknowledging missing Romanian words (to a much lesser extent, as is generally the case for pupils in Year 4, this is also an experience Bianca has in English, even though she is a very confident learner and one of the three or four students who contribute most to the classroom talk).

Bianca's confident admission, 'How can I know that?' (Line 175), can also be understood as responding to another aspect of her experience as a bilingual speaker in the classroom. She comments as someone who has just been asked to explain something to Sonia and Adriana, the two girls with whom she shares the Romanian language. While being bilingual and speaking Romanian in school can be seen as largely unmarked and 'normal' for Bianca, other situations where she is asked to *explain* something in Romanian can disrupt this normalcy. Bianca hinted at this during the language portrait activity when she and Silu were talking about the different sizes of areas coloured in their silhouettes:

32 Silu: That is how much you speak of it. So I do exactly half of it.
33 Bianca: I don't speak loads of it.
34 Silu: You could explain to Sonia, you could explain to Adriana.
35 Bianca: Yeah, most of the time, I don't like it.
            (Activities 1, Castle Primary Y4, 8 March 2017)

With 'How can I know that?' (Line 175), Bianca appears to respond to such tension by adopting the position of a bilingual speaker while simultaneously claiming ownership over the meaning that being a bilingual speaker has for her. She achieves this by ensuring that not having balanced knowledge in both languages is included in this position. That is, the child's positioning contains a disalignment from such a demand towards supposedly balanced bilingual speakers. The EAL teacher represents such a position symbolically because she had sent the two girls over to ask Bianca, even though, in all probability, the teacher does not hold such a view.

In Line 180, I take the opportunity to talk about bilingualism by asking, '*Do you speak Romanian?*'. This was the first day of the participant observation, and when I had previously asked the children in Bianca's table group whether they spoke another language apart from English, she had not mentioned Romanian (Fieldnotes Y4, Castle Primary, 10 January 2017: Lines 113–114); hence, the question is genuine. Instead of simply answering 'yes', which might have been possible, Bianca responds by developing the previous stance-object 'bilingualism' further into another, which can be understood as 'speaking Romanian'. The nine-year-old child positions herself as a Romanian speaker with 'I speak Romanian' (Line 181), using the first person, and continues to emphasise her subjectivity in 'I speak it but I am born in England. I am from Oxfordshire, from a nice little village' (Lines 181–182). Following up on her previously articulated position as a *bilingual speaker with ownership over what being bilingual means*, this can be understood primarily as another statement by her regarding why she cannot be a balanced bilingual – in this instance, why she cannot possibly know 'bizarre' in Romanian. To mention her place of birth is, from this perspective, just a further way for her to emphasise her previously held position. Being asked in the portrait activity group whether she could answer the question about having or not having a favourite language, Bianca replied, 'I can answer it – my answer is English, I was born here, I lived here all my life, I just lived in a different country only for one or two years' (Activities 1, Castle Primary Y4, 8 March 2017: Lines 280–281).

Bianca's precise words, however, suggest that it is appropriate and useful to add a further interpretation, which draws attention to a parallel positioning taking place by saying, 'I speak it, but I am born in England' (Line 181). With the conjunction 'but', Bianca signals that she is familiar with the assumption that a speaker of Romanian is not also 'born in England' and 'from Oxfordshire'. In other words, she shows an awareness of the fact that being such a speaker in the UK is a contested subject position within political discourses around immigration, and someone who is taking it up is therefore at risk of not, or at least 'not really', belonging 'here'. Although it is impossible, of course, to pinpoint exactly what motivated Bianca to state, 'but I am born in England …' (Lines 181–182), her explicit references to birthplace, country and county evoke issues of geographical origin, place and belonging. Bianca is again claiming a position as a *bilingual speaker with ownership over what bilingual means*, but now over what being a bilingual speaker of Romanian *and* English means. Pointing out her birthplace – and evoking the imagined Englishness of the picturesque countryside – allows her to challenge a discourse that positions Romanian/English speakers as 'not belonging here'. For the research process of the present study and approaches of multilingual pedagogies in the primary school, it is relevant that the utterance 'I speak Romanian. I speak it, but …' (Lines 181–182) was prompted by a question about Romanian language use. It highlights the necessity to handle questions around linguistic repertoires, language use and language experience sensitively, given that such questions are inescapably interwoven in contemporary and, therefore, lived power relations. In other words, the vignette shows how the theme of 'speaking a language' and plurilingual children's experience of the often ambiguous ways in which 'language' can become part of 'nationality and ethnicity talk' (Zhu & Li, 2016) highlights that it is essential for pedagogical approaches to avoid any resemblance to othering processes that characterise dominant discourses around language, nation and migration. Here, othering is understood as '[d]iscursive *Othering* [that] produces different subjects – Others – onto which "difference" is ascribed as an attribute' (Thomas-Olalde & Vehlo, 2011: 37, emphasis in original), and often based on a dichotomy between an inside and an outside, intersecting with practices such as racialisation, minoritisation and anti-immigration politics, which are embedded in and updated by political discourses and those within the media. The perspective of othering is helpful in this context as an analytical instrument because it 'takes into account the ambivalences of actions (also of actions intended to be counter-hegemonic) within dominant discourses' (Thomas-Olalde & Vehlo, 2011: 47). Thus, the school's symbolic multilingualism, which is well-intentioned but relies heavily on the representation of multilingualism and languages by national flags, can be usefully seen as a case in point of pedagogical actions that are meant to contradict hegemonic monolingualism without reflecting on their embeddedness in broader societal discourses. Children like Bianca are inevitably othered through such representations, even though the school aims at making their plurilingualism visible.

5.2.4 The normalcy of lived multilingualism

In all groups of the participatory activities, the children started eagerly on the task and talked while colouring their silhouettes. For example, they chipped in with phrases in different languages, talked about the first words they had learnt in their languages, enjoyed playing with accents or described how they translate during computer games. All this was done with ease and together with how the children presented their language portraits, can best be described as an expression of a plurilingual 'well-being' (Gogolin, 2015: 294). It could be said that the way the children talked about their experiences mirrors the normalcy of the multilingualism they live. Another aspect of this normalcy was addressed by Shriya, who, having Marathi and Gujarati in her own repertoire, explains:

25   Me and Archita, we are very close friends, so we know each other's
26   language very well. My – she doesn't know Marathi. But she knows my mum,
27   so she hears loads and loads of Marathi, so she knows some.
(Activities 1, Bird Primary Y3/2, 22 January 2018)

Her friend Archita confirmed this when presenting her own portrait, 'and this [Gujarati] and this [Marathi] I know a bit from Shriya (Activities 1, Bird Primary Y3/2, 22 January 2018: Line 49). The children include here a wide range of what 'knowing Marathi' means

(Line 26, 'She doesn't know...'; Line 27, 'so she knows some'; Line 49, 'I know a bit'). However, the short extract portrays how the children's experience is embedded in the normalcy of the multilingual environment in which they live and where, along with their own plurilingualism, they participate in the plurilingual world of their friends.

Another extract provides an exemplary illustration of how, during the activities, the pupils talked expertly about their experiences. The group of pupils from Ellie's Year 4 had talked about negotiating their use of language at home, and Silu and Emilija shared their familiarity with another experience:

50	Silu:	When you go to a native [...] The house where the most the
51		family is and then when you start speaking your language, most of the time, they just
52		laugh at you or they giggle.
53	Emilija:	Or sometimes when you are like speaking English and you are in a different country
54		and most people they can't speak English, you know, your mum is always like
55		'Please speak!' the whatever the language is because they can't understand you
56		but then again, I don't get it right *(laughs)* I want them to understand it

(Activities 1, Castle Primary Y4, 8 March 2017)

Silu and Emilija recount situations in which they felt self-conscious. The experience they share with each other could be seen as almost the opposite of their usually experienced normalcy when they address here the experience of not speaking 'the language' – Telugu or Lithuanian, respectively – in the same way as those speakers who live in an environment where they use it for all contexts and purposes. Yet, this extract not only effectively illustrates well the lively and dialogical communication during the language portrait activity but also shows how the children talked not so much about 'languages' but rather about their language practices and lived experiences as plurilingual speakers. As Nayr Ibrahim (2019: 41) observes in her study on children's representation of their multilingualism in an out-of-school English literacy class in Paris, 'children made constant reference to real people, tangible places and relevant experiences when asked about their languages'. Similarly, Busch (2022: 229) describes how primary school children, talking about their language portraits, related languages to places that had their respective language regimes. Thus, it can be seen as part of the normalcy of lived multilingualism to negotiate sometimes and in certain situations around the use of a language – as mentioned before by Amelija regarding her complementary school attendance and by Bianca in the extracts above. It is relevant for (teacher agency in) multilingual pedagogies within the primary school to see children as experts in this kind of experience, too. To listen to children's 'superdiverse voices' requires educators – and researchers – simultaneously to be sensitive to the normalcy of multilingualism in children's lives while also being cognisant of (potential) situations where meanings are negotiated or in which a child's ownership of normalcy might be interrupted.

5.3 A Stopover: A 'Pedagogical Space' of Multilingual Pedagogies

In this section, I discuss some inferences from the findings around the monolingual norm and the children's superdiverse voices presented in this chapter and introduce as the fourth element of the study's framework of interconnected elements a 'pedagogical space' that can contribute to the achievement of teacher agency in multilingual pedagogies.

The monolingual norm configures how the children's language experiences and repertoires come into contact with the ways in which the school acts out language ideologies. As the episodes from Ellie's class have shown, the norm is established for pupils new to English while confirmed for the other children. In this way, the dividing line between the classroom's official language and those not considered relevant for learning is reproduced. These processes occur not so much as an imposition but as a form of production and – within the school's microculture – they convey a *pedagogical* message (Alexander, 2008; Apple, 1982). The norm in the classroom is confronted with the normalcy of children's 'superdiverse voices', while the pupils, in turn, encounter the monolingual norm as the school's pedagogical normality. In this sense, the monolingual norm has been described as part of the classroom's working consensus, and it has been pointed out that such a consensus is initiated by the teachers, with whom the greater power lies.

Achieving teacher agency in multilingual pedagogies requires educators to relate and pedagogically respond to the monolingual norm and the children's superdiverse voices as opposite facets of the status quo. Teachers need to be reflective about the norm and simultaneously aware of the various meanings that languages/elements of linguistic repertoires have for children. The examples in this chapter show that pupils assign multiple meanings to the elements of their language repertoires and, consequently, are positioned differently when they come into contact with the school's monolingual norm. While the school constitutes a space where all children can be involved in negotiating the significance those repertoires might have in school, their different

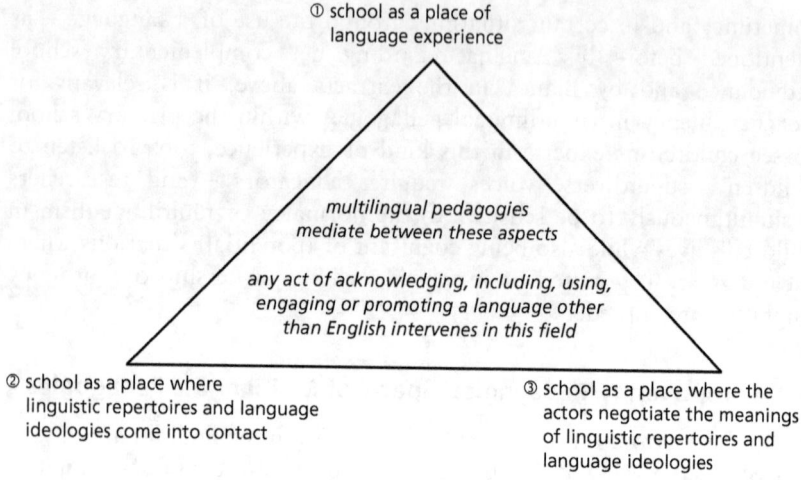

Figure 5.3 The mainstream primary school as a place for multilingual pedagogies

positions influence what they can or may want to invest in such negotiations.

The mainstream primary school that intends to forge multilingual pedagogies needs to acknowledge and reflect upon the central role it plays in mediating between children's language experiences, their encounters with the school's language ideologies, and the opportunities children have for negotiating the meanings of their language repertoires in the classroom (Figure 5.3). Given the status quo, it is the primary school's pedagogical task and challenge, to design approaches, formats and settings that respond to *both* the monolingual norm and the children's superdiverse voices. The *pedagogical space* which I delineate and advocate here builds on this understanding. It relates to the three aspects of the school as a place for multilingual pedagogies, to the specific setting of a given school or classroom, and to practical approaches that override the monolingual norm. Conceptualising a 'pedagogical space' for multilingual pedagogies in the linguistically very diverse primary school parallels, to some extent, notions of an 'interpersonal space' or 'pedagogical space' (Cummins, 2000: 42–50; Cummins *et al.*, 2011a: 31), which are used to describe the generation of knowledge and negotiations of identity in the interaction between teachers and students. However, the notion of a 'pedagogical space' proposed here addresses more explicitly the diversity of children's language repertoires, i.e. a diversity that includes the variety of meanings pupils assign to their languages alongside the number of different languages spoken by the children in one classroom. Thus, the 'pedagogical space' reflects that 'educators [should] plan carefully the ways in which all the students' home languages and their linguistic practices are *acknowledged, included,* and *used* in the classroom' (García & Flores, 2012: 242, emphasis added). As the fourth element of the framework of teacher agency in multilingual pedagogies – alongside the classrooms as part of the institution of school, children's linguistic repertoires and voices, and teachers' professional subjectivities – the 'pedagogical space' foregrounds the necessity to see *all students* as addressees of multilingual pedagogies (García & Flores, 2012: 242) and to contextually ground such pedagogies in the routines and pedagogical practices of the primary school classroom. The pedagogical space envisioned is a shared conceptual space for multilingual pedagogies and primary school pedagogy.

The extracts in this chapter show that there are, within the same classroom, pupils who have the same named language but assign different meanings to them in their repertoire. Such a constellation is most evident with Adriana, Sonia and Bianca. However, it is also apparent in the accounts of the other children for whom a 'first'/'second language' divide is no longer meaningful. One of the tasks and challenges for the pedagogical space would be to accommodate what I have portrayed as the range of meanings of speaking a language in the children's descriptions of their language practices. The pedagogical space needs to be designed as *responsive* to this diversity and as *dialogical*. From a pedagogical perspective, the notion of 'superdiverse voices' points as much to the *diversity* of languages and of meanings they have for children as it is about *children's voices*, and in school, those 'superdiverse' meanings can only be articulated in a dialogic way. The pedagogical space for multilingual pedagogies in primary school would not only need to respond conceptually to the monolingual norm and the diversity of children's language repertoires but would create – as a *constitutive part* of these pedagogies – opportunities for children and educators to explore (their) multilingualism. Such opportunities and explorations link the pedagogical space of multilingual pedagogies dynamically to other elements of the study's framework for teacher agency, namely to children's repertoires and voices and teachers' evolving professional subjectivities.

While pupils bring their language(s), and the meanings they attribute to them, as experiences to school, it is in this very context of the school that (a part of) these meanings are confirmed and valued, or questioned, ignored and devalued – or met with responses on a spectrum between these poles. The findings reported around the monolingual norm, EAL discourse and symbolic multilingualism in the five classrooms all illustrate how pedagogical practices shape which meanings are ascribed to children's linguistic repertoire in school and for learning. In fact, hardly any pedagogical practice is neutral concerning children's language experiences and, consequently, any activity of multilingual pedagogies – any act of acknowledging, including, using, engaging and promoting the student's plurilingual repertoires – can be seen as *intervening* in the nexus of the school as a place of language experience, where repertoires and ideologies meet, and where students and educators negotiate the meanings that these have in school. In other words, any element of multilingual pedagogies potentially modifies pupils' and teachers' language experience, the contact between their repertoires and language ideologies and how they (can) negotiate what these mean in school. The significance and inclusion of pupils' language experiences, the emphasis on students' voices and agency and the exploration of multilingual identities are all, in different educational contexts, important components of multilingual pedagogical approaches, such as Identity Texts (Cummins *et al.*, 2011a), cooperations between primary and complementary schools (Kenner & Ruby, 2012) and Multilingual Digital Storytelling (Anderson & Macleroy, 2016). They also relate to wider perspectives, such as critical multilingual language awareness (Hélot *et al.*, 2018b) and reciprocal multilingual awareness for multilingual citizenship (Windle *et al.*, 2023). However, this study's insights from the classroom and the participatory activities show that it is helpful for further developments in the primary school under superdiverse conditions to have – on a conceptual level – *a lens* for the evaluation of how various approaches, formats and activities can have different functions for acknowledging, promoting, including, using, engaging and promoting pupil's plurilingual repertoires. Educators need to be able to evaluate approaches and activities when making their choices, taking stances on their pedagogical work and intervening in a given status quo. The pedagogical space as such a conceptual lens constitutes, together with corresponding pedagogical and sociolinguistic knowledge, a precondition for achieving teacher agency in multilingual pedagogies in superdiverse primary schools.

A further facet of the pedagogical space emerges from Sonia's and Bianca's ways of negotiating their multilingualism. The episodes reported in this chapter show the workings of the monolingual norm. However, they can also be interpreted as situations where the pupils appear to actively resist marginalisation on account of their multilingualism: Sonia refuses to be marginalised in the classroom as an unsuccessful learner, whereas Bianca appears to oppose marginalisation in wider society, calling into question the legitimacy of bilingual Romanian/English speakers 'to belong here'. In contrast, the engagement and pleasure that many pupils displayed when talking during the participatory activities about their plurilingual experiences and skills might be seen not so much as directly defying the monolingual norm but as voicing an alternative. Chapter 7 will report how the children talked about their ideas for multilingual activities. As argued before, various positions and out-of-/in-school language experiences (can) exist simultaneously in one classroom. Such simultaneity, where pupils express their multilingual skills while others choose to downplay them or feel coerced to do so, underlines the mediating role that multilingual pedagogies play between children's language experiences in out-of-school contexts (understood as both children's home environment and their experiences in broader society and its political discourses) and the context of school. Consequently, the primary school is asked to clarify what it intends to pursue *pedagogically* and what it considers to be the teaching/learning practices, pedagogical values, motivations and reasonings it brings to the shared conceptual space for multilingual pedagogies and primary school pedagogy. Central pedagogical strands referred to in various projects and approaches of multilingual pedagogies are the critical, learner-centred and democratic traditions of Célestin Freinet, John Dewey and Paulo Freire, or Douglas Barnes and advocates of critical literacies like Hillary Janks (2010) (see e.g. Anderson & Macleroy, 2016; Cummins *et al.*, 2011a; Little & Kirwan, 2019).

Sonia's and Bianca's positionings can be instructive in relation to the general pedagogical perspectives of primary school. Given the entwined effects of EAL discourse, monolingual norm and symbolic multilingualism that devalue children's non-English language repertoires, the two girls' association of multilingualism with marginalisation cannot come as a surprise, as such a devaluation and hierarchisation of languages is one of those pedagogical messages conveyed in the microculture of school. As orientation for the pedagogical space that can be inferred from those very different constellations – on the one hand, fear and refusal of marginalisation due to multilingualism, and on the other hand, the well-being and enjoyment associated with it – it is productive to ask what approaches and activities would be experienced by the pupils as *empowerment*. The concept of 'empowerment' is, of course, a salient feature of approaches located in the tradition of Critical Pedagogy and Transformative Pedagogy (see e.g. Macleroy, 2021). A focus on the question of what might be seen as empowering from the point of view of plurilingual children is also vital for primary school pedagogy in general, as it strengthens a perspective that is neither necessarily limited to academic learning nor restricts itself to the merely symbolic acknowledgement of symbolic multilingualism. Thus, a guiding orientation for empowerment in the superdiverse primary school could be the provision of affordances that enable plurilingual children to experience 'language-as-a-resource' (Ruiz, 1984/2017) and as doing something for learning in school. Following the line of analysis adopted in this chapter, this perspective conjoins with pedagogical considerations on the question of which subject positions might be made available for different students by the various approaches of multilingual pedagogies.

In many accounts on multilingual pedagogies, the emphasis seemed to be more often than not either on students who are described as emergent bilinguals and/or as belonging to socially marginalised groups. Multilingual pedagogies in the superdiverse primary school, however, require an additional angle, actively involving all pupils. In this regard, the fact that the notion of linguistic superdiversity refers to individuals with biographical experiences of migration *and* plurilinguals, for whom multilingualism is simply a condition of their life, is crucial. Indeed, there exists a dilemma within the efforts to bring multilingual pedagogies into the pedagogical mainstream: If multilingualism remains exclusively associated with 'migration', such efforts are not only susceptible to anti-immigration discourses in media and politics but struggle to override the very logic on which historically and currently dominant monolingualising pedagogies rest. Multilingualism needs to be considered and acknowledged as normalcy without an explicit or implicitly imagined reference to 'migration' and the 'immigrant child'. While schools under superdiverse conditions seem, in principle, in a good position to establish this normalcy, they appear nevertheless – like the classrooms in this study – to be characterised by a paradox. On the one hand, a normalisation of diversity is a typical and salient trait of those schools, where labels like 'migrant' or 'non-migrant' students are no longer seen as a relevant distinction. Paul Gilroy's (2004) concept of conviviality is cited in the context of superdiversity and sociolinguistics (Blackledge *et al.*, 2018: xxx), referring 'to the processes of cohabitation and interaction that have made multiculture an ordinary feature of social life in Britain's urban areas and in postcolonial cities elsewhere' (Gilroy, 2004: xi). Representing it as much as contributing to it, primary schools are a vital part of conviviality. On the other hand, schools that respond to students' multilingualism with practices like the monolingual norm, EAL discourse and symbolic multilingualism, give their advantageous position away. Not unlike the ways described in the context of the EAL discourse, the normalisation of multilingualism is diminished when multilingualism is associated only with emergent bilingual children and is disrupted when reified in symbolic multilingualism, most notably in the representation of languages through national flags in the school environment. In both cases, multilingualism is linked to the theme of international migration, and thus the dichotomous distinction between 'migrant' and 'non-migrant' that is largely overcome in the schools' everyday practices surfaces once more.

Numerous accounts of multilingual pedagogies foreground the overall social justice perspective. Exemplarily, García and Flores (2012: 242) highlight its relevance for the development of multilingual pedagogies, '[b]ecause languages are spoken by groups of people who are situated differently socially, attention to social justice is paramount'. Such attention is vital for more equity for emergent bilingual students, and the children Daniel, Sonia and Adriana from the classrooms explored so far are cases in point. Yet, the classroom and interview extracts show not only how plurilingual children are perceived merely as EAL learners or English-speaking students, but also that the EAL discourse allows educators to see the school's monolingualism within an understanding of social justice. It is, therefore, helpful to ask how the 'pedagogical space' might be seen in relation to social justice. Nancy Fraser reminds us that we do not know 'what justice is in the abstract. I think we only learn – over time and through the process of struggle and critical thinking – that conditions we live with are unjust. The sense of injustice comes first, we react and [... t]he overcoming is a step towards justice' (Fraser, 2017). Fraser (2008) understands parity of participation as the most general meaning of justice and combines the axes of socioeconomic redistribution, legal and cultural recognition and political representation, i.e. the possibility to make claims for justice that *are heard*. The insistence on monolingualism within the EAL discourse of mainstream pedagogy might be best seen as prioritising the participation perspective – in that English language skills are indispensable for successful participation in education and thus, in the long term, in society. Such understanding of participation is inevitably limited by its own monolingual perspective, and participation is offered at the expense of a recognition of the child as a plurilingual speaker and learner. This is the restriction that Sonia appears to be aware of in the classroom vignettes presented, while her friend Adriana must be seen as largely silenced by the given pedagogical setting. In terms of social justice and Fraser's (2008, 2017) third axis – the political representation of all voices in the framing of the collective decision making in democratic institutions – newly arrived pupils like Sonia and Adriana or other children like Maimouna in Chapter 1 are simply not involved in decision making about the monolingual pedagogy they encounter. I would like to argue that it is in this context of recognition and non-recognition that multilingualism becomes a major question for primary school pedagogy. Before entering formal education, children continuously extend their language and languaging by participating in a growing number of social contexts in which they are recognised and respected as speakers and where, by using their language skills, they experience their capacity to act within these contexts. Such processes of participation and recognition are central to children's (language) experiences and interactions in the classroom, too, where every child must find their voice for interactions and learning to be successful.

As research in the realm of multilingual pedagogies is expanding in Europe, research projects explore and document developments in the system of mainstream primary schools, involving school settings that include, apart from the language of instruction, for example, the official languages Frisian and Irish, respectively (Duarte & Günther-van der Meij, 2018, 2022; Little & Kirwan, 2019). These intervention studies and school development projects move the focus of multilingual pedagogies closer to a pedagogy for all primary schools. However, the main point I want to make here is that it is necessary for further developments in schools under superdiverse conditions to foreground explicitly a frame of pedagogical motivations and rationales for multilingual pedagogies that can complement the overall social justice orientation, which is often primarily related to the theme of migration and emergent bilinguals. Importantly, those pedagogical perspectives need to be articulated and developed in school settings, where children's (and teacher's) plurilingualism *is legitimised per se* and not necessarily via the presence of more than one official language.

What I have called in this stopover section 'pedagogical space' is seen as both a conceptual lens and a concrete and practical reservoir. From the children's point of view, it would need to be a 'space' – approaches, teaching/learning formats, settings and activities – where they can make their plurilingual voices heard and experience their languages as resources for learning. This includes affordances where they can explore the meanings that languages or elements of their linguistic repertoire have for them. From the perspective of the educators and to support their achievement of agency, however, it needs to be a frame that is *flexible* enough to appreciate the 'small spaces' for decisions made in their planning and classroom, while also being sufficiently *systematic* to enable teachers to link their decisions and choices to a broader pedagogical repertoire or framework. In other words, it would be perceived by the teachers as structured in such a way that they would know, following García's phrasing (2014: 4), what to do 'strategically' with children's languages other than English. Or – following the formulation Priestley *et al.* (2015: 141) use in their definition of teacher agency – in such a way that educators would be able to choose in a given situation between different options and to judge which option is the most desirable in the circumstances of their classroom.

This chapter looked in greater detail at the classrooms in relation to monolingualism and multilingualism. The monolingual norm established for pupils new to English and maintained for the other plurilingual children helps teachers reduce the complexity of their classrooms while constituting a hindrance to teacher agency in multilingual pedagogies. However, a teacher's reflection on a homework project has drawn attention to the significance of reflexivity as a *constitutive component* of such agency in a setting shaped by a monolingual norm. The findings from the participatory activities highlight that the awareness of superdiverse voices and knowledge about the different meanings that speaking a language has for different pupils needs to be seen as an integral part of multilingual pedagogies in superdiverse primary schools, and thus as another *constitutive component* of teacher agency in this domain. A 'pedagogical space' has been suggested that would respond conceptually to the monolingual norm and, simultaneously, to the diversity of children's language repertoires, creating opportunities for children and teachers to explore their multilingualism. Within the model of teacher agency, the pedagogical space provides *different options* from which teachers can choose in response to the contexts of their classrooms, while it combines a developmental perspective to advance such pedagogies with a localised angle that aims at tailoring those approaches to particular circumstances.

6 Teachers' Perspectives in Busy Multilingual Classrooms

The first part of this chapter looks at the workplace school as an important and ambivalent context for teacher agency, and the following parts centre, within the framework of teacher agency in multilingual pedagogies, on the teachers' professional subjectivities. By exploring teachers' perspectives on their workplace and professional identities and asking how they thematise multilingualism, the chapter addresses how teachers' professional knowledge, experiences and attitudes can function as affordances for multilingual pedagogies.

6.1 'A teacher's life is hard': The Workplace School

The school as a workplace is highly relevant as a backdrop for situating teacher agency. Ultimately, agency in the classroom can only be achieved when supported by the workplace school, whose conditions afford and frame that classroom. Thus, the following findings complement the enquiry into the teachers' general agency presented in Chapter 3. Yet, these conditions can both facilitate and hinder teacher agency. Within the complexity of the institution of school, it can be challenging to define which aspects to incorporate in a description of 'conditions' and how to determine where the boundary lies between conditions of a specific school and wider circumstances of educational policy. The funding for children with special educational needs, as mentioned regarding Hira's classroom, and the precarious position of the EAL coordinator in her school, as stated by Ellie, are cases in point. The main focus here is, however, on the workplace, as described by the teachers. This is conceptually relevant, as such conditions impact teacher agency, yet such a description was also required in the research process. That is, to proceed to an exploration of teacher agency in multilingual pedagogies, it was important to ensure that the workplace conditions of the five teachers were, on the whole, comparable. It was essential to establish that no teacher found themselves in a situation where their general agency is negatively affected by the workplace conditions in such a way that it would become nearly meaningless to explore agency in relation to multilingual pedagogies – although it is highly unlikely that such an educator would have volunteered to take part in the study.

In this section, I present data on relationships, roles and scope/influence as three connected aspects of the workplace school. 'Relationships' are seen in the ecological approach as a component of social structures of the workplace school within the practical-evaluative domain that contributes to the achievement of teacher agency. Since relationships are closely linked with workplace culture, it seemed valuable to leave it up to the teachers to decide at which point during the interview they would choose to thematise them. Both 'role' and 'scope or influence' were explicitly addressed within interview questions.

The next extracts are instructive because Ellie and Heather not only describe the atmosphere but also point to vertical and horizontal orientations within relationships in their workplace, that is, to two dimensions which impact teacher agency (Priestley *et al.*, 2015: 92–104). Vertical relationships represent workplace hierarchies, whereas horizontal relationships exist between educators collaborating on the same plane. Those orientations are not necessarily mutually exclusive, and vertical relationships may also include reciprocity and dialogue. In addition, 'strong horizontal ties [...] appeared to facilitate (or at least be indicative of) a collegial and collaborative culture in the school' (Priestley *et al.*, 2015: 103). To understand Ellie's agency, it is useful to look at each of the following three extracts separately and consider how aspects are linked across the three following excerpts.

184 If we have got monitoring and we have got feedback, then I would be
185 checking after that that this is happening [...] in the different
186 classes. And really focusing on consistency [...]
188 that everyone is delivering sort of the same skills [...]
189 And that just comes through PPA and discussing things and
190 actually in this year group we are being really, really reflective. We work really
191 well together and we are very honest with each other and actually that 'that
192 activity in maths, no that didn't work at all, wasn't teachable, how do we
193 change it?' and I think that's being really good. Because I have been in year
194 groups where people [...] they were quite resistant to
195 change or they take it very personally [...]

(Interview, 8 February 2017)

The theme 'relationships' emerges as Ellie talks about her role as a year group leader and mentions her involvement in vertical relationships that come with this role (Lines 184–186). Yet, she also emphasises the importance of horizontal ties in Lines 189–193. In Line 189, she refers to their shared PPA time; that 10% of their timetabled teaching time that is set aside for planning, preparation and assessment, to which teachers are entitled. Moreover, the teacher contrasts her current experiences with those in her previous school, where she worked for seven years and was also a year group leader (Lines 193–195). As is also evident from other interview passages, the act of comparing is relevant to her assessment of the current conditions at her workplace. For example, Ellie values the fact that she can teach her class all day – as opposed to her previous school, where children were taught in 'ability' groups from Year 1 onwards – enhancing her flexibility regarding time management during the school day and her rapport with the children (Interview, 24 March 2017: Lines 185–191). Such evaluations can be understood within the iterational dimension of teacher agency (see p. 31). In other words, the achievement of agency is influenced by the teacher's professional history, which includes experiences in another workplace and contributes to her assessment of presently encountered conditions. 'Relationships' resurfaces elsewhere in Ellie's interviews:

288	TQ:	[...] Which kind of decisions do you influence or make?
289	Ellie:	[...] we get the curriculum and a lot is mapped out already
290		and that is sort of due to the position the school is in that it 'requires improvement'.
291		A lot of things like in maths is all per week plotted out what you ought to
292		deliver – down to topic, I mean it's not day by day. So, currently, I am
293		planning topic [...]
294		Ajit is doing maths, Martha is doing literacy [...]
295		we make the decision what to do
296		and how. We have a lot of discussion anyway. [...]
297		And we are really dealing – you
298		know as a team we would do that.

(Interview, 8 February 2017)

Major elements of British education policy feature prominently in the description, where teachers 'get the curriculum and a lot is mapped out already [...] due to the position the school is in that it "requires improvement"' (Lines 289–290). In my view, the fact that Ellie mentions these indicators of education policy in response to the question about decisions she is involved in is significant in that they point to the overall parameters of curriculum domination and accountability to Ofsted inspections, within which the school as a workplace, its relationships and teacher agency operate. Thus, the teacher's description chimes with two assertions referred to in Section 2.5: that the dominance of the curriculum in the English educational discourse has 'tended to make pedagogy subsidiary to curriculum' (Alexander, 2008: 47) and that '[t]he neoliberal reconstruction of the professional role has thus impacted radically on the possibilities for agency' (Priestley et al., 2015: 126).

Ellie, however, juxtaposes this overarching context with a reiteration of her earlier description of horizontal relationships, which consist, in her year group, of alternately planning for the various subjects (Lines 292–294) and include factors of reciprocity and symmetry: 'we make the decision what to do and how. We have a lot of discussions anyway [...] And we are really dealing – you know as a team we would do that' (Lines 295–298). Two aspects are relevant here: first, Ellie's teacher agency, achieved in the classroom, as described in Chapter 3, by maintaining the working consensus established with her class and by making small choices within teaching routines, is fostered by horizontal relationships, collaboration and the collegial atmosphere in her team. These supportive relationships are relevant for achieving her teacher agency. Second, such relationships are embedded in the institution of school that constitutes both a workplace and a context where education policy is played out for educators. This almost self-evident constellation is important for exploring teacher agency because it points to the fundamental fact that a teacher needs, ultimately, to come to terms with the conditions of the workplace as generated by that policy (for the phase when the role of primary school teachers in the UK was radically redefined, see e.g. Jeffrey & Woods, 1998, and Ball, 2003). Therefore, Ellie appears to describe how education policy directs her work (Lines 289–292), while also stating 'we make the decision what to do and how' (Lines 295–296). This may appear, at first glance, to be contradictory. However, I would contend that it is more usefully understood as precisely the moment when the teacher points to the room that she can claim for her agency. This is the scope 'where agency is seen as emerging from the *interaction* of individual "capacity" with environing "conditions"' (Priestley et al., 2015: 22, emphasis in original). An explicit acknowledgement that teacher agency is inevitably situated within the framework provided by education policy in England is significant for cautioning against overstraining or overstating the individual teacher's agency vis-à-vis the constraints that underlie the everyday experiences of teachers. As they state, 'I think time is just a big factor. You know we have so much to squeeze in. We are just like "go, go, go…" and everything has to be taught in a very tight time' (Interview Ellie, 24 March 2017:

Lines 298–300) or, as already quoted in Section 1.2, 'the curriculum is so jam-packed [...] if we ever have a bit of spare time, we are doing something that they, you know, giving them some free time sometimes if they have behaved well. But given the jam-packed curriculum...' (Interview Hira, 27 June 2017: Lines 558 and 561–564).

All five teachers described supportive relationships, with an emphasis on either organisational arrangements like shared planning or the cooperative atmosphere of the workplace culture, which was consistent with the fieldnotes. Furthermore, Ellie's account can shed light on how vertical and horizontal relationships might be perceived as related and how teacher agency features at this juncture. Such a connection emerged as I asked Ellie whether recent changes in teaching practices concerning guided reading and maths had been already established when she joined the school or whether she and her colleagues could still influence ongoing developments.

```
319   Most of it was in place already because I know in July, everybody
      brought sort
320   of their own from the year, 'So this doesn't work', [...] 'we would
321   suggest that thing for next year'. So we'll this year, we'll make,
      sort of make
322   decisions for the next year as to what works and quite a lot of . .
      sort of .
323   reflecting reflecting on what works [...]
324   how can we do better? And I think as a school, they
325   are quite open to feedback and actually they want to know what
      can be
326   different or then [headteacher] asked me quite a few times about
      things, you
327   know 'What did you do in your old school?' compared – they were
328   an outstanding school [...] and I think as a
329   SMT [senior management team] they are very open to that and
      they are quite willing to give things a go.
```

(Interview, 8 February 2017)

The teacher describes here and elsewhere a work culture and relationships that appear to meet the criteria of reciprocity and generative dialogue (Priestley *et al.*, 2015: 103), also within the school's vertical relationships. Yet, Ellie's repeated use of the phrase 'what works' (Lines 322 and 323) or 'this doesn't work' (Line 320) shows the entanglement with the framework of education policy where '[t]eachers [...] are required to produce measurable and "improving" outputs and performances, what is important is *what works*' (Ball, 2003: 222, emphasis in original).

The teacher's description mirrors the 'value' of what works, which has been identified as one of the discursive interventions into UK education policy and the public sector more widely used since the mid-1990s (Ball, 2003: 217–219). Moreover, she describes how the headteacher consults her, as she has the expertise of having taught and been a year group leader in a school judged by Ofsted as 'outstanding' (Lines 326–328). This chimes with her position at a kind of juncture of vertical and horizontal relationships that she addressed elsewhere when describing the school's efforts to develop the role of the year group leader, 'previously I have done a lot more of data and being really accountable [...] And I said, "You know I don't feel like people, like SMT sort of make the most of year group leaders [...] that's something that I would be able to offer"' (Interview, 8 February 2017: Lines 233–239).

262	Ellie:	[...] I think it's good to be year group leader and have
263		a class because it is easy to lose sight of what class teachers are actually doing
264		on a daily basis
266		[...] I think with assistant heads
267		and those leaders, they are not in class and they easily lose sight of people
268		actually saying 'We need it now'. With, you know, teachers in class the
269		priorities are different [...] I am in a good position
270		because I know, I know instantly what is going on in each room, whereas when
271		you are not in here day-to-day, you are not as aware

(Interview, 8 February 2017)

Ellie's account illustrates what Stephen Ball (2003: 219) has called 'deeply paradoxical' developments at the workplace school within the culture of performativity. On the one hand, changes were often portrayed as moving away from centralised forms of employee control, and managerial responsibilities were delegated with problem-solving and initiative was highly valued; on the other hand, mechanisms of very direct surveillance and self-monitoring were established. A comparable tension occurs in Ellie's description: When being addressed by the headteacher because of the role she held in her previous school (Lines 326–328) and when taking the initiative to develop her current role further (Lines 231–239), the teacher expands her possibilities to influence routines and makes choices regarding her work and role in the school. In other words, she moves beyond agency in her classroom, taking up a more powerful position in the workplace. This position as a year group leader, however, is part of the education policy context. Consequently, Ellie mentions an element of surveillance: 'I know instantly what is going on in each room' (Line 270). Simultaneously, she contrasts her role with that of 'assistant heads and those leaders, they are not in class and they easily lose sight of people actually saying "We need it now…"' (Lines 266–268), and in doing so, she foregrounds her own role as a class teacher. This constellation is instructive for understanding teacher agency in general and, by extension, within multilingual pedagogies. A role and area of responsibility in school enhances the teacher's agency beyond the classroom but can be seen as still anchored in it and the supportive relationships with other class teachers. This was also evident when Heather, who is Lower Key Stage 2 lead and also responsible for well-being in her school, was asked about the scope of her influence:

263   We are very lucky because everybody respects everybody here, it is such
264   a lovely environment to work in, […] I feel like, I do
265   have an influence and I would say people do listen to [me] but I feel like that for
266   everybody we all listen to each other. So, like well-being and other things I
267   have ownership on, I have a huge influence because I am – you are like an
268   expert in your field. And people will come to me for help and advice.

(Interview, 12 January 2018)

She describes reciprocity and dialogue as features of her school's workplace culture. As with Ellie before, Heather's roles – 'things I have ownership on' (Lines 266–267) – increase her agency in terms of vertical relationships while it remains embedded in horizontal ties with her colleagues. When asked what would happen if someone advocates 'a new idea', Heather mentions the limitations of this agency:

286   We are very lucky, everyone is open-minded, everyone knows that we
287   only want the best – hm we don't want any more hard work [imitating
288   intonation] we don't want any more paperwork to do, we are just doing it –

(Interview, 12 January 2018)

In Line 286, the teacher confirms her earlier depiction of the workplace's atmosphere. However, she also describes the limits of new developments that, from the perspective of her colleagues – and as a class teacher and within these horizontal relationships, Heather is one of them – should not cause 'any more hard work' (Line 287). The theme of workload also emerged when Hira was asked whether her colleagues would support the idea of occasionally having a day 'to bring the other languages in':

657		[…] I think everybody would be willing as
658		long as it is not extra work... and .. do you understand what I mean?
659	TQ:	Yeah
660		That is the first thing so, you know, when you have changes so when you want
661		to do something you have to think about 'Okay is that the most reduced
662		work, is there not something extra added for someone' . because yeah
663		a teacher's life is hard […]

(Interview, 27 June 2017)

Hira addresses here the overall conditions of the workplace school, where teachers need to shield themselves from additional work that may result from suggested changes. Given that the average workload of primary school teachers in England is one of the highest internationally (e.g. OECD, 2019), it is crucial to acknowledge the conditions that the two teachers refer to as the fundamental circumstances of their workplace. Those passages, along with the strategies employed here to describe the situation (imitation in Lines 287–288; a semi-rhetorical question in Line 658), point to tensions around new practices in schools and are highly significant for exploring teacher agency, as they highlight that '[a]gency can manifest itself in various ways, not merely as entering into and suggesting new work practices, but also as maintaining existing practices or struggling against suggested changes' (Eteläpelto *et al.*, 2013: 61). Since the goals and contents of multilingual pedagogies cannot be retrieved directly from the curriculum, and given that the workplace is framed by the dominance of a performativity culture, such pedagogical approaches will be 'extra work' for class teachers, whose 'life is hard', to use Hira's words. This poses a considerable dilemma because those teachers play a central role in further developments, where, as argued in Section 5.3, the classroom must be seen as a point of departure for multilingual pedagogies for various reasons, such as the required reflexivity on language ideologies, knowledge about students' superdiverse voices and the necessary development of transitions from current monolingual practices to the inclusion of pupils' plurilingual resources. All of these requirements are processes that require time, and the accounts of all five teachers show that this time is currently not provided in the mainstream primary school in England.

The findings reported here might be helpful when assigning the part of meso-level actor for multilingual pedagogies to an individual school. While not a substitute for decisions on the macro level of education policy, such a move could be considered, given the lack of local institutions that function as meso-level actors by providing guidance and resources. At the school level, decisions need to be made collectively to engage with multilingual pedagogies in the classrooms. Consequently, it can be useful to ask which roles in school may adopt a meso-level responsibility. In all three schools, the EAL coordinators combined their roles with other positions as Early Years or Key Stage 1 teachers. While they were responsible for the EAL domain across the whole school, they were inevitably situated at a certain distance from the everyday workings of numerous other classrooms. Two suggestions can be inferred from these descriptions around agency and workplace. Both seek to move from an understanding of multilingual approaches as temporary support for pupils at an early stage of learning English to approaches within a primary school pedagogy which engages with the fact that many children are plurilingual speakers.

The first suggestion refers to the 'pedagogical space' that was outlined in primarily conceptual terms in Section 5.3. In practical terms, this space would need to be organised in such a way that class teachers can become sufficiently involved to feel ownership over their choices in their classrooms while also being able to rely on their supportive professional relationships, similar to what Ellie described as 'we make the decision what to do and how'. Arguably, the dilemma around the workload remains, and this needs to be clearly acknowledged in a study on teacher agency in English primary schools. A second suggestion relates to the question of how procedures for planning and realising activities around multilingual pedagogies might be supported by roles in school and areas of responsibility. It might be worth considering the possibilities associated with various roles, which are at the juncture of vertical and horizontal workplace relationships, as described by the teachers above. It would be desirable to assign an area of responsibility for multilingual pedagogies to a role that entails a closer involvement in day-to-day practices and contents of the classroom than that of the EAL coordinator, drawing, in a sense, on Ellie's assessment that '… those leaders, they are not in class and they easily lose sight of people actually saying "We need it now"' (Lines 267–268). Thus, it is useful to allocate responsibility for multilingual pedagogies not only to EAL coordinators but also to teachers who have a coordinating role within year groups or key stages and are, importantly, still working in the classroom. This suggestion follows the perspective of relational agency, where the individual's professional agency is enhanced by working 'with others to expand the object that one is working on by bringing to bear the sense-making of others and to draw on the resources they offer when responding to that sense-making' (Edwards, 2007: 4). It is desirable to establish a setting in which the capacities and knowledge of the EAL coordinators and the year group or key stage leads could come together with the day-to-day knowledge of class teachers and their running of the classrooms.

6.2 'Knowing the children': Professional Subjectivities

The following two extracts by Kelly and Hira indicate two professional priorities and values mentioned by all teachers: the significance of children's learning experience and the teacher's rapport with the pupils. Simultaneously, they point to the connection all teachers made to their own educational experiences. Kelly explains:

85 [...] I need to make sure that
86 the children have understood the lesson – have actually learnt something
87 from every lesson [...] [she gives the previous maths lesson as example]
93 That is really important to make sure that the children really
94 understand rather than just ploughing on [...]
95 [...] and [that] the children enjoy learning. I really like learning
96 stuff [...] I love learning things and
97 I want the children to love learning. Having been either to other schools or
98 having seen my children going to other schools, where it's just the process
99 they turn up there, have known something and they go home. There
100 is no real enjoyment from learning, no curiosity. [...]
102 [...] I want them to come away from here loving
103 learning because I think if you go through all your primary years and they
104 don't come out loving learning, it is very difficult to then, to begin to go into all
105 those subjects you learn in secondary school.
(Interview, 29 November 2017)

In Lines 85–94, Kelly describes her responsibility for children's learning, which includes 'that the children really understand rather than just ploughing on' (Lines 93–94) and refers to the previous maths lesson and its formative assessment, in line with her and Heather's routine to give feedback and mark towards the end of lessons. Then, she points to the pupils' enjoyment of and love for learning (Lines 95 and 97). Kelly juxtaposes her view of a desirable learning experience on the part of the children with her own current experiences of learning (Lines 95–96) and contrasts it with her previous experiences both as a teacher in another school and as a mother (Lines 97–100). The teacher makes such connections in other interview sections, too, and here they lead, in all likelihood, to her assertion that primary school should be the foundation for 'loving learning' (Lines 103–105).

Hira responded to the question about the priorities of her work:

14 The children, first of all, that the children are having a safe environment like
15 knowing that they can make mistakes [...]
19 [...] I want children to feel happy when they come to the
20 classroom – so when I see my room, I like all the work coloured and the deco – [...]
22 because I like children to feel happy and as a child,
23 I can remember my primary school being very vibrant, and a happy face and
24 the colours [...]

224 [...] bring a smile on the children's face, like you know
225 having this relationship with them because sometimes they might need to talk
226 about something that they can't with their parents or that they need to tell
227 someone. I want to build that rapport with them where you know it feels
228 safe for them to speak about it

(Interview, 27 June 2017)

Similar to the other teacher, Hira first addresses the children's learning process and links it to the safe environment that she provides in her classroom (Lines 14–15) before mentioning the children's overall learning experience more explicitly: 'I want children to feel happy when they come to the classroom' (Lines 19–20). She associates her way of designing the classroom with her own experience as a pupil (Lines 20–24). Talking about the scope of her influence, Hira restates her commitment to the children's overall well-being in school (Line 224, 'bring a smile on the children's face'), linking it to her rapport with the children (Lines 225–228). The five teachers mentioned their relationship with the children and 'knowing the children' from different angles. I would argue, however, that Hira's description illustrates specifically how this rapport is interwoven with a concern for the whole person of the students (Adams et al., 2020; Biesta & Miedema, 2002) – literally including their voice – in a classroom where 'it feels safe for them to speak ...' (Lines 227–228).

The other teachers also addressed the learning experience of pupils and the rapport with them: 'I wanted to – I guess give back and make sure that children who might not be quite as privileged have really an exciting year in there in my class. [...] to make sure that every child first of all enjoys staying, but also you are meant to acquire the skills required ...' (Interview Mike, 30 January 2017: Lines 9–13). Elsewhere, he looks back at his own experience as a student: 'I always used to categorise teachers as always either being the fun ones which children enjoy spending time with, or the strict ones that wouldn't allow the child to move in their chair. But actually, you can do both. You can be strict [...], but you can also be fun and creative and interesting as well' (Interview Mike, 30 January 2017: Lines 35–39). This resonates with the active atmosphere that the teacher creates in his writing lessons, as described in Chapter 3. Furthermore, he addresses 'knowing the children' as part of his professional competence: 'knowing the children, you know, if you know that someone is emotional then you are on the warn yet [...] there are children [...] if they are coming after a tough break time, I know I need to speak to them [...] they know that I am there for them' (Interview Mike, 30 January 2017: Lines 106–110).

Ellie also mentioned knowledge about the individual child and engaging with them when asked about her professional priorities: 'I would just say knowing the children, like knowing them as individuals, is really like something I really try to do [...] knowing them and also knowing their ability, so knowing where they are, you know, what we are aiming for, where we try to get them to' (Interview, 8 February 2017: Lines 8–19). While this has connotations of differentiation and data monitoring in line with Ellie's role described previously, she also takes a broader pedagogical perspective: 'generally just to listen to them, in the morning quite a few have things they just want to tell you [...] paying an interest, I think it is' (Interview, 8 February 2017: Lines 31–37). This theme comes up again when she talks about her experience as Scouts leader, a role Ellie had started before becoming a teacher, and where she meets 7–10-year-olds who experience school quite negatively, '"oh we don't like school" [...] and I think through that sort of more relaxed sort of approach that I take to teaching [...] hopefully they are a bit more willing to come in – and then they tell me about all sorts of things [...] important to them and they want to share it [...] making the effort to make time to listen to them' (Interview, 8 February 2017: Lines 115–120). This description is consistent with the findings on Ellie's working consensus, and it also chimes with Hira's account quoted before, in which she links her rapport with the children to her willingness to listen to them.

The descriptions of children's learning experiences, teachers' rapport with pupils and the links to their own educational experience featured in all interviews when teachers talked about their priorities and values, and it helps advance teacher agency in multilingual pedagogies to incorporate these points in some questions of orientation: How might such pedagogies influence or change children's experience in school? How might they influence or change teachers' rapport with children? And how might multilingual pedagogies be linked to educators' own educational experiences? These questions are helpful for further reflections on multilingual pedagogies and attempts to thematise them in schools because they can connect to the existing knowledge and professional values of primary school teachers and what they experience as vital facets of their professional identities.

The connection that teachers saw to their personal experiences or interests was evident in describing choices and efforts to develop or change certain school practices. This might best be understood as personal experience and professional investment – 'investment' used here not as 'functional for', say, moving up the workplace hierarchy, but in the sense that those choices require a conscious and agentic decision on routines or practices. It is for that reason that personal experiences are relevant for teacher agency. Mike's interest in writing and his practice of teaching it, along with Ellie's experience as a Scout leader and the connection she makes to her working consensus, are cases in point.

At the time of the fieldwork, many primary schools started to change their approach to the daily guided reading lessons from a carousel model, where children read texts of their respective level of difficulty and move through different tasks during the week, to an arrangement in which all pupils read and work with the same book. Kelly and Mike were both involved in these changes in their schools. Kelly, who had repeatedly stated her passion for reading books, criticised the traditional model for disadvantaging pupils whose reading skills would currently still prevent them from a more profound reading experience and explained how her classroom initiative merged with the idea of the headteacher (Interview, 29 November 2017: Lines 373–459). Mike also referred to his personal experience in his description of how he was, together with the deputy head, responsible for rolling out the new approach in school: 'I am extremely passionate about this because I never really understood reading until I was fifteen, sixteen' (Interview, 20 March 2017, Lines 40–42). Kelly and Mike can resort for their professional investment to the official debate about teaching reading that provides legitimacy for the transformed practice. In this respect, guided reading differs considerably from the domain of multilingual pedagogies. The point to make, however, is that both teachers mentioned their personal experiences in the context of their professional investment. Such links are, in all probability, multifaceted and not linear, and for an exploration of teacher agency, they might be best understood if those experiences are seen as a kind of potential or possible resource for making choices and taking stances on teaching/learning practices. An additional question of orientation could thus be formulated: How can teachers' personal experiences become a resource for multilingual pedagogies?

6.3 Language Experiences and Reflexivity: Teachers' Positions

As shown in Chapter 4, all five teachers in the study mentioned their own language experiences when talking about the fact that many pupils were multilingual, and the following interview passages allow for an exploration of teachers' language experiences that might be relevant for achieving – or not achieving – agency in multilingual pedagogies. In addition, it is beneficial to look at the following extracts from the interviews with Mike, Hira and Heather in terms of how their thematisation of multilingualism points to different ways in which their experiences are positioned in relation to society's linguistic power relations. When asked whether his perspectives on multilingual children have changed over time, Mike replied:

448   It is completely inspiring for me to stand there and to realise that these children
449   have two and three and four languages [...] I am
450   jealous and there is a fair amount of admiration there. I think probably, at the
451   start of my career I had no idea, I came from a very sheltered background
452   where no one spoke another language. And when you are thrust into an Inner
453   London City primary school and you are suddenly exposed to all these
454   different languages [...]
455   for me it was like 'wow', quite shocking to start
456   with. But now, ya, I think just now – I don't even notice right now. I obviously
457   try and ensure that there is enough provision for the children who are
458   struggling [...]

(Interview, 30 January 2017)

The teacher repeats his description reported in Section 4.3, choosing the same picture (Lines 448–449, 'completely inspiring for me to stand there ...'). His choice of emotional language (Lines 449–450, 'I am jealous and there is a fair amount of admiration there') indicates his own language experience. He also mentions two juxtapositions: first, his family socialisation, where 'no one spoke another language' (Line 452), contrasting it with the moment he was 'thrust into an Inner London City primary school' (Lines 452–454). This experience, nine years ago, is then contrasted with 'just now – I don't even notice right now' (Line 456) before Mike makes, in line 456, another transition to children's EAL learning needs, analysed in Chapter 4 as characteristic of the 'EAL discourse'. In conjunction with Mike saying he is unaware of the languages his pupils speak (p. 87), this description of 'being inspired' by the children's multilingualism seems to confirm the power differential between teacher and plurilingual pupils. In fact, Mike's formulations, intensified by descriptions of distance – 'when I am standing there and there are –...' (p. 86, Lines 291–295) and 'for me to stand there' (Line 448) – seem to highlight and reproduce, or at least do not go beyond, the dividing line that exists in the classroom between the official English language and the children's plurilingual repertoires. From this angle, the mere acknowledgement of the fact that children speak more than one language does not result in what has been portrayed in work on the concept of 'lived experience of language' as a shift from a third-person to a first-person perspective (e.g. Busch, 2017b), and within 'translanguaging' theory as taking the perspective of bilingual speakers themselves (García & Kleyn, 2016b).

Mike's extract also chimes with his interview passage in Chapter 1 (pp. 19–20). In both extracts, his way of thematising multilingualism reproduces – somewhat paradoxically because the teacher intends to express his admiration for those repertoires – the dividing line between the classroom's official English and the children's plurilingual repertoires. He emphasises his own language experience vis-à-vis his plurilingual students, but his principal point of reference for acknowledging multilingualism is foreign language learning. This might best be understood as concurrently resulting from his own language experience and the monolingual lens that stems from this experience and the norm in school. Mike's extracts, therefore, help to understand how a teacher's own language experiences and the monolingual lens in the classroom can become interrelated. It cannot be the aim to identify linear connections between a teacher's language experience and practices around multilingual pedagogies. Yet, for understanding teacher agency and how teachers' experiences and attitudes might (or might not) function as affordances in this pedagogic domain, it is useful to see a teacher's particular experience around languages as relevant to the perspective from which they participate in the triangle that characterises the school as a place for multilingual pedagogies. In other words, Mike's example suggests that a teacher brings their own language experience into the constellation around multilingualism in school when negotiations about meanings of repertoires and ideologies occur. On the one hand, in line 456, Mike expresses, 'I don't even notice right now', that teaching multilingual children represents the normalcy of everyday routines for him. On the other hand, his wording epitomises a status quo, where the monolingual norm has become dominant and operates by hiding its own processes (see Chapter 5). Exploring the teacher's positioning and how it is linked to his language experiences within the school's status quo highlights the dilemma and inconsistency of a dominant monolingual position that expresses admiration for plurilingual children while simultaneously lacking the awareness of which languages they speak.

The next extracts can be read with a view to understanding Hira's language experiences and agency and her positionality around multilingualism. When asked about biographical or professional information, Hira said that she had always lived in London:

83   [...] It gives me an edge on the children because
84   I understand their background because also I also come—I come from a similar
85   background to the kids, so they can relate to me in many aspects and I think
86   also the fact that I am [...]
87   quite young. I can relate to them further [...] I know the
88   latest things and they know the latest things, so in that sense [...]
89   they can relate to me when speaking about things. It is easier to build
90   some rapport sometimes if you have things in common with the children. And
91   I think I have that. [...]

(Interview, 27 June 2017)

Hira describes it as beneficial for her work that she is familiar with the background of many children (Lines 84–85) and sees this identification as a mutual process (Line 85, 'so they can relate to me in many aspects'; Line 87, 'I can relate to them further'), linking it to her pedagogical theme of rapport with the children referred to before (p. 148). She mentions her familiarity with youth and popular culture as another aspect in common with her students (Lines 87–89). Her phrase 'if you have things in common with the children...' (Line 90) summarises this passage, where some 'things' are 'many aspects' of a 'similar background' and some are 'the latest things'. When asked what she means by 'background', the teacher continues:

94   Like where I come from. Not from a rich family, you know, I am coming from
95   an Asian background growing up with an – the customs that children have now
96   that was what my parents were like – not having like, for example, the
97   bedtime stories, in our culture that is not a big thing […]
99   […] I never had that, it
100 is not in my culture. So it is not that I missed out on these things, it's just that
101 it didn't happen […] I am not from
102 a particularly rich family, just working class, so I have all of those experiences
103 and obviously, being at school as a working-class child; that is what most of
104 my children are in the classroom, their parents are working class.

(Interview, 27 June 2017)

The teacher refers to the socioeconomic situation of her own family and to 'an Asian background', and she identifies with the children who would have the same customs as she had in her primary socialisation (Lines 94–95). As an example, Hira mentions the absence of bedtime stories (Lines 96–101) before returning more explicitly to the issue of class (Line 102). Here, she also expresses identification with her pupils, 'so I have all of those experiences' (Lines 102–104). These extracts include issues that would have benefited from more probing in the interview. Yet, it seems useful nonetheless to draw attention to three points: First, the teacher mentions multiple identifications, and describes her own and the children's background in terms of intersectionality, featuring class and ethnicity. Second, there might be various reasons for Hira's choice to illustrate customs through an absence of bedtime stories. However, it is noteworthy that she follows the dominant paradigm of early literacy, which understands the experience of the home story-reading (with a 'good book') as a vital precondition for future school success (see Gregory & Williams, 2000). Although Hira highlights her personal experience, ensuring it against a potential deficit interpretation (Lines 100–101), she appears to speak primarily as a teacher who does not acknowledge other literacy practices in the family. Third, she does not mention her linguistic resources at this point in her description of what she sees as a background shared with her pupils.

The teacher thematised her own bilingualism when I asked – picking up on the issue of the families' economic situation when Hira mentioned the unemployment of many parents – whether children would tell her if, say, their father had lost his job.

111 [...] a big thing like that they would tell me, they
112 would. Just as a conversation, because they would trust me with that. And also
113 I have – because I can speak another language and most of my parents are of –
114 have a language that I can speak. So I can communicate with them, even if
115 they can't speak English, but I can communicate with them to help their
116 children out, you know, explain to them things that they wouldn't understand
117 in English [...]
(Interview, 27 June 2017)

At various moments, all the teachers pointed to the importance of good contact with the children's parents. In Lines 111–114, Hira brings together conversations with the children, the trust stemming from her rapport with them and her relationship with their parents. She describes her Bengali language as important for talking to parents to support children's learning (Lines 115–117, 'to help their children out'). Foremost, her Bengali becomes relevant here as a resource for conversations with parents and thus enhances Hira's general teacher agency when she decides to address certain issues with them ('most' is not used literally here as Bengali-speaking children represented about a third of her class).

After Hira mentioned the problem of the 'jam-packed' curriculum (pp. 24–25), I asked whether she would like to do something with the languages the children speak.

573 [with emphasis] Yeah, I would love to do things
574 like that. [...] I'd love to – like have a day where maybe all you can
575 teach them is Lithua – Romanian, then another child could teach them and
576 we all could learn. I think it would be a really, really nice environment because –
577 and give them a chance, you know, show something – show a part of them
578 because that [...] language is part of them. So, it's a kind of
579 being proud as well, you know, I can speak another language is really
580 important. [...] we are lucky that we can speak two languages [...]
(Interview, 27 June 2017)

Hira stresses the desire to include the children's languages, suggesting a setting where pupils would teach each other (Lines 573–576). She foregrounds the interactive aspect, and by 'we' appears to include herself in the setting: 'we all could learn' (Line 576). In addition, in Line 576, the teacher links the envisioned setting to the theme of a 'safe stimulating environment', mentioned before when she talked about professional priorities (p. 148). Significantly, in 'and give them a chance... show a part of them' (Line 577), she points to the child as a bilingual speaker and reinforces this perspective in the following lines. Her identification with the experience of bilingual children becomes evident in that 'language is part of them. So it's a kind of being proud as well', and 'I can speak another language is really important. [...] we are, we are lucky that we can speak two languages' (Lines 578–580). The shift in pronouns from the third person 'them' to the first person 'I' and 'we' might be seen as referring to the children in her class as much as to the teacher herself. When asked what she means by 'it's part of them', Hira explains:

588 [...] it makes them them, it is part of
589 them. Like I would say, a part of me is being Bengali and, you know, I wouldn't
590 just say, I am British, I would say I am Ben – I am Bangladeshi-British because
591 that's my language and that is my culture [...]
593 I am sure, obviously all of them – that's part of them. And if we speak at home
594 we speak you know our language and that is a kind of telling them you know
595 it's okay, you kind of don't mind, it's home and school together. So that is part
596 of what makes them who they are. [...] I am
597 sure if you asked them who they are, they would say I can speak English, I can
598 speak Romanian, that's what they would do [...]

(Interview, 27 June 2017)

The teacher indicates her own experience in 'Like I would say a part of me is being Bengali' (Line 589). Then she explains this further but modifies the frame of reference from what might be seen as cultural and linguistic identifications ('Bengali') to an identification that draws chiefly on 'nations' (Bangladeshi-British), 'I would say I am Ben – I am Bangladeshi-British because that's my language and that's my culture' (Lines 590–591). What looks like a slip of the tongue – which, of course, it could be – can also be understood as indicative of how, in society's discourses, 'language', 'culture' and 'nation' reference each other in variable and often contested ways. Thus, Hira implicitly mentions various related aspects in those short passages: she evokes how language and culture are interwoven in the general and educationally relevant sense that by learning a language through interaction with others, the child enters 'the linguistic community – and, at the same time, the culture to which the language gives access' (Bruner, 1983: 19). Furthermore, the passage suggests a network of multiple identifications. Hira formulates her cultural and linguistic identifications (Line 590, 'I would say...'), while there appears to remain a certain friction when she corrects herself to 'Bangladeshi-British'. (In the UK, 'Bangladeshi' is the official term, since 'Asian/Asian British' – as one of the five official 'broad ethnic groups' – is itself subdivided chiefly based on nation-states.) Thus, this episode sheds light on some of the processes by which – dependent on the societal context – 'the dialogic relationship between language and ethnic identity is (re)produced, contested or modified' (Lytra, 2016: 135). However, it also shows how the teacher articulates and claims her ownership over what it means for her to be a bilingual speaker. Finally, the extract refers to an awareness that such processes take place around what it means to speak a language and that they are potentially intertwined with questions of belonging. These three aspects go beyond the mere fact that the teacher speaks Bengali and English and expresses experiences of 'being bilingual', which enables Hira to advocate the perspective of pupils as plurilingual speakers. I would suggest that the normalcy that the teacher emphasises when returning to her previous assertion that children's languages and bilingualism are 'part of them' (Line 593), 'part of what makes them who they are' (Lines 595–596), and the emphasis she puts in her repetition 'if you asked them who they are ...' (Lines 597–598), chimes with the conclusion from the participant activities about the normalcy of children's plurilingualism in Chapter 5. Moreover, Hira described the normalcy of her own plurilingual experience in school when asked about using Bengali with other teachers: 'Yes, yeah [laughs] – *Why is that?* – 'I don't know, they obviously know the same language, so we have – we joke in that language and [...] it's mixed, it's not just Bengali, it's mixed, I mix up English and Bengali all the time' (Interview, 14 July 2017: Lines 183–187).

It seems instructive to consider another part of the last extract: 'And if we speak at home we speak you know our language and that is a kind of telling them you know it's okay...' (Lines 593–595). This wording acknowledges the languages spoken at home in a somewhat guarded way (Line 595, 'you kind of don't mind') before stating the educational maxim 'it's home and school together'. This passage does not need to be seen as contradicting Hira's perspective on the children as plurilingual speakers but might be perceived as expressing her awareness or a realistic evaluation of the classroom's monolingual prevalence, which she had described before (p. 78). From this angle, Hira's extracts complement her previous description that she would sometimes speak with a newly arrived pupil in Bengali but would not use it otherwise around learning activities. Given the absence of a pedagogical framework, it does not come as a surprise that the teacher's language experiences and the resultant positionality alone do not translate into multilingual approaches or decisions about what to do 'strategically' with the children's non-English languages. It is important to eschew any deterministic understanding when including teachers' language experiences and their positions in relation to society's linguistic power relations within an exploration of teacher agency in multilingual pedagogies. However, Hira's extracts illustrate that her experiences enable her to articulate the perspective of the children as plurilingual speakers and attribute normalcy to them. Therefore, the teacher's own language experiences can offer a different starting point for participating in the school's nexus around multilingualism. Concurrently, the institutional context, including the culture of performativity, the curricular status quo and the monolingual norm, sets robust limitations for achieving more agency.

Heather describes her own schooling in a village where 'everyone spoke English. Just a really white British school' (Interview, 12 January 2018: Lines 532–533). Other excerpts from her interviews have demonstrated how she reflects on the tension that she talks with her students about their languages but does not make their plurilingual resources and voices heard (p. 79). There is also tension regarding how she addresses that two pupils had not included their reading in languages other than English in a homework task (pp. 111–113). Here, she offers further reflective perspectives in an extract from the context presented in Chapter 4, where she describes her insights into the families' linguistic constellations:

438 [...] I am aware because as teachers we have to know everything about
439 each child and then, language-wise, I mean children tell me [...]
445 I talk with them about their lives and
446 the different languages they speak and the countries they visit and their
447 families. And I do ask, 'Do you speak to your...?' Like 'Can you communicate
448 with your nan?' Because personally, my friend is – her dad is Italian, her mum is
449 English, and she never learnt Italian and she cannot communicate with her
450 grandparents. [...]

(Interview, 16 March 2018)

Heather sees her knowledge of the children's linguistic repertoires as part of her professional task (Lines 438–439). As previously in Section 4.1, she includes the perspective of the children and mentions a friend's experience as a personal motivation that underscores this angle. Heather had explained before that occasionally she would become aware of more details of a family's linguistic repertoire and illustrates this with the example of Khalid's family, where 'his mum is fluent in five different languages and so is his older brother' (Interview Heather, 12 January 2018: Lines 406–407) – Khalid is the child who said in the participatory activities that he speaks Italian and English all the time at home, and the other languages of the mother are Berber, Arabic and French. However, the teacher contrasts the situation of this family, which she sees as confidently living their plurilingualism, with other children in school and explains the circumstances of newly arrived families: 'Their parents speak their home language but then they bring them here and put them in an English-speaking school, the parents then feel like they have to speak English to their children which they absolutely don't' (Interview Heather, 12 January 2018: Lines 411–413). Heather describes the approach of her school to encourage these parents to speak their home languages, pointing out that it would not support the children's English learning if the parents could not be role models. I asked her where, in her view, this coercion would derive from:

431   I don't think it is from school. I think it is from thinking that they are in an
432   English-speaking country so they have to fit in or speak that language. That is
433   what I have observed because when we say to them 'Please, please continue
434   to speak your home language!', then 'Oh, okay…' And then like – so they are
435   sort of shocked that you are encouraging – I think they just think from society
436   that they have to not speak their language [...]
(Interview, 12 January 2018)

The teacher thematises linguistic power relations in this extract, although she does not use such a term. It is instructive for understanding Heather's reflexivity that she links her observation from conversations with parents to her assessment of the discourse of assimilation (Lines 431–432, 'from thinking that they are…'; Lines 435–436, 'they just think from society…'). Elsewhere, Heather more directly addresses society's dominant discourse that associates monolingualism with assimilation, in other words, with a concept that in and of itself articulates power relations.

551   [...] I do think there is that sort of
552   divide. But I think we should encourage different languages – I do feel like
553   it's really, I don't know, if the right word is – like racist – is it racist if you are like
554   'This is an English-speaking country, you should be speaking English'?
560   [...] I think in Britain, we are like [imitating aggressive intonation] 'Why
561   don't they speak English?' And I think that does divide because – and especially,
562   I see the parents, they are quite vulnerable and then they might think, they
563   are doing the wrong thing by talking in their home language. [...]
565   And also why should they not – it is
566   their culture [...]

(Interview, 16 March 2018)

The teacher explicitly distances herself from what she considers a divisive discourse (Line 552, 'But I think...'). Remaining a bit cautious about naming the power relationships inherent to this discourse (Lines 553–554, 'I don't know, if the right word is – like racist...'), Heather links her stance again to her interactions with parents, problematising the pressure they feel vis-à-vis such discourse and empathising with their uncertainty about how best to support their children (Line 562, 'I see the parents, they are quite vulnerable...'). Then, she returns to the right of the parents to speak their home language, rejecting the discourse of assimilation (Lines 565–566). Heather also mentions Khalid's mother, recalling that the parent perceived English as the 'weakest' language in her repertoire and spoke with her about conversations with other teachers some years ago, in which the mother had felt she was not being taken seriously because of her English. In such situations, Khalid's mother turned to two teachers who spoke French (Interview Heather, 16 March 2018: Lines 647–651). Heather's account illustrates how the teacher, in her reflections, combines insights from her professional experiences with the children and perceptions from her interactions with parents. Importantly, these extracts chime with the reflexivity Heather showed previously in those interview passages in which she attempted to see certain situations from the plurilingual children's perspective. In her reflection and critique of the linguistic power relations to which the parents are subjected, Heather strives – just as in the earlier extracts – to see the constellations from the perspective of plurilingual speakers. In this sense, these passages also confirm the relevance of the teacher's reflexivity as an important precondition for achieving agency in multilingual pedagogies.

Chapter 6 showed the workplace school as a context for teacher agency that is considerably framed by the everyday workload and the time constraints of the curriculum, resulting in 'two poles' of teacher agency: it can manifest itself in the maintenance of current practices, and in making choices towards changing them. The findings also confirmed the educators' supportive relationships with their colleagues as an important aspect of their general teacher agency (see Priestley *et al.*, 2015: 103). It has been proposed to assign responsibility for multilingual pedagogies not only to EAL coordinators but also to roles with a coordinating brief more closely linked to the everyday classroom, such as year group or key stage leaders. The professional values and priorities mentioned by all five teachers have been translated into four questions of orientation that can help, in schools, to thematise and reflect on multilingual pedagogies, thus potentially facilitating teacher agency in this domain: How might multilingual pedagogies influence or change children's experience in school? How might they influence or change teachers' rapport with children? How might multilingual pedagogies be linked to educators' own educational experiences? And: How can teachers' personal experiences become a resource for multilingual pedagogies?

The different ways in which the teachers thematised their own language experiences when talking about their pupils' multilingualism provide a further aspect that potentially facilitates this agency. However, it is important how those experiences are included in the overall consideration of teacher agency. In fact, the experiences described by the teachers differed considerably, and it has been suggested that the educators' own language experiences provide various points of departure for their participation in the school's nexus around multilingualism. When addressing agency, it is vital to consider teacher's experiences without assigning a status that essentialises them. While the teachers have various language experiences and different positions concerning the linguistic power relations operating in society and school, it is not only or not necessarily the language experience that potentially facilitates teacher agency in multilingual pedagogies, but rather the reflexive stance teachers take vis-à-vis multilingualism and their own positionality.

7 Towards Possibilities of Multilingual Pedagogies

This chapter returns to the 'pedagogical space' as an element of the framework for teacher agency in multilingual pedagogies. In the two parts of the chapter, the 'pedagogical space' is approached in relation to two other elements of the framework: the teachers' professional subjectivities and the children's linguistic repertoires and voices. As I have argued in Section 5.3, the 'pedagogical space' needs to be sufficiently flexible to connect to 'small' spaces of teachers' decisions and classroom routines and systematic enough to provide a frame of reference for decisions and developments. Drawing chiefly on the teacher interviews in the first part, the second part of the chapter presents findings from the second participatory activities that show how pupils' and teachers' experiences could come together to develop (teacher agency in) multilingual pedagogies in the classroom further.

7.1 'And perhaps, if we had a bit more time, we would be a bit more creative': Teachers' Views on Possibilities

The 'pedagogical space' is understood as both conceptual and concrete/practical, and, correspondingly, the following findings form a sequence that leads from more conceptual to more practical orientations, namely, from a focus on teachers' *pedagogical motivation*, via their *ideas*, to the question of helpful *resources*. The section addresses possibilities as they emerged from the interviews, and the excerpts chosen here reflect the earlier finding that 'small' choices and decisions constitute an important part of teachers' agency (see Chapter 3). Crucially for the question of how multilingual pedagogies can be integrated into mainstream settings, where they need to be legitimised *per se* and not via bilingual programmes or particular circumstances in officially bilingual regions, the excerpts enable a contextualisation in relation to issues generally relevant to primary school pedagogy, such as the 'whole child' perspective and the issue of time.

7.1.1 Pedagogical motivation

The following extracts from Ellie can be linked to the episodes and themes reported previously and refer both to pupils new to English and other plurilingual children. The teacher had explained, 'I don't think we encourage the use of their home language' (see p. 78), and had been asked whether she would like to do so:

248   Yeah, I think it would be good. I think, personally, probably why I don't do it,
249   is because you don't have a clue about what they are saying. [...]
250   then they might not be speaking about what
251   they are supposed to be speaking about. And how do you assess what they
252   have done because you don't know what it says? Ahm, like with Adriana and
253   Sonia – I got them to write in their home language when they first came.
254   I didn't have a clue what it says [laughs] but they wrote a whole page in
255   Romanian but I didn't know what it says. So I think it would be nice.

(Interview, 24 March 2017)

Firstly, acknowledging that such encouragement 'would be good' (Line 248), the teacher describes in Lines 248–252 the lack of control over children's talk and her chance to assess their work as reasons why she does not encourage the use of pupils' non-English repertoires. This appears to contradict her working consensus, which is based chiefly on trust ('if you listen to them, they are talking about the work in most cases', see p. 60) and, to a lesser degree, on control ('if people are talking about what they had for dinner... they do need to go and turn their cards', see p. 60). In fact, this contradiction can itself be seen as a manifestation of the strength of the monolingual norm: the consensus – pupils may talk with each other during phases of individual work – is overridden by the rule that this needs to be done in English. Although the teacher is, in all likelihood, aware that children sometimes talk about non-task-related issues, she describes her lack of control over conversations in another language as a concern that prevents her from encouraging students to use their whole language repertoire. Yet, in Lines 252–255, Ellie refers to an occasion she had mentioned in the first interview, where she had asked Adriana and Sonia to write

645   the story in Romanian at the beginning of the year [...]
646   they only did it for a couple of lessons because
647   I just felt they needed that time to show what they can do [...]
650   Bianca could read it, she read it through and said, generally it's okay
653   [...] And you can see their frustration, you

654   know, 'We don't understand what they are saying'. So it was quite
655   draining really for them and when they read their story then, 'We can do it'.

(Interview, 8 February 2017)

Ellie pursued a particular pedagogical goal more explicitly when encouraging the use of Romanian, giving the children the chance to 'show what they can do' (Line 647). In the first extract, she did not genuinely explain why she deems it pedagogically valuable to include the home language. Instead, she foregrounded at its end again the challenge she faced (Line 254, 'I didn't have a clue what it says'). Her laugh may indicate some uncertainty or self-irony provoked by the fact that the usual power differential between teacher and pupils is questioned by suspending the monolingual norm. On the whole, Ellie points to the pedagogical aspect of pupils' empowerment as a rationale for encouraging the inclusion and use of the two children's first language. Yet, she considers such empowerment on the general level of Adriana's and Sonia's well-being in their new class rather than within a teaching/learning design that enables them to make links between languages or to use their existing skills for more independent learning. Consequently, the teacher did not follow up on the initial inclusion of Adriana's and Sonia's – and Bianca's – Romanian for learning purposes and did not engage further with their language repertoires.

When asked about her possible pedagogical motivation to include other languages, Ellie answers, 'I think just seeing a different side of them' (Interview, 24 March 2017: Line 271), recalling an encounter on the playground:

277   [...] they were just talking, I think it was at playtime,
278   they were chatting away in Lithuanian and I, 'Oh my goodness!'. And they went
279   like, 'What?!' – 'I never heard you speak like that!' So I think it's quite
280   nice to see the other side of them [...]

(Interview, 24 March 2017)

Ellie's description resembles Hira's 'language is part of them' (see p. 155) and asserts the pedagogical motivation to include the 'whole child'. In the context of the 'pedagogical space', I have argued that creating opportunities for children and educators to explore multilingualism needs to be seen as a constitutive element of multilingual pedagogies in the superdiverse primary school. The encounter, which Ellie retells vividly here as a kind of 'dialogue of astonishments' – can be understood and employed as such an opportunity, leading to questions such as, 'Do we want our teacher to know more about our language (practices)?' or 'How would such knowledge, on my part as a teacher, change my pedagogical approach in the classroom?'. The situation itself and Ellie's way of describing it illustrate how crucial the lens of 'voices being heard' is for a reflection of a 'whole child' perspective. In her retelling, the children's voices are literally heard and experienced by the teacher as the voices of plurilingual children.

Mike hinted at a similar 'whole child' perspective when I asked whether he could envision ways to link pupils' other languages to their learning after having told him how Brayden had expressed his wish to learn about Vietnamese or Chinese medicine during the participatory activities. The teacher highlighted the pressure he feels to meet the targets, which would not leave room to include other languages, at least not in English, and continues:

302	[…] it is self-esteem. I can tell with Brayden, you
303	know, he needs that, I guess, to talk about how he uses languages. And
304	even the fact that he speaks another language is a massively important thing
305	for him […]
308	yeah he gives some very articulate answers and some quite
309	ambitious answers […]

(Interview, 20 March 2017)

This might seem to contradict what has been described earlier as Mike's tendency to merely acknowledge pupils' multilingualism without considering the standpoint of the child as a bilingual speaker. However, given that it is neither apt nor possible to assume linear connections between the monolingual status quo, a teacher's own language experience and multilingual practices, Mike's statement should not necessarily be seen as contradicting the previous analysis of his position but as displaying – within his broader professional experience – an awareness of the complexity involved in 'speaking as a pupil'. As before, with the five teachers' careful attention to children's learning experiences as part of their professional values, what comes into view in terms of possibilities of multilingual pedagogies is a more holistic perspective of primary school pedagogy. The 'whole child' perspective is multifaceted and has been frequently advocated as the main principle of primary education in the submissions to the Cambridge Primary Review (Alexander, 2010: 184). It also mattered to the teachers in the present study when, for example, Hira pointed out:

200 [...] I can think of a handful of kids in my class who
201 don't like English and maths that much, and they are amazing in music,
202 singing, dance, drama [...]
203 sometimes during lessons, 'Oh, I am not that clever, I don't have nothing else'
204 but when you have drama or music, they can show themselves that they
205 actually have that [...]
206 [...] I think that is good for them.

(Interview, 27 June 2017)

As with her description of pupils' multilingualism, Hira articulates a holistic angle, following the children's standpoint (Line 203, 'I am not...') and her perspective as a teacher (Line 206, 'I think that is good for them'). Her observation chimes with the long-lasting assertion in the broader educational debate that the development of schools and sustainable improvements of students' attainment not only need to aim for children's empowerment but also to include creative and performing arts with their educative potential to foster confidence, cooperation and learner autonomy (Alexander, 2022: Ch. 12; Wrigley, 2000). Principles of a 'whole child' perspective and of 'pupils' empowerment' are common and essential features of research projects on multilingual pedagogies (e.g. Anderson & Macleroy, 2016; Cummins *et al.*, 2011a; Kenner & Ruby, 2012) and in accounts of whole-school developments (e.g. Little & Kirwan, 2019; Wrigley, 2000). In the present study, the teachers also implicitly expressed such perspectives as aspects of a pedagogical motivation for multilingual pedagogies. Yet, none used these terms explicitly (with one exception, where Kelly used 'whole child' when talking about some parents who would judge schools on inspection reports instead of 'thinking about a whole child'), and this appears relevant for teacher agency in multilingual pedagogies, as it highlights the precarious nature of the current situation. Considering that multilingualism was only addressed, if at all, as 'EAL' in their initial training and that schools did not provide further guidance, it is hardly surprising that the teachers did not articulate a more explicit or conceptually formulated rationale. Moreover, it is argued that the general climate in education, where schools and their teachers are evaluated primarily on performance data, does not consider the whole child (Adams *et al.*, 2020: 863), and a study on initial teacher training provision in this domain concluded that 'the high stakes inherent in the performativity discourse can mean that the holistic takes second place in practice even if it is held in high value by trainers, trainees, and teachers alike' (Adams *et al.*, 2015: 213).

Against this backdrop, the implicit and somewhat hesitant articulation of a holistic perspective appears to represent the kind of constellation that was described regarding teacher agency in Chapter 3, where I argued that a classroom configures the priorities a teacher has and that, following Wertsch *et al.*'s (1993) concept of mediated agency, the formulation of particular problems and the possibilities to follow them up with actions is shaped by means of the mediation employed. In other words, to act upon certain demands and dilemmas, teachers need to perceive them as such, and multilingual pedagogies – as a set of pedagogical rationales, values, concepts and teaching approaches – would need to constitute such mediational means. However, the observation of the implicit and cautious formulation of a holistic perspective is instructive for exploring the possibilities of (teacher agency in) multilingual pedagogies for two reasons. First, it shows how the teachers hinted at the broader pedagogical context of a holistic perspective *on the basis of their experiences* with the children, and this professional knowledge on the part of the teachers is 'already out there' in the classroom. Second, the holistic considerations emerging from the teacher interviews might be seen as a perspective that potentially *connects* primary school pedagogy with developments of multilingual pedagogies. In this sense, the shift from a third-person to a first-person perspective of plurilingual children that is fundamental to translanguaging pedagogy (García & Kleyn, 2016b) and to work with primary school children instigated by the language biographical research perspective (Busch, 2022) corresponds to and intersects with the multifaceted pedagogical debates around holistic approaches and the empowerment of the 'whole child' (e.g. Adams *et al.*, 2020; Alexander, 2010: 184–185).

7.1.2 Teachers' ideas for multilingual activities

Like the 'River of Reading' activity mentioned in Chapter 3, the following task belongs to the domain of homework projects that explicitly aim at linking learning in school and at home. As the boundaries between these two sites of learning become less distinct, aspects of parents' involvement and children's multilingual literacy skills can come into view. In Ellie's Year 4 class, pupils were asked to create, over the half-term break, a presentation 'about the country you are from' in formats like leaflets or posters. Other options for the children were a recount of a visit to the Museum of London, a 'Guide to Paris' or a collage/short text as preparation for an upcoming Art Week. The task was planned as linked to the construction of a class wiki, which was the computing topic of the half term, and students were supposed to hand in their work by the end of the term. Following up on the 'cultural week', as quoted in Section 4.1, Ellie continues,

168 Teacher Agency in Multilingual Pedagogies

227 [...] They don't really get that much chance to . speak about their
228 home language within lessons. At the moment they have with this wiki page
229 and we did these city guides for homework and they had to produce like a
230 presentation on their own home country [...]
232 But the majority did posters on – like Khadija's over
233 there and she put all facts on there and her little things.

(Interview Ellie, 24 March 2017)

The teacher appears to suggest a direct association between 'country' and 'language' (Line 228, 'At the moment they have with this wiki page...'). However, when asked whether the children would include other languages in their work, she replied, 'They haven't included any other language, just facts about their home country' (Interview Ellie, 24 March 2017: Lines 242–243). In Lines 232–233, Ellie refers to a poster where Khadija has drawn a map showing the provinces and cities of Italy with facts and personal experiences written around it (Figure 7.1).

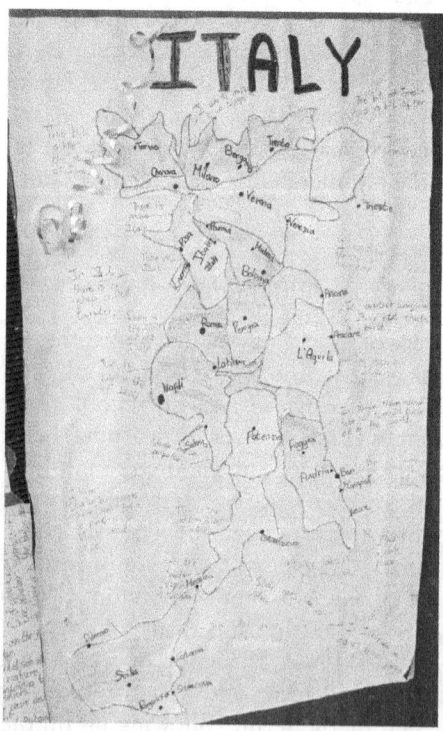

Figure 7.1 Khadija's homework poster

How the task was set and which essentialising concepts of 'culture' and 'home country' were implicated deserves further analysis. The children, however, mentioned this task and the wiki project when asked in the second participatory activity whether they had ever translated a story or a text, either at home or in school. Nojus explained:

196   I always translate to my mum and dad, because they don't really talk English, they can't
197   really understand English so I always translate it in Lithuanian. Like I – like I've done
198   a website I have done the – that about my city – the city, I have done it. And my mum asked
199   me like 'What did you write?' So I first said it in English and then I said it in Lithuanian.
(Activities 2, Castle Primary Y4, 15 March 2017)

Nojus here refers to writing about the capital of Lithuania as part of the class wiki. In Lines 196–197, 'I always translate…', he describes translating as an everyday practice from the viewpoint of a child whose language repertoire differs from that of his parents regarding the registers he and they can access in Lithuanian and English. Khadija, too, described the use of two languages during the homework project:

215   Actually we had to write some facts. I wanted to write in Italian, but my mum said not –
216   I found – I searched for it and something that I already know about it, I searched some things
217   and I searched for it, so it came in Italian. But my mum said not to write that. But I really
218   wanted to – so I had to – I know how to translate that into English. So I wrote that in English.
(Activities 2, Castle Primary Y4, 15 March 2017)

Khadija explains how she wanted to use in her homework 'something that I already know' (Line 216), which she had inserted in Italian into the search engine. She describes how the negotiation with her mother arose when she intended to write in Italian on her poster that would go on display in the classroom (Line 215, 'But my mum said not –'; Line 217, 'But my mum said not to write that'). While the child negotiated with her mother at home, the focus is on the question of whether Khadija's Italian skills can have the status of a language for learning in school, and the constellation can be seen as a reproduction of the classroom's monolingual norm in the context of the homework. However, contrary to the 'River of Reading' task, where the two boys said that they had forgotten to add their reading in Polish and Romanian (see Section 5.1.3),

Khadija clearly indicates her intention to include Italian (Line 215, 'I wanted to write in Italian'), and her emphasis 'But I really wanted to –' (Lines 217–218) can be understood in reference to both the inclusion of the facts and the use of Italian when writing them on her poster. The negotiation ended with the child translating the information into English (Line 218). That is, while Khadija's participation in the entire task had not been at stake, it could be argued that it was her recognition as – and her subject position of being – a plurilingual student that was at stake and conceded.

Nojus's and Khadija's accounts are relevant for the possibilities of multilingual pedagogies, as they point to the children's bilingual practices during their homework and wiki projects. For both children, the normalcy of their bilingual – or, in Khadija's case, plurilingual – language use is evident, understood as *'multiple discursive practices* in which bilinguals engage in order to *make sense of their bilingual worlds'* (García, 2009: 45, emphasis in original): Nojus uses Lithuanian to *involve* his mother in his homework, and Khadija uses Italian and English for completing the task, i.e. for *learning* (in this situation, she does not mention Bengali, which she describes elsewhere as her primary language of communication with her parents, see p. 115). To envision the next steps for including the children's plurilingual repertoires, it is useful to scrutinise at which points those language practices do not transfer into Khadija's poster and Nojus's work for the wiki page, in other words, into the official classroom. I would argue that this is even more important, as activities like the homework and the class wiki are intentionally designed to reach out to what is seen as the children's interests and personal motivations, using variable and multimodal formats, which allow for a greater variety of ways in which pupils may respond. It seems, therefore, almost a paradoxical effect that interest and multimodality are included in the task set by the teacher, whereas what is not included are the languages the two children used when working on the poster and the wiki page. In the homework 'River of Reading', the 'forgetting' appeared to follow the hidden workings of the monolingual norm. Khadija's recount, however, indicates that her Italian language resources are actively excluded, and it is at this point that her learning activity – or at least how her learning activity is acknowledged and presented in the classroom – becomes monolingual. For Nojus, by contrast, his literacy skills constitute the hurdle to including his bilingual repertoire. Since the range of children's literacy skills was one of the dimensions of diversity identified in all groups of the participatory activities (see p. 122), it is helpful to explore this in more detail. Nojus explains that his parents would sometimes give him 'a Lithuanian newspaper to read because I can't really read Lithuanian so I can have some practice' (Activities 2, Castle Primary Y4, 15 March 2017: Lines 223–224), and he returns to this theme:

231	Nojus:	[...] I actually like – we read this type of thick Lithuanian newspapers.
232	TQ:	Are you sitting together with your parents or...?
233	Nojus:	Yeah.
234	TQ:	Do you like it?
235	Nojus:	It is because hm . I actually learn more Lithuanian like because I only know easy words I don't
236		know some hard words.

(Activities 2, Castle Primary Y4, 15 March 2017)

Nojus describes his literacy skills, 'I can't really read Lithuanian' (Line 223) and 'I only know easy words...' (Lines 235–236) in relative instead of absolute terms, and his use of 'really' resembles the previous 'they don't really talk English, they can't really understand English' (Lines 196-197, p. 169) when describing his parents' language skills in English. Such evaluations are simultaneously embedded in the child's lived experiences and dominant language ideologies.

As suggested in Section 5.2.4, negotiations about language use in certain family situations are part of some children's experiences as plurilingual speakers. For possibilities of multilingual pedagogies, the question arises of how homework could be designed to draw on the linguistic repertoires of all participants. That is, the next steps in the constellations reported here could be an opportunity for Nojus's parents to expand their involvement in the homework by supporting their son's literacy skills in Lithuanian and some guidance for Khadija's parents regarding the use of Italian in her daughter's homework. At the end of the interview section, Ellie concluded, 'But that would be nice, and that could be something we could do in our homework projects. Try write something, like as a challenge try to include something in your home language, even if it is just a caption on a picture' (Interview, 24 March 2017: Lines 382–384). She suggests the possibility of including the children's 'home language' in existing homework routines in a way that is responsive to the diversity of their literacy skills. Moreover, the teacher uses her practical pedagogical knowledge, namely, how to use the 'challenge' routine and set the task on a small and feasible scale. As with the holistic perspective, I would like to suggest that also, within this context, the links to the teacher's experience and proximity to her routines – and her 'small' decisions – can be usefully understood as facets of, or starting points for, teacher agency in multilingual pedagogies.

Similar flexibility to include children's plurilingual literacy skills was facilitated in a postcard activity Kelly had designed for her previous Year 3 for the 'European Day of Languages' or 'Languages Day', as renamed at her school. Children were asked to write postcards either in English or another language they speak or write, and the teacher deemed the task successful because the children could combine their creativity with varying degrees of literacy skills. She remembered their pride when they read aloud and translated their texts, whose length varied between a 'Hello!' and four lines (Interview, 7 December 2017). Yet earlier, when asked whether she would 'like to do more with the children's other languages', Kelly replied, 'Not especially. Not that I think they are not important [...] I don't think there is time in the day' (Interview Kelly, 9 March 2018: Lines 374–376). Thus, when asked whether she knew which of her current pupils had some literacy skills in another language than English, the teacher replied, 'No, I don't actually, I should do, shouldn't I? (Interview, 7 December 2017: Line 918). Regarding teacher agency, her description highlights the problem of a one-off activity, where the teacher had been agentic in the previous year but did not transfer the opportunity to gain insights into pupils' literacy skills and to engage with them in a routine for the next Year 3 classroom.

Asked about spaces 'to give children the opportunity to do something with the languages', Heather mentioned several ideas related to religious education lessons and to the cross-year-group activities, where once a week, children from Key Stage 2 classes come together in groups of ten for 20 minutes and, led by Year 6 pupils, address various topics, '[it] would be really good to look at the different languages in your family circles with the aim of like teaching each other something from your own language. That would be really nice, actually, I might put that idea forward' (Interview Heather, 16 March 2018: Lines 702–705). When talking about possibilities, Heather appeared to speak in her role as well-being lead teacher and mentioned routines that already exist, where teachers plan activities in the realm of personal and social learning. She referred to the provision of personal, social, health and economic education (PSHE), where currently languages were mentioned in units like 'Being Me', though only as very brief comments – 'just that "I speak that language" or "I am learning", like Hajar "reading the Quran"' (Interview, 16 March 2018, Lines 591–592) – but where Heather also saw possibilities to address multilingualism within other units around personal identity. Thus, her suggestions offer spaces for exploring multilingualism that might develop into further explorations and potentially into multilingual practices closer to everyday classroom routines.

The 'pedagogical space' is, under present circumstances, always a 'space' that needs to be found and created. The contested issue of time runs through all the teacher interviews and is crucially important for understanding the connection between such space, possibilities of multilingual pedagogies and teacher agency. Given the lack of curriculum guidance and, subsequently, of defining resources and supporting meso-level actors, teachers' contentions around time need to be included explicitly here. This was most clearly articulated by Ellie: 'And perhaps, if we had a bit more time, we would be a bit more creative' (Interview, 24 March 2017: Lines 300–301). Both the 'pedagogical space' and how educators develop it require time.

At first glance, a *designated space* for multilingual pedagogies that would be set aside specifically for them might seem to be in tension with the earlier emphasis on the proximity of possibilities of such pedagogies to the teacher's classroom routines. Both elements, however, must be seen as complementary approaches to developing possibilities that transcend the status quo of the 'currently possible'. To further explore such possibilities, it is necessary to understand better which opportunities could emerge if teachers had teaching/learning time set aside for this purpose, e.g. in the weekly, fortnightly or monthly timetable, and how such ring-fenced time would help educators to develop and tailor approaches to their classes. Ultimately, the problem of time refers to the broader issue of the curriculum and questions about the knowledge and learning it legitimises. Presently, possibilities of multilingual pedagogies are neither mentioned in the National Curriculum nor technically excluded, as 'there is time and space in the school day and in each week, term and year to range beyond the national curriculum specifications' (DfE, 2013: 6). The fact that this vague formulation does not facilitate multilingual approaches beyond the status quo suggests that it is useful for further discussions to draw on what the Cambridge Primary Review conceptualises as a 'protected local element in the curriculum' (Alexander, 2010: 259). It proposes a 70/30 division between a 'national' and a 'local component' within an envisioned curriculum, aiming for a balance between global, national and local concerns and opportunities within each teaching/learning domain. The content of the locally designed element would increase the responsiveness of schools' curricula to their specific contexts (Alexander, 2010: 251–277).

In this sense, such designated space for multilingual pedagogies would be located within the teaching/learning time that is institutionally approved for this purpose. It would neither clarify how teachers respond in detail to a linguistically highly diverse context nor address issues of resources. Yet, in relation to the projective dimension of teacher agency, it would allow for a legitimised frame onto which teachers could project their agency without facing competing demands. In the official education policy in England, an acknowledgement of the issue of time and perspectives of including the 'whole child' or providing for pupils' broader development are mentioned in Ofsted's inspection framework (2019). Its criterion of 'quality of education' and advocacy of a broad and rich curriculum (Ofsted, 2023) alongside the evaluation of 'leaders' [...] intent to provide for the personal development of all pupils' (Ofsted, 2023: para. 323) could, in principle, be interpreted as a point of reference for time and space set aside for multilingual pedagogies. However, as long as the rigid system of inspections and its grading system remain in place, such space is very hard to envision.

The homework situations reported above point to the involvement of parents and the relevance of children's literacy skills as two elements of multilingual pedagogies. Educators responded positively when asked about potential reactions on the part of parents. I had sketched a fictitious task, where – following the writing of an adventure story in English at school – children would be asked to render (part of) the story in another language, and I asked Ellie whether, in her opinion, parents would support their children with such a task. The teacher mentioned that during parent evenings, many parents showed a lack of confidence in English and explained, 'So I think if they would do it in their home language, they probably would be more enthusiastic perhaps or we'd have a higher parent engagement [...] I think they probably would' (Interview, 24 March 2017: Lines 418–421). This chimes with Hira's consideration when – following up on her idea to have children bring in books – she was asked what this might mean for parents: 'I think [...] more involving. They would feel happy [...] because it's their culture and their language' (Interview, 14 July 2017: Lines 263–267). Heather also assumed that parents would be willing to come into school to talk about their languages, as they had done for the 'Languages Day' before.

Like Ellie, other teachers also offered ideas regarding their pupils' multilingual literacy skills. Drawing on Probal's description that he writes in Bengali and reads poems, I asked Hira about the possibility 'to do something around different types of texts', and her response illustrates the complexity of the classroom situation as seen from the teacher's perspective:

62 As in different kinds of texts of different cultures or different kinds of texts in
63 different languages? [...]
67 Because if we did it with different texts in different languages, it would be very
68 difficult for other children that don't [...] know that and obviously
69 it has to be specifically linked to the topics that we are doing in English or the
70 topics that we are doing in topic [transdisciplinary lessons] or science or whatever it may be. So that
71 link, it always has to have [...] if it was texts from different cultures
72 bringing in – that's definitely – that's more doable I think than texts with the
73 language specific.

(Interview, 14 July 2017)

Overall, Hira points to the numerous languages the children speak and to the tight framework set by the curriculum. When I told her how Darius had explained that he enjoys reading books in Romanian and asked the teacher what it could imply for the school to try to acknowledge such reading, she spoke of the possibility of having children bring in books from home (Interview, 14 July 2017: Lines 114–123). Yet, not unlike Kelly's explanation reported earlier that she is not aware of who among her pupils has literacy skills in another language than English (p. 172), Hira replied that she was 'not sure' which children in her class attended a complementary school. By bringing in the texts they read, Hira's pupils would make their skills visible and audible in the 'official' classroom and have the chance to explore this aspect of their multilingualism with their teacher and peers. Regarding 'possibilities' and the projective dimension of teacher agency, this may potentially initiate further developments.

Heather addresses children's plurilingual literacy when asked about her ideas for homework that has 'to do something with language',

854 […] we could easily give a sort of homework where
855 they could write a story with their – I mean it depends whether they can write
856 in their language, I guess, but read a story or write or just write something or
857 take pictures when – like Hajar, when she goes to the mosque having Quran
858 reading, like that. Just to bring what they do with their language back […]

(Interview, 16 March 2018)

Importantly, and as described before in the context of Ellie's homework, Heather also mentions *a range* of tasks, from writing or reading a story to shorter homework tasks like 'writing something' or documenting language and literacy skills by taking photographs. Her example (Lines 857–858, 'take pictures when…') foregrounds the acknowledgement of children's plurilingual literacies and corresponds to the fact that Heather encouraged Darya to record the reading in her Quran lessons in her reading journal.

The ideas put forward by the teachers share three features. First, the suggestions invite the children's families to participate and thus respond to an important question concerning multilingual pedagogies under superdiverse conditions: Who can support multilingual activities with their language/literacy knowledge? Second, the ideas can function as initial steps, opening the official classroom for children's plurilingual repertoires and facilitating further activities. Third, the proposals involve activities that educators would initiate but which they control considerably less than other teaching/learning routines. The students would bring their linguistic/literacy knowledge into the classroom and jointly construct with their teachers a pedagogical space where they offer insights into their plurilingual repertoires. Considered within the framework for teacher agency in multilingual pedagogies (see Section 1.3), these features underline how the framework's elements – classroom, children's linguistic repertoires and voices, teachers' professional subjectivities and the 'pedagogical space' of multilingual pedagogies – need to be appreciated as closely interconnected. The pedagogical space is linked to the classroom, the children's repertoires/voices and teachers' professional subjectivities. Simultaneously, it is the interplay of all four elements that supports the achievement of teacher agency in multilingual pedagogies.

If multilingual pedagogies are broadly defined as acknowledging, including, using, engaging and promoting children's plurilingual repertoires, then the teachers' suggestions roughly fall into the (overlapping) categories of acknowledgement, inclusion and engagement. They acknowledge the children's individual practices and include them in the respective context of learning, i.e. the homework/wiki (Ellie), general reading (Hira) and homework as an umbrella task for presenting various literacy skills (Heather). Given multilingual possibilities and the projective component of teacher agency, these categories allow educators to 'strategically' explore and plan for what could be respective next steps towards using and promoting children's entire linguistic repertoire within the classroom's teaching/learning activities.

7.1.2.1 Resources for the classroom

Ideas and concepts form only one part of the 'pedagogical space' that could support teacher agency. When asked about helpful resources for including children's multilingualism, the educators listed a variety of suggestions: Ellie mentioned in-service training and – expressing her uncertainties around pronunciations in languages other than English and different scripts – easily accessible one-click audio resources (Interview, 24 March 2017: Lines 479–482). In her response, Hira followed up on two aspects she had previously pointed out: the necessity to link activities to curriculum topics and the number of languages the children speak, namely, 'specific books related to specific topics. That would help us with our topic [...] and with our English, so it's specifically linked, so it's easier maybe to plan for [...] Maybe more audio things, like audio stories from Romanian or the languages the children speak [...] Audio can be really useful' (Interview, 14 July 2017: Lines 210–222). Heather explained that she would like to get more ideas for including children's multilingualism: 'how we sort of appreciate it more [...] how we can talk to other children about their language beyond like recognising they are EAL and doing stuff to support them' (Interview, 16 March 2018, Lines 825–828).

Although the question of resources was not addressed in more detail in the interviews, two points seem instructive in relation to multilingual possibilities and the enhancement of teacher agency. First, the resources mentioned here belong to the meso level of guidance and support (in-service training and 'ideas') and the micro level of material resources ('one-click audio resources', specific books and audio stories). In the sense of agency as 'individual(s)-operating-with-mediational-means' (Wertsch *et al.*, 1993), educators rely on conceptual *and* material artefacts for achieving agency in a given pedagogical domain. Second, regarding the micro-level resources, the teachers pointed to hurdles for implementing multilingual approaches: the accessibility of help with pronunciation, the availability of resources linked to the curriculum as a precondition for planning accordingly and the availability of audio recordings of stories in various languages. The latter might be usefully understood as a possibility for pupils to listen to, for languages to become audible in the classroom, and, potentially, for the teacher to develop pedagogical settings where children work in personalised ways on multilingual tasks. Such hurdles shed some light on the challenges teachers experience when accessing the 'pedagogical space' and the type of resources that may support them.

The examples given by teachers and children point implicitly to a rather obvious distinction that is nevertheless very relevant to developments within the primary school: it is helpful to distinguish between artefacts *of plurilingual speakers,* such as Nojus's 'thick Lithuanian newspapers' or the books Hira would ask the children to bring in, and artefacts *for multilingual pedagogies,* like Ellie's 'one-click audio resources' or Hira's specific books and audio stories. There exists an overlap between these two types of artefacts, e.g. dictionaries, bilingual books or topic-specific books. Yet, for enhancing (teacher agency in) multilingual pedagogies, the distinction is conceptually useful. It allows for an exploration of how various activities and formats require different types of resources. It invites the question of how the material and conceptual resources on the part of the teacher/classroom can *interact* with those resources that pupils, families and complementary schools can bring to the pedagogical space – resources that, in addition to material artefacts, comprise meanings, linguistic knowledge and literacy skills, among others.

7.2 'Our ideas': Children's Views

The second participatory activity arose from talking with the children about their language experiences, acknowledging them as experts in their own multilingualism. As multilingual pedagogies need to include the various meanings children ascribe to the elements of their linguistic repertoire, it is neither possible nor justifiable to explore the possibilities of multilingual pedagogies without consulting their views. The following extract from the end of the language portrait activity with six children from Mike's class captures well the atmosphere and the children's opinions:

298 TQ: Did you enjoy the activity?
299 all: Yeah.

When asked why they had enjoyed it, Mariana and Brayden replied:

309 Mariana: So being in a group because we are not like in a school. I like to be in a little
310 group, I like to discuss [...]
311 it's like – it is really good because like you do learn more things like that. So I think it's
312 really good.
313 Brayden: Yeah, I haven't really talked about different countries, about languages and things
314 like that and, yeah, you never really get to talk to – go into a group and talk about
315 languages [...] you don't really think about languages
316 TQ: So you mean you have not been talking a lot about your languages in school so far?
317 all: No.
318 TQ: Is that something you would like to do?
319 all: Yeah.

(Activities 2, Castle Primary Y5, 9 March 2017)

Mariana describes what, in her view, sets the participatory activity apart from the dominant classroom talk setting and points to her preference for talk done in a small group. Brayden – as quoted at the beginning of the introduction – emphasises that multilingualism has not been thematised in school (Lines 313–315), and his third affirmation (Line 315, 'you don't really think about languages') might be seen as describing this exact situation in a classroom, where only monolingualism can prevail, normalised by 'not thinking about languages'. The extract expresses the enjoyment the children showed during the language portrait activity, which gave them an opportunity to share their experiences of being plurilingual speakers.

The group of six children from Ellie's class talked about their use of languages in school. After Nojus had described how he would sometimes ask Emilija for help using Lithuanian, Khadija explained:

158	Khadija:	[…] I help myself talking in Italian […] with all
159		the subjects but not art because art – I don't need to think Italian – I think English
160		because art is only drawing
161	TQ:	But what do you mean by you help yourself with the Italian?
162	Khadija:	[…] hm I am giving just an example of maths. Like now, we are learning the angles. I just –
163		some activities like these, we have already done it in Year 3 in Italy. So like the angles like
164		acute, obtoos… ehm obtuse like those I know them […] so first
165		I check talking with myself in Italian and after I try to understand it in English.

(Activities 2, Castle Primary Y4, 15 March 2017)

After around six and a half months in an English primary school and, in all likelihood, benefitting from having learnt English as a foreign language in the Italian primary school, Khadija speaks confidently about her learning. The Year 4 pupil almost seems to give descriptions of concepts like the BICS/CALP distinction (e.g. Cummins, 2000: 53–111) and translanguaging (e.g. García & Kleyn, 2016b) when talking about her experiences in Lines 158–159, 'talking in Italian', 'to think Italian' and 'I think English', respectively, appear to point to the inseparable nature of talk and content learning in school. In Line 162, 'I am giving just an example…', the child uses a phrase that is itself typical of communicating successfully in school and refers then to mathematical notions that are cognates in English and Italian and whose concepts she had learnt before (Lines 163–164). Khadija's specific words (Line 158, 'I help myself talking in Italian'; Lines 164–165, 'so first I check talking with myself in Italian and after…') point to processes that would be called in the Vygotskian perspective 'inner speech' (Vygotsky, 1986; e.g. Wells, 1999: 116–118). Her description is also significant in relation to the dynamics around the classroom's norm that 'English is the only official language for learning'. By explaining how her Italian language is a resource for learning – for accessing previous content knowledge and learning the corresponding notions and concepts in English – Khadija offers insights into her learner identity. As observed and described by her teacher, the child participates actively in lessons, and though 'inner speech is not overt and what is said is accessible to the speaker alone' (Wells, 1999: 118), what Khadija displays is a plurilingual learner identity, where she uses the Italian element of her linguistic repertoire in a private and inaudible way for learning. This 'private' use resembles the episodes where Sonia uses Romanian 'privately' to explain a task to Adriana (see p. 102), even though this language does not gain official status for learning in the classroom. In both cases, the 'private' use for learning does not suspend the dividing line between official English and the 'unofficial' other languages on which the monolingual norm is based. The main question for possibilities of multilingual pedagogies emerging here would be: what kinds of options or activities around multilingualism, plurilingual identities and 'doing something with languages for learning' would go beyond this partition and give the children's language practices a role and a status in the 'official' classroom? In principle, this could be any activity that renders a child's language or language practice audible or visible. While such a general description does not address issues of frequency or the integration of other languages into existing tasks and many others, interactive tasks like 'teaching my language' or 'giving a presentation' were often mentioned by the children when asked about their ideas.

Talking with children about a fictitious task of describing an invented machine – a genre addressed recently in literacy – a brief exchange with Leon occurred. He had explained elsewhere that he speaks primarily Polish with his mother at home, that his father had taught him Spanish as a toddler and that he watches cartoons in Catalan to learn it.

87	TQ:	You have a machine and you explain that in English. And let's pretend, someone is coming
88		and says 'oh Leon, could you explain that machine in another language? Does your machine
89		have a button for a Polish translation?
90	Leon:	Tak
91	TQ:	or 'zak' for a Spanish translation?
92	Leon:	Sí, that means 'yes'.
93	TQ:	Sí, cómo funciona?
94	Leon:	oh
95	TQ:	Cómo, cómo funciona la maq... How do you say 'machine' in Spanish?
96	Leon:	I don't know...
97	TQ:	La máquina?
98	Leon:	But I know how to say it in Polish: maszyna. (Kacpar and Luiza agree)
99	TQ:	maszyna? That is very similar –, ... Do you know what it is in German? 'Maschine'.
100	Leon:	Now it is confusing. Maschine . maszyna...
101		(Children play around with the words – indiscernible)

(Activities 2, Bird Primary Y3/1-1, 31 January 2018)

Within a few spontaneous, slightly playful moves between linguistic repertoires, the child and the adult display both knowledge and uncertainty before discovering the cognates. The miniature here serves to illustrate how such instances require a *pedagogical and linguistic interaction* in which both participants acknowledge that they have only some partial knowledge of these languages.

Instances that bring private plurilingual practices into the 'official' classroom and activities that are designed for language comparisons are also relevant from a spiral-curricular and long-term angle as their regular inclusion in the orality of primary classroom communication can help lay the foundations for expanding plurilingual approaches into literacy practices (Little & Kirwan, 2019). For such moves between languages and between orality and literacy to happen, 'teachers must trust the pupils to know how to make use of their linguistic resources' (Little & Kirwan, 2019: 40). In the interviews, teachers pointed implicitly to the importance of interactions, audibility and reciprocity as potential steps towards instances in which language awareness is facilitated. For example, Heather reflected on how pupils might not see her interest in their languages because she never asked them explicitly to make their plurilingual voices audible in the classroom (see p. 79). When asked about instances of including other languages, Kelly explained that she had 'not really thought about it'. As with other teachers, Kelly mentioned her own language experiences and described her uncertainties:

391   I don't really speak any other language, I mean, a bit but I wouldn't ever go –
392   never write on a form 'Oh yes, I speak a little French' [...]
393   Or I did two years of German at school – I would never say I speak German.
394   Perhaps I would be more confident
395   if I spoke other languages [...] if other languages were a bit more
396   a comfort zone for me.

(Interview, 9 March 2018)

What appears to emerge here, with some relevance for teacher agency in multilingual pedagogies, might be usefully seen as a kind of *reciprocity*. In other words, when creating or joining linguistic interactions around multilingualism and multilingual language awareness, teachers and pupils must use their language knowledge but equally acknowledge uncertainties, partial knowledge or lack of knowledge. Indeed, a theme that runs implicitly through those interview passages, where the teachers mentioned their own language experience, and which can also be found in Kelly's extract here, is the fact that the interaction with plurilingual children seemingly requires teachers to reflect on their own linguistic repertoires and language experiences. Thus, I would like to argue that this aspect of 'reciprocity' is also relevant to the possibilities of multilingual pedagogies. Given the apparently underlying experience of some disappointment described by Mike (see pp. 19–20), Heather (see p. 96) and Kelly (above), it could be productive to ask what these teachers would gain if they explored for themselves those perspectives that do not conceptualise language as an entity, which someone does or does not possess, but evolve around different contexts for language use and the notion of the linguistic repertoire among others. The situation in an English primary school differs from the settings where a second official language can serve as a catalyst for plurilingual, more integrated approaches (e.g. Duarte & Günther-van der Meij, 2018; Little & Kirwan, 2019). However, teachers' reflections on such reciprocities when generating instances of multilingual language awareness may prove beneficial for teacher agency. It allows teachers to enter multilingual interactions, knowing that they are responsible for the pedagogical design of a situation – either spontaneous, routinised or planned – but, borrowing from Kelly (Lines 394–396), also aware that they can be confident and in their comfort zone, because they are permitted to bring not only their linguistic knowledge into these interactions but also their uncertainties, partial knowledge or lack of knowledge. Thus, educators should trust themselves, too, when designing activities that encourage children to bring their experiences as plurilingual speakers and their linguistic knowledge to the pedagogical space.

7.2.1 'Would you like to do more with your languages in school?'

In the second participatory activity, the children voiced their experiences and ideas. These children are eminently present in their classrooms, and even though the specific constellations of their linguistic repertoires are individual and unique, by considering their experiences it becomes possible to ask what these voices may entail in the development of multilingual pedagogies. The first extract from pupils in Heather's Year 3 follows a passage where the children had described plurilingual literacy experiences: Shriya remembered how, on a visit to India, her grandmother read to her in Gujarati and helped her with a Gujarati writing book; Radut recalled how his parents read stories to him when he was younger; and Florin, who had said earlier that he learnt to read and to write, mentioned that his mother had brought him an audio device on which he could listen to a book in Romanian.

| 139 | TQ: | Would you like to do more with your languages in school? Would that be a good idea? |
| 143 | Shriya: | [...] 'yes' because you can like – . because everyone can hear your language and what you |

144		can do with it and like learn from the language and stuff . so . and you can also read and
145		learn about that
146	TQ:	You can learn to read in the language you mean?
147	S.:	Yeah.
148	TQ:	Would you like to do that more?
149	S.:	Yeah.

(Activities 2, Bird Primary Y3/2-1, 31 January 2018)

Shriya points to what might be understood as the child's description of the audibility of a language in the official classroom (Line 143, 'because everyone can hear your language') and of the contexts in which she uses the language (Lines 143–144, 'and what you can do with it...'). She then addresses literacy learning (Lines 144–145). I would argue that regarding 'possibilities', this move from audibility to literacy skills is the point where personal learning would begin for Shriya, who does not share her Gujarati with anyone in her class but uses it with two children in Years 2 and 5, as she had explained elsewhere. Khalid's response, however, refers to a different aspect:

151	Khalid:	I think 'no' because some people might [...] not really like – like the language –
152		like or understand it
153	all:	*(talking over each other, indiscernible)* [...]
155	Shriya:	you could learn about it
156	Khalid:	hm – or maybe they can learn
157	TQ:	Or Shriya could do something with her Gujarati and at the same time you could do
158		something with your Italian.
159	Khalid:	Oh yeah

(Activities 2, Bird Primary Y3/2-1, 31 January 2018)

Khalid seems to foreground an interactional aspect when anticipating 'some people might...' (Lines 151–152). Shriya replies by arguing that, in such a situation, 'you could learn about it' (Line 155), after she had described elsewhere how she learnt from others in informal situations. Khalid appears to agree in Line 156, while I suggest that children could also pursue personalised tasks with different languages (Lines 157–158). The extract also shows that while the vast majority of children saw it as 'a good idea to do more with their languages in school', a few children in the Year 3 classes had concerns related to such interactional experiences.

The next extracts are from pupils in Kelly's Year 3 class and illustrate once again the superdiverse conditions of the classrooms. Nylah explained that when she went with her parents to India, an uncle 'taught me a bit of Hindi and a bit of Urdu. And my mum kept on talking Hindi, and so I learnt to understand what Hindi is and then I started speaking it (Activities 1, Bird Primary Y3/1-2, 24 January 2018: Lines 135–136). She was then asked by Joana,

147	Joana:	So like – do you enjoy doing it – like learning all these languages? Like learning how to
148		speak Hindi and English and languages?
149	Nylah:	I like doing it but when I talk, I feel like I get something wrong, so it's like – my mum says it's
150		fine, fine to do but I still talk like I am not ready. She says I can only talk to her like this
151		because she can teach me again if I get it wrong.

(Activities 1, Bird Primary Y3/1-2, 24 January 2018)

This passage exemplifies many instances during both participatory activities when the seven- and eight-year-olds engaged among themselves in a dialogue about experiences as plurilingual speakers. It also allows for a return to a facet of children's plurilingual experiences mentioned previously in Section 5.2 on 'superdiverse voices' and could be noticed throughout the activities in all groups. The passages from Probal about arriving in the Italian school and later the English school (see p. 39), from Amelija about learning Russian from her mother and attending the Lithuanian complementary school (see pp. 116–117), from Sana about learning French as an MFL and reading Arabic in the mosque (see p. 120), and the experiences described by Nojus, Shriya, Florin, Joana and Nylah in this chapter all show in various ways how experiences of plurilingual children frequently include *experiences of learning*. The children often articulated their *confidence* in learning languages/literacies and *ambivalences* around such experiences. In Nylah's case, when she was asked if she would like to do more with her languages in school, her response appeared to show both ambivalence and confidence in learning. Referring to her Arabic class, she described it as sometimes 'actually quite embarrassing when you say the wrong words [...] so, I mean, the sentence doesn't make sense' (Activities 2, Bird Primary Y3/1-2, 29 January 2018: Lines 42–46). Yet, about Hindi, the child foregrounded her confidence:

50	TQ:	Would it be good to do more with [...] Hindi in school for you?
51	Nylah:	I think it would be easy to learn the language for everyone. Because my mum normally
52		speaks in that language at home, I normally, I normally understand it, so I just get the right

53		words – they are in the proper sentence. But once they get the words, they'll know where it
54		is because Hindi is quite easy to learn.
55	TQ:	My question was not so much about whether you would like to start teaching the other
56		children in Hindi but whether you would like to learn more Hindi and maybe do that in
57		school as well?
58	Nylah:	Yeah.

(Activities 2, Bird Primary Y3/1-2, 29 January 2018)

Nylah addresses the question in relation to teaching other children the language. She referred to her own learning in everyday situations with her mother, describing learning processes around words and syntax (Lines 52–53, 'I normally understand it...'). The child presents herself as a *confident plurilingual learner*, and her evaluation quoted before, 'I feel like I get something wrong [...] I still talk like I am not ready' (Lines 149–150) does not necessarily contradict that description but, instead, could be seen as the child's awareness of the learning involved.

The element of 'learning' might seem a matter of course, as language repertoires are not fixed but constantly evolving. Yet, I would argue that dialogic talk or other activities about children's experiences of *being a plurilingual learner* are important when exploring and creating possibilities for multilingual activities in a classroom and belong to the component of multilingual pedagogies, where children and educators explore their multilingualism, preceding further developments, as described in Section 5.3.

The notion of the 'plurilingual speaker' has been used throughout the chapters for children who have, through their family socialisation and/or migration trajectories, more than one (named) language in their repertoire. To complement this perspective with an emphasis on the *plurilingual learner* is, in my view, useful for the possibilities of multilingual pedagogies within the primary school. It enables teachers to allow for a variety of plurilingual speakers in their 'superdiverse' classrooms: emerging bilinguals like Sonia, Adriana and Khadija; pupils with varying degrees of plurilingual literacy skills (those who attend complementary schools, like Amelija or Brayden, or those who sometimes learn with parents or other family members, like Nojus or Destiny, who borrows books in Twi from the local library); children, who learn a language which they had not acquired originally via their family socialisation but started to learn later in this context like Nylah and Amelija (see p. 184 and pp. 116–117); and pupils who do not fit into any of these groups of learners. Thus, within an analytical lens of subjectivation in a classroom that is characterised by a monolingual norm, an emphasis on the plurilingual *learner* can potentially provide teachers with a criterion to decide which tasks, activities or settings may offer a child or a group of children the subject position of the *successful plurilingual learner who uses their entire linguistic repertoire for learning*.

Furthermore, the emphasis on the plurilingual *learner* enables teachers to be more responsive to the many children who are *not* emerging bilinguals and for whom it is important to keep their ownership over what being bilingual means for them, or – as the episode from Bianca has shown (see Section 5.2.3) – who might be wary of losing this ownership. Children like Nojus (p. 169), Bianca, Shriya, Khalid, Nylah (above) or the three girls in Ellie's playground encounter (p. 164) are all successful monolingual *pupils* in their respective 'official' classroom, who live the normalcy of their plurilingualism outside the classroom. It would be the teacher's pedagogical responsibility to design 'possibilities' without causing harm to the children's experience of normalcy. Such caution appears even more important because – as Bianca's episode has also shown – children are aware of wider society's discourses, which tend to link languages other than English with immigration. They can anticipate the discriminatory effects this might have. Thus, the emphasis on the plurilingual *learner* offers teachers an opportunity to thematise among themselves and with their students the knowledge/skills transfer between languages, developments of metalinguistic skills and other facets of what may be portrayed as the normalcy within evolving plurilingual repertoires. These features are, in fact, important when developing tasks for and with those children who have acquired (and are continuously acquiring) more academic language skills in spoken and written English than in other components of their repertoire. The thematisation of learning on such a metacognitive plane could potentially take multilingual activities beyond the acknowledgement of multilingualism and closer to learning as the key activity in school. It allows us, in a sense, to thematise certain language hierarchies, which are inevitably part of children's experiences and can open ways of bidirectional transfers between children's languages or their literacy skills in different languages that play an important part in the dynamics of learning and learner autonomy documented in whole-school developments of multilingual pedagogies (Little & Kirwan, 2019).

Another reason why it appears important to complement, for all children, the perspective of the plurilingual *speaker* with an explicit emphasis on the plurilingual *learner* is closely related and provides valuable long-term perspectives. From the angle of plurilingual children, the start of Reception class marks a beginning, when they learn what 'is done' and how learning works in school. They acquire an understanding of how the new interactional environment responds to their dispositions and skills and, as part of those, to their language practices. As a key principle of primary school, long-term or spiral-curricular orientation is relevant for the learner regarding both possible *multilingual-specific* activities and other *more general pedagogical* features within multilingual pedagogies. As Little and Kirwan (2019) documented for one primary school, the inclusion of children's whole language repertoires throughout the primary years needs to be embedded in approaches of dialogic teaching and writing as self-expression, and pedagogical principles in the tradition of Dewey, Freinet and Freire feature prominently in approaches of multilingual pedagogies (e.g. Anderson & Macleroy, 2016; Cummins *et al.*, 2011a; Schreger & Pernes, 2014).

Regarding this study, I would suggest that the three features that emerged as common denominators of the ideas put forward by the teachers Ellie, Hira and Heather – inviting the families to participate, enlarging the periphery of the official classroom, and pointing to activities where educators have considerably less control than in other teaching/learning activities – can be usefully understood as falling into the latter category of general pedagogical features. Although they can be found in many intervention or whole-school-development studies (e.g. Hélot *et al.*, 2014; Kenner & Ruby, 2012; Little & Kirwan, 2019) – and are not limited to multilingual pedagogies either, they point to challenges in primary education and to developments around multiliteracies pedagogies (e.g. Pahl & Rowsell, 2012; Pahl & Burnett, 2013) – it is relevant for the 'possibilities' of multilingual pedagogies and teacher agency that the three features emerged here from the ideas and experiences of the teachers. An emphasis on the plurilingual *learner* may allow educators to foreground more explicitly that long-term and spiral-curricular considerations are important not only for the multilingual-specific activities themselves but also in relation to more general pedagogical features that underpin them. Three of the five teachers in this study taught in Lower Key Stage 2 classes (Years 3 and 4), and what they considered as the 'currently possible' is inevitably influenced by the approaches that preceded this phase and by those that follow in Upper Key Stage 2 (Years 5 and 6). In other words, how families' knowledge is being included, how children are encouraged to make their out-of-school literacies and interests 'official' and 'normal' in the classroom, and how teachers design activities in which pupils' agency and autonomy increase while their own control decreases, are all pedagogical considerations that would benefit from consistency as they require growth and some routine – on the part of the teachers and the pupils as plurilingual learners. On the whole, from the learner's perspective, these features would be part of what 'is done' and how learning works in school, and what is possible in the middle years of primary school depends to a considerable extent on long-term perspectives throughout the primary phase. What seems self-evident is worth mentioning in the context of 'possibilities' and teacher agency. Although a spiral-curricular angle cannot, in itself, fill the gap left by the negligence of multilingualism in the current curriculum in England and the resultant lack of meso-level guidance, it can strengthen the projective dimension of teacher agency in multilingual pedagogies over the course of the primary school years.

The mind map activity (see Section 2.4.3) was designed to acknowledge the children as experts in their plurilingual repertoires without expecting them to present their ideas in pedagogical formats. The ideas, which the children put forward, can be usefully considered in four groups: interactive activities, explicitly literacy-related learning, multiliteracies and others. These headings are used only for an overview here, and there are also overlaps between the groups (if no other reference to the audio recording is given, the following quotations refer to the activity sheet; the spellings have been corrected). Interactivity is a shared element of those ideas, where children wanted to teach the language, ranging from 'to share with friends' and 'trade with people' (Khalid, Florin) via 'teach people' (Brayden) and 'I would play a game and teach important words' (Mason, Activities 2, Castle Primary, 15 March 2017: Line 294) to Sana's explicit 'be a teacher, teach people'. In all groups, many children mentioned games, for example, 'I would play a game to teach what this word or that means and then I translate it into English and then there it will be in Telugu and English, and then they can try to match it' (Silu, Activities 2, Castle Primary, 15 March 2017: Lines 272–274). Audibility – as described before by Shriya, 'everyone can hear your language' (see p. 182) – was a common element of all those activities. It also featured in 'presentations' about their languages, which four children from Ellie's Year 4 suggested, along with Sana's suggestion to tell stories. On a somewhat smaller scale, children from Heather's class mentioned talking to another child who also speaks Farsi (Darya) or 'tell your teacher your language' (Antonina). Others mentioned video games, some of which they would play in languages other than English.

The second group of ideas relates explicitly to literacy learning, used here in the 'traditional' reference to reading and writing. However, this may include technical devices, as the children described their use at home. Pupils from Ellie's class wrote to 'learn more' (Emilija, Bianca), and other suggestions included 'read stories and say them out loud and write stories and [...] tell the story' (Rasa, Y5) and 'to read books and then make your own book' (Mariana, Y5). Books featured in many other ideas the children put forward: Kacpar wrote about 'books in Polish and Spanish and lots of other languages'; Joana suggested 'reading books, using a Portuguese thesaurus or dictionary' and 'Make a book out of Portuguese'; and Khalia mentioned 'A Twi handwriting, Twi dictionary and Twi book'. Other ideas around writing were 'write a story, poem' (Khalid) and 'Do some recipes in Italian and Bengali' (Khadija). Children from Hira's Year 3, (see pp. 120–122), wrote 'get a Bengali teacher and teach everybody' (Sana) and 'I will get a teacher, an Urdu one, and just talk with her, and if I learn I will know it and I will learn so much' (Azayiz). Nadia wrote, 'Instead of French we would have a teacher for every language we have in school. The teachers would pick the children who speak the same language'.

The children's ideas in the third group about *multiliteracies* related to projects they were working on or had completed recently. All six children from Ellie's class suggested creating a wiki. A class wiki was their current computing topic, and Ellie described how this type of format appeals to both for her and the pupils, who enjoy accessing their peers' pages at home and commenting on each other's work. Shriya suggested an animation movie, like one they had made recently in Kelly's class using the stop motion technique:

240	TQ:	What would you do with your Gujarati and the animation movie?
242	Shriya:	[...] The imovie is the same as *The Iron Man* and what you would do
243		is, you have to take pictures [...]
244	TQ:	And what would you do with the language?
245	S.:	With the language I think ... I don't know, you – I am not sure
246	TQ:	What would you do? Would you do subtitles? Or would you just take
247		your voice and tell the story in Gujarati?
248	S.:	I think – just take your voice [...]

(Activities 2, Bird Primary Y3/2-1, 31 January 2018)

This extract points to an almost self-evident aspect that is nevertheless very relevant for conceptually understanding the relationship between children's ideas and teacher agency for the creation of 'possibilities'. As with the wiki pages, Shriya's and other children's suggestion to make a movie demonstrates that multiliteracies formats are highly motivating for pupils. However, while Shriya is positive about the inclusion of Gujarati in school activities (see pp. 182–183), her indecisiveness in Line 245 'With the language I think ... I don't know, you – I am not sure' underlines the need for some pedagogical facilitation on the part of the teacher to modify or extend the format that Shriya experienced so far, to include children's multilingualism. On the whole, the observations around the 'River of Reading' (see Section 5.1.3), the wiki (see pp. 167–170) and *The Iron Man* stop motion movie, where in all instances the monolingual norm had not been suspended, chime with the assertion that 'in practice multilingualism has not been fully integrated into a multiliteracies pedagogy' (Macleroy, 2016: 74).

Finally, the children wrote 'other' ideas, in which language featured in conjunction with other subject areas or topics, for example, 'history because so we will know what happened in the home language' (Mariana, Y5), 'learn Vietnamese/Chinese medicine' (Brayden, Y5), 'I would like to do a science experiment' (Anna, Y5); many children also referred to art: 'Learn about Portuguese artists' (Joana) or 'Do something arty from it' (Bianca). Through the ideas reported here as 'others', the children primarily expressed their individual interest in certain topics. Implicitly, they also thematised more fundamental insights, showing not only the awareness that all topics could be potentially accessed through the languages whose foundations they had learnt in their families but also that there were topics whose knowledge could be accessed more profoundly through those languages.

Teachers and children came up with many ideas – the teachers somewhat more cautiously, and the children more freely when filling in the silhouette diagram for a second time. Some of their ideas were presented in this chapter. It also explored how possibilities of multilingual pedagogies can emerge, how teacher agency might be enhanced and how the 'pedagogical space' can be further conceptualised for this purpose. In addition to the previous suggestions that it needs to be conceptual *and* concrete/practical, sufficiently flexible to connect to teachers' 'small' choices and sufficiently systematic to provide orientation for their decisions, the insights from this chapter allow us to understand further how the 'pedagogical space' can be created and supported. The findings highlight that the possibilities of multilingual pedagogies in a primary school under superdiverse conditions could and should be seen as *co-constructed* by teachers and their pupils. That is, on the one hand, teachers would contribute not only with practical/concrete decisions and actions but also with their pedagogical motivation grounded in holistic and empowerment perspectives. Although these perspectives were formulated somewhat hesitantly, it is significant that for the educators, they arose out of their experience of working with the children. Therefore, this pedagogical knowledge can be seen as 'already out there' in the classroom and as providing a link to teachers' professional identities. On the other hand, the pupils would contribute to this pedagogical space with their experiences as plurilingual children – speakers and learners – with all the meanings the languages in their repertoires have for them, with their language and literacy skills and with their ideas of what to do with those languages in school. Considering how the teachers talked about children's plurilingualism – for example, Mike's 'standing there' (p. 86) or Heather's 'I talk with them about their lives and the different languages they speak' (p. 79 and p. 158), but also Hira's and

Kelly's lack of knowledge about children's complementary school attendance and literacy skills, respectively (p. 175 and p. 172) and the enjoyment and normalcy the children showed in the participatory activities – it appears relevant to appreciate how teachers' and pupils' experiences could and should come together, literally as an *interaction*. This is especially important for activities where children and teachers explore their multilingualism, which should be a constitutive part of multilingual pedagogies. The superdiversity of children's voices – their different languages and the range of meanings they have for the children – requires dialogic approaches, and those can emerge best if teachers have the opportunity to listen and children the chance to feel being listened to in a dialogue that might not yet take place very often around multilingualism. As Brayden put it, 'you never really get to talk [...] you don't really think about languages' (p. 1). The features described before as a common denominator of the teachers' ideas notably include an interactive angle, too: if the teacher intends to invite families to share their plurilingual knowledge, it is necessary to establish and sustain communication and trust with the families. If the teacher inspires pupils to bring into school their out-of-school language and literacy experiences in the sense of enlarging the periphery of the official classroom, such encouragement also requires interaction.

To summarise further how possibilities can emerge in the linguistically highly diverse school, I would like to draw attention to three other points to take away from this chapter. First, the three teachers' pedagogical motivations and ideas point, on the whole, to a willingness to engage with multilingual pedagogies and to exert some agency in this regard. Even the two teachers who did not express their readiness, citing a lack of time, deemed a previous one-off activity successful (Kelly, see p. 172) and considered the acknowledgement of a child's bilingualism as important for his or her self-esteem (Mike, see p. 165). Although the educators expressed their 'whole child' and empowerment perspectives implicitly, I want to contend that this angle can represent a sustainable link to primary school pedagogy as a whole. Thus, it refers to what was described in Section 5.3 as a desideratum for the 'superdiverse' school to clarify what it wants to pursue *pedagogically*, complementing the social justice orientation with a reference frame for all plurilingual pupils.

Second, the teachers suggested their ideas cautiously and mentioned a need for fundamental ways of support, such as in-service training, and access to more ideas and resources that link to curriculum themes. It is, therefore, important for the 'pedagogical space' to include a kind of pool of approaches, formats and activities, from which teachers could choose and to which, at the same time, they could contribute. Such a *pool of practical possibilities* might be usefully linked to teachers' 'small' choices and classroom routines while also providing a more conceptual frame of reference for decisions, e.g. regarding the distinction between acknowledgement, inclusion, use, engagement with and promotion of the languages other than English or concerning the interplay between activities in a classroom, in a year group or on the level of a school's broader ethos. Moreover, such a 'pool' could refer to the various aspects that are relevant within the workings of a primary school, such as different teaching/learning formats and resources, subjects, orality/literacy foci and, importantly, the spiral-curricular orientation.

Third, while the children put forward many ideas, it would be the educators' role to make choices and develop further pedagogical formats, with the institution of school having the task of supplying resources. Simultaneously, creating possibilities in the 'superdiverse' primary school requires that children are given an active role in choosing from and developing possibilities, and thus the 'pool' could also have a mediating role between children's ideas, families' or complementary schools' involvement and teachers' and schools' professional knowledge and resources – which returns us, in a sense, to the perspective of a co-construction of possibilities of multilingual pedagogies.

This chapter has addressed the teachers' pedagogical motivations, grounded in 'whole child' and empowerment perspectives, as *potentially facilitating* their agency in multilingual pedagogies. This wider pedagogical concern, which the teachers articulated based on their experiences with their pupils, can constitute a sustainable link between their professional values and multilingual pedagogies, and the teachers' pedagogical motivation and ideas point to their willingness to engage with such pedagogies and practice agency regarding this domain. Yet, the fact that they articulated this link somewhat implicitly and put their ideas forward with caution highlights the precarious nature of the connection between their pedagogical views and agency in multilingual pedagogies. Thus, the teachers' pedagogical motivation emerged as *potentially facilitating* this agency. At the same time, their references to the need for more resources, and for support on the meso level, for example, through continuous professional development, further underscores the insecure character of teacher agency in this pedagogical domain. Throughout the chapter, possibilities of multilingual pedagogies were explored, with a focus on the activities suggested by the teachers and on the plurilingual experiences and ideas shared by the children. The findings are also relevant to teacher agency. The proposed reciprocity between teachers and pupils in their interactions around multilingualism, an acceptance on the part of the teachers to have only partial knowledge and features common to the teachers' ideas – inviting family participation, amplifying the periphery of the official classroom and accepting they would have less control than in other activities – all point to the relational character of teacher agency in multilingual pedagogies. Thus, the 'pedagogical space' for such pedagogies should be seen as co-constructed by teachers and their pupils. In addition to the conceptual aspects introduced in Chapter 5, this space would also need to provide in practical terms a pool of approaches, formats and activities, from which educators could choose and to which they could contribute. That is, to *facilitate* teacher agency, the pedagogical space needs to be seen as a whole that integrates conceptual, practical and temporal components.

8 Teacher Agency in Multilingual Pedagogies: No Guarantees

With the concluding chapter, it is time to leave the five classrooms and ask how the study's findings can be assembled and usefully included in further developments within the mainstream primary school. The exploration of teacher agency in multilingual pedagogies was guided by the assumption that it is beneficial to commence with the schools' everyday workings and investigate the five classrooms as they present themselves to teachers, for whom they are the context and point of departure regarding agency in this pedagogical domain. The enquiry focused on the two emergent phenomena of teacher agency and multilingual pedagogies in parallel and in relation to each other while taking neither as a given. It was set in the context of mainstream education which, regarding multilingualism, has been generally described as characterised by a 'monolingual habitus' (Gogolin, 1997), an overall failure of UK education to surmount monolingualising ideologies and a failure to value children's plurilingualism as a learning resource (Anderson, 2016: 18). More recently, there has been a sizable gap between the state-of-the-art in research and the mindset still dominant in many educational settings (Duarte & Günther-van der Meij, 2022: 452). However, amid these somewhat sobering general monolingual scenarios, studies within language policy research have foregrounded the leeway for policy negotiations within classroom practice as 'it is', in the words of Kate Menken and Ofelia García, 'ultimately educators – particularly classroom teachers – who are the final arbiters of language policy implementation' (2010: 1). Teacher agency in multilingual pedagogies can be seen as located between these various scenarios. It shows the reciprocal and complex ways in which professional contexts and professional identities remain constantly linked to each other and are ultimately inseparable when it comes to further developments in multilingual pedagogies within mainstream education. As Priestley *et al.* (2015: 54) put it, 'beliefs and values are not held in a vacuum but are themselves the result of the range of influences, demands, and pressures that structure the settings – the particular ecologies – within which teachers think and act'.

This final chapter begins with an overview of features that were identified in the previous chapters as *constituting*, *hindering* and *potentially facilitating* teacher agency in multilingual pedagogies. Drawing on their analysis, I will then discuss how teachers' professional knowledge and identities can function as affordances for multilingual pedagogies, in what conditions agency can be achieved or enhanced, and how possibilities for multilingual pedagogies can emerge in the mainstream primary school classroom. Finally, these considerations will be linked to developments in teacher professionalisation.

The following features have been identified as *constituting* teacher agency in multilingual pedagogies: (1) general teacher agency, which includes supportive relationships at the workplace; (2) reflexivity derived from a teacher's pedagogical motivations, professional experiences and language experiences, etc.; (3) knowledge about multilingualism, multilingual learning and learners; (4) awareness of and knowledge about pupils' linguistic repertoires and the various meanings that speaking a language can have for them; (5) the capacity to make conceptual choices within multilingual pedagogies; and (6) the concomitance of possibilities for making practical choices.

Further features emerged as *potentially facilitating* teacher agency in multilingual pedagogies: (1) a teacher's pedagogical motivation and knowledge; (2) their everyday routines and small decisions; (3) opportunities to reflect on questions that thematise multilingual pedagogies – for example, how such activities may influence children's experience in school or teachers' rapport with their pupils; (4) a rapport with children, families and educators in the community; and (5) a 'pedagogical space' with conceptual, practical and temporal components.

Finally, the findings point to six *hindrances* to such agency: (1) a workplace school characterised by the culture of performativity; (2) the lack of references to multilingual pedagogies in the school curriculum, resulting in (3) a lack of support, resources and conceptual guidance; and the features of (4) a monolingual norm in the official classroom, (5) the dominance of an 'EAL discourse' and (6) the prevalence of a merely 'symbolic multilingualism' (Figure 8.1).

The professional knowledge, experiences and attitudes of teachers emerge from the study as *potential* points of departure and affordances for multilingual pedagogies, connecting to their general teacher agency and related aspects, such as their working consensus or classroom routines, and their professional and personal interests. Yet, under the current circumstances, there are no guarantees that these facets of educators' professional knowledge and identities will indeed evolve into affordances for multilingual pedagogies. On the contrary, the findings highlight the precarious nature of teacher agency in multilingual pedagogies – a fragility that mirrors the official status of these

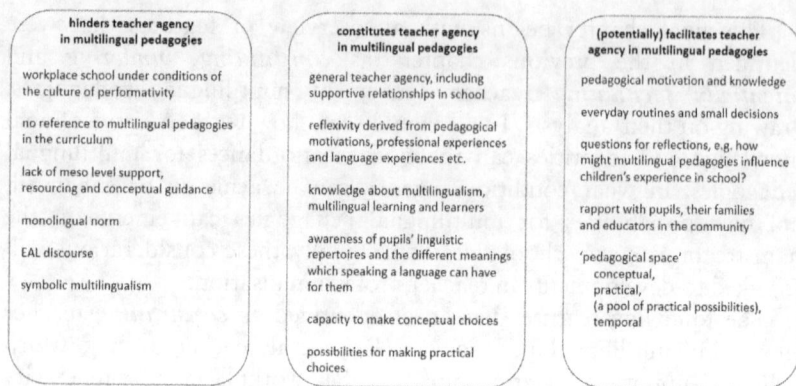

Figure 8.1 Features that hinder, constitute and (potentially) facilitate teacher agency in multilingual pedagogies

pedagogies and the pressures around them. As described above, the latter include a monolingual habitus, monolingualising ideologies and dominant mindsets in schools.

The ethnographic research approach was well suited to exploring the currently tenuous character of teacher agency in multilingual pedagogies. It showed that the link between teachers' knowledge/experiences and multilingual pedagogies is particularly relevant for realising these pedagogical approaches in superdiverse primary classrooms. As part of their knowledge of local conditions, teachers need to develop knowledge about the multifaceted diversity of children's linguistic repertoires to which multilingual pedagogies must respond. In this context, two other fields come into view simultaneously: the status of multilingual pedagogies within primary school pedagogy and, by extension, in teacher education. Insights from the five classrooms suggest that teachers must move beyond the restricted perspectives currently offered by the EAL discourse and the merely symbolic acknowledgement of multilingualism in order to be able to draw for multilingual pedagogies on their general professional resources. Teachers need to be able to address multilingualism within broader pedagogical considerations. Given that professional knowledge and identities are, to a considerable extent, mediated by teacher education, teachers can only make use of their knowledge, experiences and attitudes as affordances for multilingual pedagogies if this domain becomes an integral part of primary school pedagogy and of teacher education mediating this pedagogy.

The concept of teacher agency allows us to consider teachers' choices and views within the contexts of their routines, motivations and experiences, and of the school as a workplace. In this regard, too, the exploration followed an approach to understanding teacher agency in multilingual pedagogies based on the everyday classroom. The findings point to the substantial constraints on this agency in an education system rooted in performativity. On the one hand, the persistent culture of performativity (Ball, 2003) interlaces the school as a workplace with teachers' professional identities and knowledge; on the other hand, 'performativity calls teacher professionalism into question' (Priestley et al., 2015: 107–108). This entanglement inevitably results in a tension between existing possibilities defined by the status quo and potential pedagogical developments. For the English primary school, the scope for language policy negotiations in classroom practices, as cited above, must be seen as very limited. In other words, negotiations (would need to) extend also to wider education policy, as educators' commitments and pedagogical motivations currently lack support from policy initiatives, guidance, resources and, crucially, the legitimisation provided by education policy for developments in mainstream schools. Considerations of how to support teachers in achieving agency in multilingual pedagogies cannot circumvent or resolve this overall tension but rather are located within it.

8.1 Achieving and Enhancing Teacher Agency in Multilingual Pedagogies

A closer examination of the features identified as *hindering* teacher agency and those *potentially facilitating* it (see Figure 8.1) shows a considerable power differential between them. The features that hinder the achievement of agency are anchored in the structures of the education system and dominant language ideologies, operating with far greater force and influence than those which (potentially) facilitate it. Thus, when seeking to enhance teacher agency in multilingual pedagogies, it is important to explore how the latter features can be fostered and how they contrast with the other features that have been identified as hindrances.

The chapters highlight the importance of considering all three types of features – hindrances, constitutive components and facilitating aspects – in future developments. The teachers spoke about time restraints, adopted, to various degrees, reflective stances on monolingualism and multilingualism in schools, and described pedagogical motivations for the inclusion of their pupils' entire linguistic repertoires – or obstacles to achieving this. Developments that strive for the achievement and enhancement of teacher agency must connect to this diverse range of experiences and positions. It is crucial to thematise all three types of features with educators, including phenomena that operate through symbolic domination (like the monolingual norm) or paradoxical effects which educators do not necessarily perceive as working within this norm, such as the EAL discourse and the mere symbolic acknowledgement of multilingualism. Furthermore, it is indispensable to thematise the school's current workplace conditions in order to connect with the everyday experiences of teachers.

Within a model for studying teacher agency for social justice (Pantić, 2015, 2017), reflexivity is conceptualised as teachers' 'capacity to monitor and evaluate one's actions and structural contexts' (Pantić, 2017: 220). In the context of professional development, this concept expands to 'expansive reflection', involving educators' consideration of circumstances and outcomes related to their collective activity (Pantić, 2021: 143). In the previous chapters, reflexivity emerged as a central constitutive aspect of teacher agency precisely because it allows educators to engage with their pedagogical experiences and motivations while simultaneously juxtaposing and contrasting them with those aspects that hinder their agency in multilingual pedagogies. It is instructive to return here to the fine-grained processes of the agency model: actors can move between their agentic orientations and recreate the configuration of the dimensions of iteration, projectivity and practical evaluation through processes of dialogue and interaction. Thus, they may enhance or reduce their capacity for invention, choice and transformation in relation to the situation in which they act (Emirbayer & Mische, 1998: 1003). This offers a fruitful perspective on reflexivity and the significance of small tensions or small decisions on the part of the teacher. The reflexivity found among teachers can respond to and start to challenge those hindrances that manifest in linguistic power relations, such as the monolingual norm, the EAL discourse or mere symbolic acknowledgement of multilingualism. Yet, while the processes initiated by teachers' reflexivity can support shifts between the three agency dimensions of iteration, projectivity and practical evaluation, it is crucial that reflexivity vis-à-vis the status quo should be expected not only – and not primarily – from individual teachers. Following Pantić's (2015) elaboration that foregrounds *collective* agency, it is ultimately the remit and responsibility of education policy and the professional field of primary school pedagogy, initial teacher education and continuous professional development to provide opportunities and time for reflexivity.

A further and, in a sense a related, strand of findings relevant to the question of how teacher agency in multilingual pedagogies can be enhanced concerns the 'two poles' of agency: maintaining practices in the officially monolingual classroom can be just as much a manifestation of a teacher's general agency as making choices and taking stances for alternative possibilities. Therefore, considerations and provisions that respond to educators' workplace experiences are important for developing teacher agency in multilingual pedagogies. These issues need to be thematised with teachers to foster practical developments. However, they also constitute a theoretical concern for broader debates in multilingual pedagogies, aiming to avoid a decontextualised approach to teachers' attitudes or options. The ambivalences around the 'two poles' were apparent in this study. The frictions related to the classrooms' monolingual status quo remain below a level where teachers perceive them as tensions requiring pedagogical responses, and the only cautiously stated motivations to link their whole child/empowerment perspectives to multilingual approaches in the classroom illustrate these ambivalences.

To enhance teacher agency, it becomes paramount to ask what teachers might need to move their choices towards a more explicit and courageous engagement with multilingual pedagogies in their classroom. It is beneficial and instructive to draw on the framework for teacher agency in multilingual pedagogies to answer this question, revisiting the constellation of the four elements *classrooms, teachers' professional subjectivities, children's linguistic repertoires and voices and the 'pedagogical space' of multilingual pedagogies*. The present study suggests achieving agency in multilingual pedagogies and creating possibilities for them requires teachers to be able to draw on all four contextual factors when making their choices and taking stances. Simultaneously, the processes involved must be seen as multidirectional and closely interrelated (Figure 8.2).

Teacher agency and possibilities for multilingual pedagogies can emerge only when educators possess sufficient awareness of children's linguistic repertoires and the diverse meanings that having a language in their repertoire might have for them. Conversely, children can contribute this knowledge only if the official classroom provides suitable opportunities and after the teacher has chosen particular approaches and formats from the 'pedagogical space'. However, teachers' choices

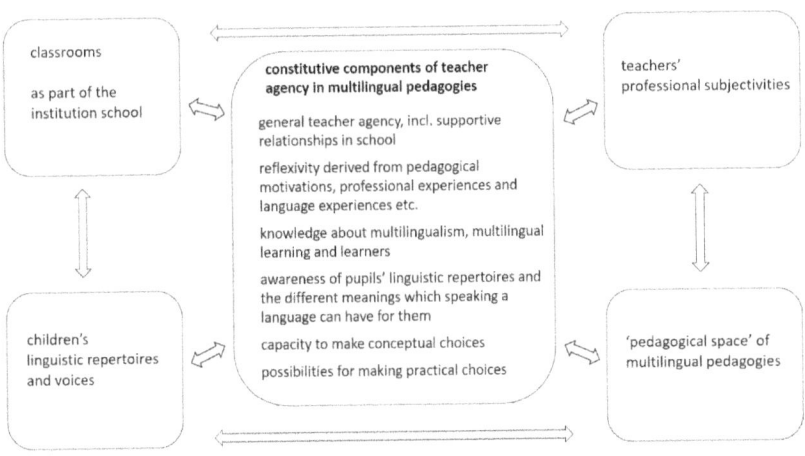

Figure 8.2 The framework for teacher agency in multilingual pedagogies

can only be made based on their reflective stances and pedagogical knowledge regarding multilingual learners. On the whole, these processes need to be grounded in a classroom where the educator has already established a working consensus and an atmosphere of cooperation and trust. In such an environment, pupils can learn confidently, enjoy linguistic interactions and share, for example, the variety of their plurilingual literacy skills. This, in turn, enhances the teacher's capacity to make conceptual and practical choices for more multilingual activities. It is important to highlight that for such possibilities to emerge, activities can begin at various points within the framework and might be initiated by teachers or children. Activities may start with the children showing their language repertoires, as in the playground encounter remembered by their teacher, Ellie, or during the 'River of Reading' homework, which another teacher, Heather, reflected upon. While various dynamics are involved, it is the educator who must be attentive to the possibilities emerging within a specific situation and who makes conscious decisions about moving such possibilities into the realm of the official classroom. The 'pedagogical space' directly supports the teacher's agency and the emergence of multilingual pedagogies by fostering educators' capacity to make conceptual and practical choices. In this study, I propose the 'pedagogical space' as a conceptual response to the status quo. However, among the four contextual factors, it remains the element that is currently least accessible for teachers and cannot be taken for granted. Analysing the status quo within a given school setting through the lens of the framework can offer a focus on particular elements and support tailored responses to strengthen teacher agency and promote further development.

8.2 Supporting and Empowering Teacher Agency in the Professional Field

The fact that there are (currently) no guarantees that teacher agency is achieved in multilingual pedagogies within mainstream primary education raises the question of how other actors in the professional field could foster and support such agency. Thus, it becomes necessary to contextualise the findings presented here within developments of teacher professionalisation. Possibilities and limitations regarding the normalisation of multilingualism in initial teacher education (ITE) and continuous professional development (CPD) are increasingly thematised (e.g. Foley, 2022; Kirsch et al., 2021; Putjata et al., 2022). Foley et al. (2022) examined the extent to which UK teacher education programmes prepare future teachers to inclusively teach students with English as an additional language. They reported a mixed situation, expressing concern that a quarter of prospective teachers, across a range of ITE providers, indicated little or no increase in EAL-related teaching strategies by the end of their programmes. Additionally, about a fifth lacked confidence in supporting EAL learners. Relevant to multilingual pedagogies, Foley *et al.* found that student teachers encountered conflicting discourses regarding the status of 'home languages' in the classroom, and some faced constraints due to 'English only' policies in their placement schools. Goltsev *et al.* (2022) investigated how teacher educators with a multilingual biography approached multilingualism in a mandatory German-as-additional-language module within ITE in the federal state of North Rhine-Westphalia, Germany. Although the researchers understood the module's framing as bolstering a monolingual mindset, the teacher educators found room to explore multilingualism with their student teachers. Goltsev *et al.* argue that such compulsory ITE elements hold considerable potential for establishing perspectives on the multilingual turn for all future teachers. Based on their intervention studies and school development programmes in Finnish, Dutch and Luxemburgish settings, Kirsch *et al.* (2021) emphasise that the complex ways in which policies, beliefs and practices of teachers and their agency are intertwined need to be considered in successful provisions of professional development for multilingual pedagogies. Their findings from CPD in Dutch primary schools (Duarte & Günther-van der Meij, 2018, 2022) apply more broadly to teacher professionalisation: '[T]eachers need to create safe spaces in which to experiment with multiple languages in the classrooms […] operationalise the various approaches for multilingual education for their own context and particular aims' (Kirsch *et al.*, 2021: 196–197).

These insights from research conducted within different education policy contexts highlight that the conditions and contents of ITE and CDP necessarily reflect national or regional education policies and the wider societal and political climate regarding multilingualism. Teacher education functions as a gatekeeper to future developments. On the one hand, this constitutes a challenge in England, where teacher education itself is under considerable pressure and risks resulting in 'adaptive learning', prioritising government and school requirements along with practical knowledge of the immediate context over theoretical and broader pedagogical knowledge (Murray & Passy, 2014). It is not possible to refer to ITE in England without drawing attention to the tight timeframe (the traditional Postgraduate Certificate of Education pathway consists of a nine-month course) and the increasingly varied routes into the profession resulting from neoliberal/neoconservative policies, which have continuously enlarged the share of school-led provision in ITE and CDP. This situation can amplify the dominance of the performativity paradigm, and 'all teacher education, wherever it is located, is still heavily policed by the presence of standards and a more severe Ofsted inspection regime' (Childs, 2013: 326). On the other hand, initial teacher education provides a context for professionalisation that combines theory and practice. It allows critical exploration, debate and shifts in professional discourses. As Yvonne Foley (2022: 103) argues, '[a] crucial step for teacher education is to enable teachers to see themselves as part of the diverse profile of the classroom in order to decentre and pluralise the monolingual, monocultural habitus that so often frames educational policies, practices, and teacher professionalism'. The five teachers in this book were, in different ways and to varying degrees, aware of their positionality vis-à-vis children's multilingualism, and perhaps not surprisingly, they began to thematise their own language experiences when talking about plurilingual pupils in their class. These educators viewed multilingualism as normalcy among the children and teaching them as the normalcy of their profession, yet did not engage with the children's plurilingual repertoires in teaching/learning processes. The present study thus clearly underscores the overall significance of the triad of policy, practices and professionalism mentioned above. It is this triad that is addressed in the request to normalise multilingualism in the institution of school. For teacher agency in multilingual pedagogies to emerge and be consistently and reliably achieved, education policy must legitimise such pedagogies at the macro level. Additionally, on the meso level, teachers need conceptual support and material resources. Crucially, education policy must guarantee that educators are allowed the pedagogical flexibility to develop such agency at the micro level of their schools and classrooms. Initiatives in continuous professional development and school development programmes, as reported in the research literature, usually involve some form of legitimisation of multilingual pedagogical approaches, for example through prior consent as a requirement for participation. However, the situation is different for contexts of initial teacher education, where – depending on national or regional conditions of education policy – such legitimisation cannot be taken as a given. Instead, ITE needs to offer broader opportunities to explore existing and alternative professional discourses. This preparation is essential for future teachers, who will work throughout their careers in various schools within an increasingly multilingual society, irrespective of whether their first immediate school context, for example in a placement school, is a 'superdiverse' or a supposedly 'monolingual' primary school, or even a setting with an overt 'English only' policy.

The features identified as constituting and potentially facilitating teacher agency in multilingual pedagogies offer – so I hope – valuable insights for settings of teacher education. They serve as points of reference to support both prospective and practising teachers, helping them build their capacities in specific domains. Conversely, those features identified as hindrances to the achievement of such agency can provide points of departure for critical, reflective explorations. In combination, the three sets of features allow for an analysis of the status quo in a given educational setting (in a group of future teachers or in a school) and for tailoring next steps of development.

In fact, both the nexus between the three sets of features and the power differential between hindering and potentially facilitating aspects need to be addressed to instigate, in the sense of collective agency, further processes of reflexivity in the professional field and among its various actors – prospective teachers, teachers working in primary schools, teacher educators, researchers and policymakers.

Inevitably, the political context – not only of education policy but also language ideologies and politics of inclusion and exclusion – comes into view. Some newly arrived children in the previous chapters spoke Romanian, others Italian and Bengali and one of the teachers, Heather, mentioned two pupils from war-torn Syria, who she had taught previously. In this regard, every ethnographic study in a primary school is – in addition to the contingent composition of a class – a snapshot that can reflect current violent conflicts and/or the contemporary immigration regime. As I was writing these chapters, hardly a week passed in Britain without headlines about plurilingual pupils being affected by governmental decisions that disrupted their education and well-being, and even potentially endangered their lives or the lives of family members through threats of deportation. Dominant discourses and counter-discourses about 'language' and multilingualism belong to these wider contestations about the kind of society we envision inhabiting. They pertain to the very question of who constitutes 'we': 'No one is an illegitimate speaker' and 'No one is illegal' are related concepts, and we are reminded that boundaries and borders are not abstract concepts but rather very concrete for those who are denied permission to cross them.

Multilingual pedagogies manifest in different places and educational settings, and 'language education finds its temporary shapes and contours by identifying with particular localities, inhabiting particular practices, and connecting with the different voices and relationships taking part in it' (Lytra *et al.*, 2022: 321). Indeed, primary schools in England represent only one of many settings for multilingual pedagogies, and under current conditions not even a dependable one. The primary school, however, plays a key role as the basis of (almost) all children's formal education. Here, official knowledge is enacted through the curriculum that defines what counts as knowledge, via a pedagogy that identifies what counts as a valid way of conveying this knowledge, and through an evaluation that determines what counts as its successful realisation on the part of the pupils (Bernstein, 1971: 47). This makes the primary school a crucial setting for negotiating and disrupting monolingual ideologies in addition to reflecting on the kind of school and pedagogy we envision for children (and teachers), and on the related questions of who is recognised as 'we' in curriculum and pedagogy along with whose voices and views are included.

School education operates within complex sociopolitical constellations, where many stakeholders can legitimately claim their 'stake' (Priestley *et al.*, 2015: 4–5). While this constellation requires finding a balance between students, parents, the state and employers, the lens of teacher agency foregrounds the importance of teachers as stakeholders with their unique expertise and experience. The Polish poet Wisława Szymborska (cited in Richardson, 2002: vii) spoke about how inspiration is not an exclusive privilege of poets or artists who work in their profession with love and imagination, but a trait that doctors, teachers and gardeners, to name but a few, have in common: '[A]nd I could list a hundred more professions. Their work becomes one continuous adventure as long as they manage to keep discovering new challenges in it. Difficulties and setbacks never quell their curiosity' (Szymborska, 1996). This portrayal is an empathic way to describe the professional agency of teachers and others. Indeed, 'imagining otherwise' is seen as a key part in literature and research on multilingualism (Pahl, 2022: 318), and its importance was also evident in this exploration of teacher agency in multilingual pedagogies. Curiosity and the capability to 'imagine otherwise', however, need to be nurtured. Individually and as members of a professional field, educators must be empowered if the primary school and its pedagogy are expected to successfully incorporate and shape their multilingual pedagogies. Seen through the lens of teacher agency, the institutional normalisation of multilingualism involves the political will to facilitate that empowerment – both politically and in terms of programmes and resources for schools, teacher education and research initiatives. Seen from the perspective of the children, these pedagogies should offer opportunities to explore their plurilingual repertoires, leveraging them for learning, and thus negotiating what these repertoires can mean in school. Seen from the teachers' point of view, multilingual pedagogies require time and space for them to listen to their pupils, to reflect on the status quo and to leverage all their professional experiences and creativity, their curiosity and their pedagogical imagination.

References

Adams, K., Monahan, J. and Wills, R. (2015) Losing the whole child? A national survey of primary education training provision for spiritual, moral, social and cultural development. *European Journal of Teacher Education* 38 (2), 199–216.

Adams, K., Lumb, A., Tapp, J. and Paige, R. (2020) Whole child, whole teacher: Leadership for flourishing primary schools. *Education 3-13* 48 (7), 861–874.

Alexander, R. (2008) *Essays on Pedagogy*. Routledge.

Alexander, R. (ed.) (2010) *Children, their World, their Education. Final Report and Recommendations of the Cambridge Primary Review*. Routledge.

Alexander, R. (2017) *Towards Dialogic Teaching. Rethinking Classroom Talk* (5th edn). Dialogos.

Alexander, R. (2018) Developing dialogic teaching: Genesis, process, trial. *Research Papers in Education* 33 (5), 561–598.

Alexander, R. (2022) *Education in Spite of Policy*. Routledge.

Alexander, R., Rose, J. and Woodhead, C. (1992) *Curriculum Organisation and Classroom Practice in Primary Schools. A Discussion Paper*. DES. See https://dera.ioe.ac.uk//4373/ (accessed August 2024).

All-Party Parliamentary Group on Modern Languages (2019) A National Recovery Programme for Languages. See https://nationalrecoverylanguages.weebly.com/downloads.html (accessed August 2024).

Althusser, L. (1984) *Essays on Ideology*. Verso.

Anderson, Ja. (2024) Translanguaging: A paradigm shift for ELT theory and practice. *ELT Journal* 78 (1), 72–80.

Anderson, J. (2016) Language and literacy. Challenging monolingual discourses. In J. Anderson and V. Macleroy (eds) *Multilingual Digital Storytelling: Engaging Creatively and Critically with Literacy* (pp. 13–41). Routledge.

Anderson, J. and Macleroy, V. (2015) Rethinking multilingualism: Trajectories in policy, pedagogy and research in the UK. In A. Yiokoumetti (ed.) *Multilingualism and Language in Education* (pp. 243–266). CUP.

Anderson, J. and Macleroy, V. (eds) (2016) *Multilingual Digital Storytelling: Engaging Creatively and Critically with Literacy*. Routledge.

Apple, M. (1982) *Education and Power*. Routledge & Kegan Paul.

Archer, M. (2000) *Being Human: The Problem of Agency*. CUP.

Arnaut, K., Blommaert, J., Rampton, B. and Spotti, M. (eds) (2016) *Language and Superdiversity*. Routledge.

Badwan, K. (2021a) Unmooring language for social justice: Young people talking about language in place in Manchester, UK. *Critical Inquiry in Language Studies* 18 (2), 153–173.

Badwan, K. (2021b) *Language in a Globalised World. Social Justice Perspectives on Mobility and Contact*. Palgrave Macmillan.

Bailey, B. (2012) Heteroglossia. In M. Martin-Jones, A. Blackledge and A. Creese (eds) *The Routledge Handbook of Multilingualism* (pp. 499–507). Routledge.

Ball, S. (2003) The teacher's soul and the terrors of performativity. *Journal of Education Policy* 18 (2), 215–228.

Ball, S. (2013a) *The Education Debate* (2nd edn). Policy Press.

Ball, S. (2013b) *Foucault, Power, and Education*. Routledge.

Ball, S. (2018) The tragedy of state education in England: Reluctance, compromise and muddle – A system in disarray. *Journal of the British Academy* 6, 207–238.
Bandura, A. (1982) Self-efficacy mechanism in human agency. *American Psychologist* 37 (2), 122–147.
Barnes, D. (1976) *From Communication to Curriculum*. Penguin.
Bernstein, B. (1971) On the classification and framing of educational knowledge. In M. Young (ed.) *Knowledge and Control. New Directions of the Sociology of Education* (pp. 47–69). Collier-Macmillan.
Biesta, G. and Miedema, S. (2002) Instruction or pedagogy? The need for a transformative conception of education. *Teaching and Teacher Education* 18, 173–181.
Biesta, G. and Tedder, M. (2007) Agency and learning in the life course: Towards an ecological perspective. *Studies in the Education of Adults* 39 (2), 132–149.
Billet, S. (2006) Relational interdependence between social and individual agency in work and working life. *Mind, Culture and Activity* 13 (1), 53–69.
Black, L. (2007) Interactive whole class teaching and pupil learning: Theoretical and practical implications. *Language and Education* 21 (4), 271–283.
Blackledge, A. (2004) Constructions of identity in political discourse in multilingual Britain. In A. Pavlenko and A. Blackledge (eds) *Negotiation of Identities in Multilingual Contexts* (pp. 68–92). Multilingual Matters.
Blackledge, A. and Creese, A. (2010) *Multilingualism. A Critical Perspective*. Continuum.
Blackledge, A. and Creese, A. with Baynham, M., Cooke, M., Goodson, L., Hua, Z., Malkani, B., Phillimore, J., Robinson, M., Rock, F., Simpson, J., Tagg, C., Thompson, J., Trehan, K. and Li, W. (2018) Language and superdiversity. An interdisciplinary perspective. In A. Creese and A. Blackledge (eds) *The Routledge Handbook of Language and Superdiversity. An Interdisciplinary Perspective* (pp. xxi–xlv). Routledge.
Blommaert, J. (2018) *Dialogues with Ethnography: Notes on Classics, and How I Read Them*. Multilingual Matters.
Bonnett, A. and Carrington, B. (2000) Fitting into categories or falling between them? Rethinking ethnic classification. *British Journal of Sociology* 21 (4), 487–500.
Borthwick, K. (2018) Support unsung heros: Community-based language learning and teaching. In M. Kelly (ed.) *Languages After Brexit. How the UK Speaks to the World* (pp. 185–194). Palgrave Macmillan.
Bourdieu, P. (1991) *Language and Symbolic Power*. Polity.
Bourne, J. (2001) Discourses and identities in a multi-lingual primary classroom. *Oxford Review of Education* 27 (1), 103–114.
Braun, V. and Clarke, V. (2006) Using thematic analysis in psychology. *Qualitative Research in Psychology* 3 (2), 77–101.
Braun, V. and Clarke, V. (2022) *Thematic Analysis. A Practical Guide*. Sage.
Brinkmann, S. and Kvale, S. (2015) *InterViews. Learning the Craft of Qualitative Research Interviewing* (3rd edn). Sage.
British Academy (2019) Languages in the UK. A call for action. See https://www.thebritishacademy.ac.uk/publications/languages-uk-academies-statement/ (accessed August 2024).
British Educational Research Association (BERA) (2018) *Ethical Guidelines for Educational Research* (4th edn). BERA. See https://www.bera.ac.uk/wp-content/uploads/2018/06/BERA-Ethical-Guidelines-for-Educational-Research_4thEdn_2018.pdf (accessed August 2024).
Bruner, J. (1983) *Child's Talk. Learning to Use Language*. Norton.
Buchanan, R. (2015) Teacher identity and agency in an era of accountability. *Teachers and Teaching: Theory and Practice* 21 (6), 700–719.
Busch, B. (2012) The linguistic repertoire revisited. *Applied Linguistics* 33 (5), 503–523.
Busch, B. (2016) Categorizing languages and speakers: Why linguists should mistrust census data and statistics. *Working Papers in Urban Language and Literacies* WP189. See https://www.academia.edu/20770728/WP189_Busch_2016_Categorizing_languages_

and_speakers_Why_linguists_should_mistrust_census_data_and_statistics (accessed August 2024).
Busch, B. (2017a) Biographical approaches to research in multilingual settings. Exploring linguistic repertoires. In M. Martin-Jones and D. Martin (eds) *Researching Multilingualism* (pp. 46–59). Routledge.
Busch, B. (2017b) Expanding the notion of the linguistic repertoire: On the concept of Spracherleben – The lived experience of language. *Applied Linguistics* 38 (3), 340–358.
Busch, B. (2018) The language portrait in multilingualism research: Theoretical and methodological considerations. *Working Papers in Urban Language and Literacies* WP236. See https://academia.edu/35988562/WP236_Busch_2018_The_language_portrait_in_multilingualism_research_Theoretical_and_methodological_considerations (accessed August 2024).
Busch, B. (2022) Children's perception of their multilingualism. In A. Stavans and U. Jessner (eds) *The Cambridge Handbook of Childhood Multilingualism* (pp. 215–234). CUP.
Butcher, J., Sinka, I. and Troman, G. (2007) Exploring diversity: Teacher education policy and bilingualism. *Research Papers in Education* 22 (4), 483–501.
Butler, J. (1997) *The Psychic Life of Power*. SUP.
Canagarajah, S. (2004) Subversive identities, pedagogical safe houses, and critical learning. In B. Norton and K. Toohey (eds) *Critical Pedagogies and Language Learning* (pp. 116–137). CUP.
Carbonara, V. and Scibetta, A. (2022) Integrating translanguaging pedagogy into Italian primary schools: Implications for language practices and children's empowerment. *International Journal of Bilingual Education and Bilingualism* 25 (3), 1049–1069.
Celic, C. and Seltzer, K. (2013) *Translanguaging: A CUNY-NYSIEB Guide for Educators*. CUNY-NYSIEB. See https://www.cuny-nysieb.org/wp-content/uploads/2016/04/Translanguaging-Guide-March-2013.pdf (accessed August 2024).
Cenoz, J. and Gorter, D. (2017) Minority languages and sustainable translanguaging: Threat or opportunity? *Journal of Multilingual and Multicultural Development* 38 (10), 901–912.
Childs, A. (2013) The work of teacher educators: An English policy perspective. *Journal of Education for Teaching* 39 (3), 314–328.
Cliff Hodges, G. (2010) Rivers of reading: Using critical incident collages to learn about adolescent readers and their readership. *English in Education* 44 (3), 181–200.
Cole, M. (1996) *Cultural Psychology. A Once and Future Discipline*. Harvard University Press.
Conteh, J. (2018) Translanguaging as pedagogy – A critical review. In A. Creese and A. Blackledge (eds) *The Routledge Handbook of Language and Superdiversity. An Interdisciplinary Perspective* (pp. 473–487). Routledge.
Conteh, J. and Meier, G. (eds) (2014) *The Multilingual Turn in Languages Education. Opportunities and Challenges*. Multilingual Matters.
Cook, V. (1995) Multi-competence and learning of many languages. *Language, Culture and Curriculum* 8 (2), 93–98.
Copland, F. and McPake, J. (2022) 'Building a new public idea about language'?: Multilingualism and language learning in the post-Brexit UK. *Current Issues in Language Planning* 23 (2), 117–136.
Costley, T. (2014) English as an additional language, policy and the teaching and learning of English in England. *Language and Education* 28 (3), 276–292.
Creese, A. and Blackledge, A. (2010) Translanguaging in the bilingual classroom: A pedagogy for learning and teaching? *The Modern Language Journal* 94 (1), 103–115.
Cremin, T. and Baker, S. (2010) Exploring teacher-writer identities in the classroom: Conceptualising the struggle. *English Teaching: Practice and Critique* 9 (3), 8–25.
Cremin, T. and Myhill, D. (2012) *Writing Voices. Creating Communities of Writers*. Routledge.

Cummins, J. (1979) Linguistic interdependence and the development of bilingual children. *Review of Educational Research* 49, 222–251.
Cummins, J. (2000) *Language, Power and Pedagogy. Bilingual Children in the Crossfire.* Multilingual Matters.
Cummins, J. (2017) Teaching for transfer in multilingual school contexts. In O. Garcia, A. Lin and S. May (eds) *Bilingual and Multilingual Education. Encyclopedia of Language and Education* (3rd edn, pp. 103–115). Springer.
Cummins, J. (2021a) *Rethinking the Education of Multilingual Learners: A Critical Analysis of Theoretical Concepts.* Multilingual Matters.
Cummins, J. (2021b) Translanguaging: A critical analysis of theoretical claims. In P. Juvonen and M. Källvist (eds) *Pedagogical Translanguaging. Theoretical, Methodological and Empirical Perspectives* (pp. 7–36). Multilingual Matters.
Cummins, J., Early, M. and Stille, S. (2011a) Frames of reference: Identity texts in perspective. In J. Cummins and M. Early (eds) *Identity Texts. The Collaborative Creation of Power in Multilingual Schools* (pp. 21–43). Trentham.
Cummins, J., Early, M., Leoni, L. and Stille, S. (2011b) 'It really comes down to the teachers, I think': Pedagogies of choice in multilingual classrooms. In J. Cummins and M. Early (eds) *Identity Texts* (pp. 153–163). Trentham.
Cunningham, C. (2019) 'The inappropriateness of language': Discourses of power and control over languages beyond English in primary schools. *Language and Education* 33 (4), 285–301.
Cunningham, C. and Little, S. (2023) 'Inert benevolence' towards languages beyond English in the discourses of English primary school teacher. *Linguistics and Education* 78. https://doi.org/10.1016/j.linged.2022.101122.
Davies, B. (2006) Subjectification: The relevance of Butler's analysis for education. *British Journal of Sociology of Education* 27 (4), 425–438.
Debono, J. (n.d.) Language of the month activities. Newbury Park Primary School. See https://www.newburyparkschool.net/lotm/activitiesbooklet.pdf (accessed August 2024).
Denzin, N. (2017) Critical qualitative inquiry. *Qualitative Inquiry* 23 (1), 8–16.
Department of Education (2011) *The National Strategies 1997–2011. A Brief Summary of the Impact and Effectiveness of the National Strategies.* HMSO.
Department for Education (2013) *The National Curriculum in England. Key Stages 1 and 2 Framework Document.* DfE.
Department for Education (2017) *School Census 2016 to 2017. Business and technical Specification.* HMSO.
Department for Education (2023a) School teacher workforce. See https://www.ethnicity-facts-figures.service.gov.uk/workforce-and-business/workforce-diversity/school-teacher-workforce/latest (accessed August 2024).
Department for Education (2023b) Initial teacher training census. See https://explore-education-statistics.service.gov.uk/find-statistics/initial-teacher-training-census#dataBlock-d7f1257a-c086-4531-8ea1-6669e30bb312-tables (accessed August 2024).
Department for Education (2024) Schools, pupils and their characteristics. See https://explore-education-statistics.service.gov.uk/find-statistics/school-pupils-and-their-characteristics (accessed August 2024).
Department for Education and Employment (1998) *The National Literacy Strategy: A Framework for Teaching.* HMSO.
Department for Education and Employment (1999) *The National Numeracy Strategy: Framework for Teaching Mathematics from Reception to Year 6.* HMSO.
Department of Education and Science (DES) (1985) *Education for All (The Swann Report).* HMSO.
Dinneen, A. (2017) *The Hampshire Young Interpreter Scheme: A Coming of Age.* Naldic.

Dirim, İ. and Mecheril, P. (2010) Die Sprache(n) der Migrationsgesellschaft [The langugage(s) of the migration society]. In P. Mecheril, M. Castro Varela, İ. Dirim, A. Kalpaka and C. Melter (eds) *Migrationspädagogik [Migration Pedagogy]* (pp. 99–120). Beltz.

Duarte, J. (2019) Translanguaging in mainstream education: A sociocultural approach. *International Journal of Bilingual Education and Bilingualism* 22 (2), 150–164.

Duarte, J. and Gogolin, I. (2013) Introduction. Linguistic superdiversity in educational institutions. In J. Duarte and I. Gogolin (eds) *Linguistic Superdiversity in Urban Areas. Research Approaches* (pp. 1–24). John Benjamins.

Duarte, J. and Günther-van der Meij, M. (2018) A holistic model for multilingualism in education. *EuroAmerican Journal of Applied Linguistics and Languages* [Special Issue] 5 (2) 24–43.

Duarte, J. and Günther-van der Meij, M. (2022) 'Just accept each other, while the rest of the world doesn't' – Teachers' reflections on multilingual education. *Language and Education* 36 (5), 451–466.

Duarte, J. and Kirsch, C. (2021) Introduction. Multilingual approaches for teaching and learning. In C. Kirsch and J. Duarte (eds) *Multilingual Approaches for Teaching and Learning* (pp. 1–11). Routledge.

Du Bois, J. (2007) The stance triangle. In R. Englebretson (ed.) *Stancetaking in Discourse. Subjectivity, Evaluation, Interaction* (pp. 139–182). John Benjamins.

Edwards, A. (2007) Relational agency in professional practice: A CHAT analysis. *Actio: An International Journal of Human Activity Theory* 1, 1–17.

Emirbayer, M. and Mische, A. (1998) What is agency? *The American Journal of Sociology* 103 (4), 962–1023.

Eteläpelto, A., Vähäsantanen, K., Hökkä, P. and Paloniemi, S. (2013) What is agency? Conceptualizing professional agency at work. *Educational Research Review* 10, 45–65.

Eteläpelto, A., Vähäsantanen, K. and Hökkä, P. (2015) How do novice teachers in Finland perceive their professional agency? *Teachers and Teaching* 21 (6), 660–680.

Fashanu, C., Wood, E. and Payne, M. (2020) Multilingual communication under the radar: How multilingual children challenge the dominant monolingual discourse in a superdiverse, Early Years educational setting in England. *English in Education* 54 (1), 93–112.

Fekete, L. (2019) *Europe's Fault Lines. Racism and the Rise of the Right*. Verso.

Flubacher, M.-C. and Purkarthofer, J. (2022) Speaking subjects in multilingualism research: Biographical and speaker-centred approaches. In J. Purkarthofer and M.-C. Flubacher (eds) *Speaking Subjects in Multilingualism Research: Biographical and Speaker-centred Approaches* (pp. 3–20). Multilingual Matters.

Foley, Y. (2022) Introduction to the special issue: Normalising difference in teacher education: National and international perspectives. *Language and Education* 36 (2), 103–105.

Foley, Y., Anderson, C., Hancock, J. and Conteh, J. (2022) Exploring the professional identity and agency of student teachers in multilingual classrooms. *Language and Education* 36 (2), 106–121.

Fones, A. (2019) Examining high school English language learner teacher agency: Opportunities and constraints. In H. Kayi-Aydar, X. Gao, E.R. Miller, M. Varghese and G. Vitanova (eds) *Theorizing and Analyzing Language Teacher Agency* (pp. 24–43). Multilingual Matters.

Foucault, M. (1971) Orders of discourse. *Social Science Information* 10 (2), 7–30.

Fraser, N. (2008) *Scales of Justice. Reimagining Political Space in a Globalizing World*. Polity.

Fraser, N. (2017) I would be thrilled to be called a dangerous woman. *The Dangerous Women Project*, 23rd January. See https://dangerouswomenproject.org/2017/01/23/nancy-fraser/ (accessed August 2024).

Gajo, L. (2014) From normalization to didactization of multilingualism: European and Francophone research at the crossroads between linguistics and didactics. In J. Conteh and G. Meier (eds) *The Multilingual Turn in Languages Education: Opportunites and Challenges* (pp. 113–131). Multilingual Matters.

García, O. (2009) *Bilingual Education in the 21 Century. A Global Perspective.* Wiley-Blackwell.
García, O. (2014) What is translanguaging? Expanded questions and answers for U.S. educators. In S. Hesson, K. Seltzer and H. Woodley (auths) *Translanguaging in Curriculum and Instruction: A CUNY-NYSIEB Guide for Educators* (pp. 1–13). CUNY-NYSIEB. See https://www.cuny-nysieb.org/wp-content/uploads/2016/04/Translanguaging-Guide-Curr-Inst-Final-December-2014.pdf (accessed August 2024).
García, O. and Flores, N. (2012) Multilingual pedagogies. In M. Martin-Jones, A. Blackledge and A. Creese (eds) *The Routledge Handbook of Multilingualism* (pp. 232–246). Routledge.
García, O. and Kano, N. (2014) Translanguaging as process and pedagogy: Developing the English writing of Janpanese students in the US. In J. Conteh and G. Meier (eds) *The Multilingual Turn in Languages Education: Opportunities and Challenges* (pp. 258–277). Multilingual Matters.
García, O. and Li, W. (2014) *Translanguaging. Language, Bilingualism and Education.* Palgrave/Macmillan.
García, O. and Kleyn, T. (eds) (2016a) *Translanguaging with Multilingual Students. Learning from Classroom Moments.* Routledge.
García, O. and Kleyn, T. (2016b) Translanguaging theory in education. In O. García and T. Kleyn (eds) *Translanguaging with Multilingual Students* (pp. 9–33). Routledge.
García, O. and Lin, A. (2016) Translanguaging in bilingual education. In O. García, A. Lin and S. May (eds) *Bilingual and Multilingual Education. Encyclopedia of Language and Education* (3rd edn). Springer.
García, O., Ibarra Johnson, S. and Seltzer, K. (2017) *The Translanguaging Classroom. Leveraging Student Bilingualism for Learning.* Caslon.
Gewirtz, S. and Cribb, A. (2009) *Understanding Education. A Sociological Perspective.* Polity.
Gibbons, P. (2002) *Scaffolding Language, Scaffolding Learning. Teaching Second Language Learners in the Mainstream Classroom.* Heinemann.
Gibbons, P. (2006) *Bridging Discourses in the ESL Classroom. Students, Teachers and Researchers.* Continuum.
Giddens, A. (1984) *The Constitution of Society.* University of California Press.
Gilroy, P. (2004) *After Empire. Melancholia or Convivial Culture?* Routledge.
Gogolin, I. (1997) The "monolingual habitus" as the common feature in teaching in the language of the majority in different countries. *Per Linguam* 13 (2), 38–49.
Gogolin, I. (2015) Die Karriere einer Kontur – Sprachenportraits [The career of a silhouette – Language portraits]. In I. Dirim, I. Gogolin, D. Knorr, M. Krüger-Potratz, D. Lengyel, H. Reich and W. Weiße (eds) *Impulse für die Migrationsgesellschaft. Bildung, Politik und Religion [Impulses for the Migration Society. Education, Politics and Religion]* (pp. 294–304). Waxmann.
Gogolin, I. (2021) Multilingualism: A threat to public education or a resource in public education? – European histories and realities. *European Educational Research Journal* 20 (3), 297–310.
Goltsev, E., Olfert, H. and Putjata, G. (2022) Finding spaces for all languages. Teacher educators' perspectives on multilingualism. *Language and Education* 36 (5), 437–450.
Gordon, T., Holland, J. and Lahelma, E. (2001) Ethnographic research in educational settings. In P. Atkinson, A. Coffey, S. Delamont, J. Lofland and L. Lofland (eds) *Handbook of Ethnography* (pp. 188–203). Sage.
Green, J. and Bloome, D. (1997) Ethnography and ethnographers of and in education: A situated perspective. In J. Flood, S. Heath and D. Lapp (eds) *Handbook of Research on Teaching Literacy through the Communicative and Visual Arts* (pp. 183–202). Macmillan.
Gregory, E. and Williams, A. (2000) Work or play? 'Unofficial' literacies in the lives of two East London communities. In M. Martin-Jones and K. Jones (eds) *Multilingual Literacies* (pp. 37–54). John Benjamins.

Greig, A., Taylor, J. and MacKay, T. (2013) *Doing Research with Children. A Practical Guide* (3rd edn). Sage.

Grosjean, F. (1989) Neurolinguists, beware! The bilingual is not two monolinguals in one person. *Brain and Language* 36 (1), 3–15.

Gumperz, J. (1964) Linguistic and social interaction in two Communities. *American Anthropologist* 66, 137–153.

Gundarina, O. and Simpson, J. (2022) A monolingual approach in an English primary school: Practices and implications. *Language and Education* 36 (6), 523–543.

Hall, S. (1992) The West and the rest: Discourse and power. In S. Hall and B. Gieben (eds) *Formations of Modernity* (pp. 275–320). Open University/Polity.

Hammersley, M. and Traianou, A. (2012) *Ethics in Qualitative Research. Controversies and Contexts*. Sage.

Harré, R. and van Langenhove, L. (1991) Varieties of positioning. *Journal of the Theory of Social Behaviour* 21 (4), 393–407.

Harris, R. (1997) Romantic bilingualism: Time for a change? In C. Leung and C. Cable (eds) *English as an Additional Language. Changing Perspectives* (pp. 14–27). NALDIC.

Hawkins, E. (1984) *Awareness of Language: An Introduction*. CUP.

Heller, M. (2007) Bilingualism as ideology and practice In M. Heller (ed.) *Bilingualism: A Social Approach* (pp. 1–22). Palgrave/Macmillan.

Hélot, C., Sneddon, R. and Daly, N. (eds) (2014) *Children's Literature in Multilingual Classrooms. From Multiliteracy to Multimodality*. Trentham/IOE Press.

Hélot, C., Frijns, C., van Gorp, K. and Sierens, S. (eds) (2018a) *Language Awareness in Multilingual Classrooms in Europe. From Theory to Practice*. De Gruyter.

Hélot, C., Frijns, C., van Gorp, K. and Sierens, S. (2018b) Introduction: Toward critical multilingual language awareness for 21st century schools. In C. Hélot, C. Frijns, K. van Gorp and S. Sierens (eds) *Language Awareness in Multilingual Classrooms in Europe. From Theory to Practice* (pp. 1 – 20). De Gruyter.

Herdina, P. and Jessner, U. (2002) *A Dynamic Model of Multilingualism: Changing the Psycholinguistic Perspective*. Multilingual Matters.

Heugh, K. (2015) Epistemologies in multilingual education: Translanguaging and genre – Companions in conversation with policy and practice. *Language and Education* 29 (3), 280–285.

Heugh, K. (2018) Commentary – Linguistic citizenship: Who decides whose languages, ideologies and vocabulary matter? In L. Lim, C. Stroud and L. Wee (eds) *The Multilingual Citizen. Towards a Politics of Language for Agency and Change* (pp. 174–189). Multilingual Matters.

Heugh, K. (2021) Southern multilingualisms, translanguaging and transknowledging in inclusive and sustainable education. In P. Harding-Esch and H. Coleman (eds) *Language and the Sustainable Development Goals* (pp. 37–47). British Council.

Hobsbawm, E.J. (1992) *Nations and Nationalism since 1780. Programme, Myth, Reality* (2nd edn). CUP.

Houlton, D. (1985) *All Our Languages. A Handbook for the Multilingual Classroom*. Arnold.

Hymes, D. (1996) *Ethnography, Linguistics, Narrative Inequality. Toward an Understanding of Voice*. Routledge.

Ibrahim, N. (2019) Children's multimodal visual narratives as possible sites of identity performance. In P. Kalaja and S. Melo-Pfeifer (eds) *Visualising Multilingual Lives. More Than Words* (pp. 33–52). Multilingual Matters.

Jaffe, A. (ed.) (2009a) *Stance. Sociolinguistic Perspectives*. OUP.

Jaffe, A. (2009b) Introduction. The sociolinguistic of stance. In A. Jaffe (ed.) *Stance. Sociolinguistic Perspectives* (pp. 3–28). OUP.

Jaffe, A. (2009c) Stance in a Corsian school. Institutional and ideological orders and the production of bilingual subjects. In A. Jaffe (ed.) *Stance. Sociolinguistic Perspectives* (pp. 119–145). OUP.

Janks, H. (2010) *Literacy and Power*. Routledge.
Jeffrey, B. and Woods, P. (1998) *Testing Teachers: The Effect of School Inspections on Primary Teachers*. Falmer.
Kayi-Aydar, H. (2015) Multiple identities, negotiations, and agency across time and space: A narrative inquiry of a foreign language teacher candidate. *Critical Inquiry in Language Studies* 12 (2), 137–160.
Kayi-Aydar, H. (2019a) A language teacher's agency in the development of her professional identity: A narrative case study. *Journal of Latinos and Education* 18 (1), 4–18.
Kayi-Aydar, H. (2019b) Language teacher agency: Major theoretical considerations, conceptualizations and methodological choices. In H. Kayi-Aydar, X. Gao, E.R. Miller, M. Varghese and G. Vitanova (eds) *Theorizing and Analyzing Language Teacher Agency* (pp. 10–21). Multilingual Matters.
Kayi-Aydar, H., Gao, X., Miller, E.R., Varghese, M. and Vitanova, G. (2019) Introduction. In H. Kayi-Aydar, X. Gao, E.R. Miller, M. Varghese and G. Vitanova (eds) *Theorizing and Analyzing Language Teacher Agency* (pp. 1–9). Multilingual Matters.
Kenner, C. and Ruby, M. (2012) *Interconnecting Worlds. Teacher Partnerships for Bilingual Learning*. Trentham.
Kirsch, C. (2021) Translanguaging pedagogies in early childhood education in Luxembourg: Theory into practice. In C. Kirsch and J. Duarte (eds) *Multilingual Approaches for Teaching and Learning* (pp. 15–33). Routledge.
Kirsch, C., Duarte, J. and Palviainen, A. (2021) Language policy, professional development and sustainability of multilingual approaches. In C. Kirsch and J. Duarte (eds) *Multilingual Approaches for Teaching and Learning. From Acknowledging to Capitalising on Multilingualism in European Mainstream Education* (pp. 186–203). Routledge.
Kounin, J. (1970) *Discipline and Group Management in Classrooms*. Holt Rhinehart and Winston.
Kozulin, A. (1998) *Psychological Tools. A Sociocultural Approach to Education*. Harvard University Press.
Kroskrity, P. (2010) Language ideologies – Evolving Perspectives. In J. Jaspers, J. Östman and J. Verschueren (eds) *Society and Language Use* (pp. 192–211). John Benjamins.
Laihonen, P. and Szabó, T. (2017) Investigating visual practices in educational settings. In M. Martin-Jones and D. Martin (eds) *Researching Multilingualism* (pp. 121–138). Routledge.
Lanvers, U. (2011) Language education policy in England. Is English the elephant in the room? *Apples – Journal of Applied Language Studies* 3 (5), 63–78.
Lasky, S. (2005) A sociocultural approach to understanding teacher identity, agency and professional vulnerability in a context of secondary school reform. *Teaching and Teacher Education* 21 (8), 899–916.
Mary, L. and Hélot, C. (2022) Multilingual education in formal schooling: Conceptual shifts in theory, policy and practice. In A. Stavans and U. Jessner (eds) *The Cambridge Handbook of Childhood Multilingualism* (pp. 82–109). CUP.
Leung, C. (2016) English as an additional language – A genealogy of language-in-education policies and reflections on research trajectories. *Language and Education* 30 (2), 158–174.
Leung, C. (2019) EAL in the mainstream: An English story. *EAL Journal* Summer 2019, 18–19.
Leung, C. and Valdés, G. (2019) Translanguaging and the transdisciplinary framework for language teaching and learning in a multilingual world. *The Modern Language Journal* 103 (2), 348–370.
Lewis, G., Jones, B. and Baker, C. (2012a) Translanguaging: Origins and development from school to street and beyond. *Educational Research and Evaluation* 18 (7), 641–654.
Lewis, G., Jones, B. and Baker, C. (2012b) Translanguaging: Developing its conceptualisation and contextualisation. *Educational Research and Evaluation* 18 (7), 655–670.

Li, W. (2014) Who's teaching whom? Co-learning in multilingual classrooms. In S. May (ed.) *The Multilingual Turn* (pp. 167–190). Routledge.
Li, W. (2018) Translanguaging as a practical theory of language. *Applied Linguistics* 39 (1), 9–30.
Li, W. and Lin, A. (2019) Translanguaging classroom discourse: Pushing limits, breaking boundaries. *Classroom Discourse* 10 (3/4), 209–215.
Little, D. and Kirwan, D. (2019) *Engaging with Linguistic Diversity. A Study of Educational Inclusion in an Irish Primary School*. Bloomsbury.
Long, R. and Daneshi, S. (2022a) *Teacher recruitment and retention in England. Research Briefing*. House of Commons Library.
Long, R. and Daneshi, S. (2022b) *Language Teaching in Schools (England). Research Briefing*. House of Commons Library.
Lytra, V. (2011) Negotiating language, culture and pupil agency in complementary school classrooms. *Linguistics and Education* 22 (1), 23–36.
Lytra, V. (2016) Language and ethnic identity. In S. Preece (ed.) *The Routledge Handbook of Language and Identity* (pp. 131–145). Routledge.
Lytra, V. and Martin, P. (eds) (2010) *Sites of Multilingualism: Complementary Schools in Britain Today*. Trentham.
Lytra, V., Ros I Solé, C., Anderson, J. and Macleroy, V. (2022) Conclusion: Language education collages. In V. Lytra, C. Ros i Solé, J. Anderson and V. Macleroy (eds), *Liberating Language Education* (pp. 321–330). Multilingual Matters.
Macleroy, V. (2021) Framing critical perspectives on migration, fairness and belonging through the lens of young people's multilingual digital stories. In L. Mary, A.-B. Krüger and A.S. Young (eds) *Migration, Multilingualism and Education: Critical Perspectives on Inclusion* (pp. 202–219). Multilingual Matters.
MacSwan, J. (ed.) 2022 *Multilingual Perspectives on Translanguaging*. Multilingual Matters.
Makalela, L. (2019) Uncovering the universals of ubuntu translanguaging in classroom discourses. *Classroom Discourse* 10 (3/4), 237–251.
Martin, J. and Rose, D. (2008) *Genre Relations. Mapping Culture*. Equinox.
Martin-Jones, M., Blackledge, A. and Creese, A. (2012) Introduction: A sociolinguistics of multilingualism for our times. In M. Martin-Jones, A. Blackledge and A. Creese (eds) *The Routledge Handbook of Multilingualism* (pp. 1–26). Routledge.
May, S. (ed.) (2014) *The Multilingual Turn. Implications for SLA, TESOL and Bilingual Education*. Routledge.
May, S. (2022a) Afterword: The multilingual turn, superdiversity and translanguaging – The rush from heterodoxy to orthodoxy. In J. MacSwan (ed.) *Multilingual Perspectives on Translanguaging* (pp. 343–355). Multilingual Matters.
May, S. (2022b) Superdiversity and its explanatory limits. *Sociolinguistica* 36 (1–2), 125–136.
Mecheril, P. (2018) Orders of belonging and education. Migration pedagogy as criticism. In D. Bachmann-Medek and J. Kugele (eds) *Migration: Changing Concepts, Critical Approaches* (pp. 121–138). De Gruyter.
Meier, G. (2017) The multilingual turn as a critical movement in education: Assumptions, challenges and a need for reflection. *Applied Linguistics Review* 8 (1), 131–161.
Meissner, F. and Vertovec, S. (2015) Comparing super-diversity. *Ethnic and Racial Studies* 38 (4), 541–555.
Menken, K. and García, O. (2010) Introduction. In K. Menken and O. García (eds) *Negotiating Language Policies in School. Educators as Policymakers* (pp. 1–10). Routledge.
Mercer, N. (2019) *Language and the Joint Construction of Knowledge. The Selected Works of Neil Mercer*. Routledge.
Miller, J. (1999) Becoming audible: Social identity and second language use. *Journal of Intercultural Studies* 20 (2), 149–165.
Miller, J. (2003) *Audible Difference: ESL and Social Identity in Schools*. Multilingual Matters.
Murray, J. and Passy, R. (2014) Primary teacher education in England: 40 years on. *Journal of Education for Teaching* 40 (5), 492–506.

Myhill, D. (2001) Writing: Crafting and creating. *English in Education* 35 (3), 13–20.
National Literacy Trust (2017) *Guidance to Using the Mapping Grid*. NLT.
Norton, B. (2013) *Identity and Language Learning. Extending the Conversation* (2nd edn). Multilingual Matters.
OECD (2019) *TALIS 2018 Results (Volume 1). Teachers and School Leaders as Lifelong Learners*. OECD.
Österreichisches Sprachen-Kompetenz-Zentrum (ed.) (2010) *Europäisches Sprachenportfolio für die Grundschule zum Einsatz an Volksschulen in Österreich. [European Language Portfolio for the Primary School for Use in State Schools in Austria]*. ÖSZ. Illustration by E. Obermüller.
Ofsted (2019) *The Education Inspection Framework*. Ofsted. See https://www.gov.uk/government/publications/education-inspection-framework (accessed August 2024).
Ofsted (2023) *School Inspection Handbook*. Ofsted. See https://www.gov.uk/government/publications/school-inspection-handbook-eif/school-inspection-handbook-for-september-2023 (accessed August 2024).
Otheguy, R. García, O. and Reid, W. (2019) A translanguaging view of the linguistic system of bilinguals. *Applied Linguistics Review* 10 (4), 625–651.
Pahl, K. (2022) Commentary for Part 4. In V. Lytra, C. Ros i Solé, J. Anderson and V. Macleroy (eds) *Liberating Language Education* (pp. 318–320). Multilingual Matters.
Pahl, K. and Rowsell, J. (2012) *Literacy and Education: Understanding the New Literacy Studies in the Classroom* (2nd edn). Sage.
Pahl, K. and Burnett, C. (2013) Literacies in homes and communities. In K. Hall, T. Cremin, B. Comber and L. Moll (eds) *International Handbook of Research on Children's Literacy, Learning, and Culture* (pp. 1–14). Wiley.
Pantić, N. (2015) A model for study of teacher agency for social justice. *Teachers and Teaching* 21 (6), 759–778.
Pantić, N. (2017) An exploratory study of teacher agency for social justice. *Teaching and Teacher Education* 66, 219–230.
Pantić, N. (2021) Teachers' Reflection on their Agency for Change (TRAC): A tool for teacher development and professional inquiry. *Teacher Development* 25 (2), 136–154.
Pearce, S. (2012) Confronting dominant whiteness in the primary classroom: Progressive student teachers' dilemmas and constraints. *Oxford Review of Education* 38 (4), 455–472.
Pollard, A. (1985) *The Social World of the Primary School*. Cassell.
Pollard, A. with Anderson, J., Maddock, M., Swaffield, S., Warin, J. and Warwick, P. (2008) *Reflective Teaching. Evidence-Informed Professional Practice* (3rd edn). Continuum.
Priestley, M., Biesta, G. and Robinson, S. (2015) *Teacher Agency. An Ecological Approach*. Bloomsbury.
Probyn, M. (2019) Pedagogical translanguaging and the construction of science knowledge in a multilingual South African classroom: Challenging monolglossic/postcolonial orthodoxies. *Classroom Discourse* 10 (3/4), 216–236.
Purkarthofer, J. (2022) And the subject speaks to you: Biographical narratives as memories and stories of the narratable self. In J. Purkarthofer and M.-C. Flubacher (eds) *Speaking Subjects in Multilingualism Research: Biographical and Speaker-centred Approaches* (pp. 21–38). Multilingual Matters.
Purkarthofer, J. and Flubacher, M.-C. (eds) (2022) *Speaking Subjects in Multilingualism Research: Biographical and Speaker-centred Approaches*. Multilingual Matters.
Putjata, G., Brizić, K., Goltsev, E. and Olfert, H. (2022) Introduction: Towards a multilingual turn in teacher professionalization. *Language and Education* 36 (5), 399–403.
Pyhältö, K., Pietarinen, J. and Soini, T. (2014) Comprehensive school teachers' professional agency in large-scale educational change. *Journal of Educational Change* 15 (3), 303–325.
Quehl, T. (2022) 'I don't think we encourage the use of their home language…': Exploring 'multilingualism light' in a London primary school. In V. Lytra, C. Ros i Solé, J. Anderson and V. Macleroy (eds) *Liberating Language Education* (pp. 23–39). Multilingual Matters.

Rampton, B. (2005) *Crossing: Language and Ethnicity among Adolescents.* (2nd edn). St Jerome.
Rampton, B., Leung, C. and Cooke, M. (2020) Education, England and users of languages other than English. *Working Papers in Urban Language and Literacy* WP275. See https://www.academia.edu/44031452/WP275_Rampton_Leung_and_Cooke_2020_Education_England_and_users_of_languages_other_than_English (accessed August 2024).
Reyes, V. (2020) Ethnographic toolkit: Strategic positionality and researchers' visible and invisible tools in field research. *Ethnography* 21 (2), 220–240.
Richardson, R. (2002) *In Praise of Teachers. Identity, Equality and Education. Six Topical Lectures.* Trentham.
Riegl, M. and Vaško, T. (2007) Comparison of language policies in the post-Soviet Union countries on the European Continent. *Annual of Language and Politics and Politics of Identity* 1 (1), 47–78.
Rosowsky, A. (2016) Heavenly entextualisations. The acquisition and performance of classical religious texts. In V. Lytra, D. Volk and E. Gregory (eds) *Navigating Languages, Literacies and Identities. Religion in Young Lives* (pp. 110–125). Routledge.
Ruiz, R. (1984/2017) Orientations in language planning. In N.H. Hornberger (ed.) *Honoring Richard Ruiz and his Work on Language Planning and Bilingual Education* (pp. 13–32). Multilingual Matters.
Schreger, C. and Pernes, S. (2014) The big world of 'Little Books'. In C. Hélot, R. Sneddon and N. Daly (eds) *Children's Literature in Multilingual Classrooms. From Multiliteracy to Multimodality* (pp. 154–170). Trentham/IOE Press.
Sinclair, J. and Coulthard, M. (1975) *Towards an Analysis of Discourse: The English Used by Teachers and Pupils.* OUP.
Smith, F., Hardman, F., Wall, K. and Mroz, M. (2004) Interactive whole class teaching in the national literacy and numeracy strategies. *British Educational Research Journal* 30 (3), 395–411.
Sneddon, R. (2014) Reading and making books in two languages. In C. Hélot, R. Sneddon and N. Daly (eds) *Children's Literature in Multilingual Classrooms. From Multiliteracy to Multimodality* (pp. 121–137). Trentham/IOE Press.
Spitzmüller, J. (2022) Ideologies of communication: The social link between actors, signs and practices. In J. Purkarthofer and M.-C. Flubacher (eds) *Speaking Subjects in Multilingualism Research: Biographical and Speaker-centred Approaches* (pp. 248–269). Multilingual Matters.
Strand, S., Malmberg, L. and Hall, J. (2015) English as an Additional Language (EAL) and educational achievement in England: An analysis of the National Pupil Database. University of Oxford, Department of Ed. See https://ora.ox.ac.uk/objects/uuid:5fe64adb-a4b8-465c-aa9c-0e80697e28bb/download_file?file_format=application%2Fpdf&safe_filename=EAL_and_educational_achievement2.pdf&type_of_work=Report (accessed August 2024).
Szymborska, W. (1996) Nobel lecture: The poet and the world. See https://www.nobelprize.org/prizes/literature/1996/szymborska/lecture/ (accessed August 2024).
Tao, J. and Gao, X. (2021) *Language Teacher Agency.* CUP.
Thomas-Olalde, O. and Vehlo, A. (2011) Othering and its effects – Exploring the concept. In H. Niedrig and C. Ydesen (eds) *Writing Postcolonial Histories of Intercultural Education* (pp. 27–51). Peter Lang.
Thompson, G., Lingard, B. and Ball, S. (2021) 'Indentured autonomy': Headteachers and academisation policy in Northern England. *Journal of Educational Administration and History* 53 (3–4), 215–232.
Toom, A., Pyhältö, K. and O'Connell Rust, F. (2015) Teachers' professional agency in contradictory times. *Teachers and Teaching* 21 (6), 615–623.
Vallejo, C. and Dooly, M. (2020) Plurilingualism and translanguaging: Emergent approaches and shared concerns. Introduction to the special issue. *International Journal of Bilingual Education and Bilingualism* 23 (1), 1–16.

Vertovec, S. (2007) Super-diversity and its implications. *Ethnic and Racial Studies* 30 (6), 1024–1054.
Vygotsky, L. (1981) The instrumental method in psychology. In J. Wertsch (ed. and trans.) *The Concept of Activity in Soviet Psychology* (pp. 134–143). Sharpe.
Vygotsky, L. (1986) *Thought and Language* (ed. A. Kozulin). MIT Press.
Wells, G. (1999) *Dialogic Inquiry. Toward a Sociocultural Practice and Theory of Education.* CUP.
Welply, O. (2017) 'My language … I don't know how to talk about it': Children's views on language diversity in primary schools in France and England. *Language and Intercultural Communication* 17 (4), 437–454.
Wertsch, J., Tulviste, P. and Hagstrom, F. (1993) A sociocultural approach to agency. In E. Forman, N. Minick and A. Stone (eds) *Contexts for Learning. Sociocultural Dynamics in Children's Development* (pp. 336–356). OUP.
Windle, J., Heugh, K., French, M., Armitage, J. and Chang, L.-C. (2023) Reciprocal multilingual awareness for linguistic citizenship. *Language Awareness* 32 (4), 582–599.
Wright, D. and Brookes, G. (2019) 'This is England, speak English!': A corpus-assisted critical study of language ideologies in the right-leaning British press. *Critical Discourse Studies* 16 (1), 56–83.
Wrigley, T. (2000) *The Power to Learn. Stories of Success in the Education of Asian and other Bilingual Pupils.* Trentham.
Yuval-Davis, N. (2006) Belonging and the politics of belonging. *Patterns of Prejudice* 40 (3), 197–214.
Zhu, H. and Li, W. (2016) 'Where are you really from?' Nationality and ethnic talk (net) in everyday interactions. *Applied Linguistics Review* 7 (4), 449–470.

Index

Alexander, Robin 7, 17, 21, 32, 33, 129, 141, 165, 166, 173
Anderson, Jason 9
Anderson, Jim 52, 194
Anderson, Jim and Macleroy, Vicky 52, 53, 132, 133, 166, 187

Badwan, Khawla 4, 39, 115
Ball, Stephen 50, 51, 52, 81, 91, 141, 142, 143, 197
belonging
  experiences of 44, 126, 132, 157, 161
  natio-racial-culturally coded order of 4, 21
  politics of 39
bilingual, notion of 37
Braun, Virginia and Clarke, Victoria 46, 47, 49
Busch, Brigitta 17, 19, 20, 38, 48, 51, 93, 105, 113, 128, 167

complementary school 22, 43, 52, 82, 85, 118, 119, 122, 129, 175, 177, 184, 185, 191, 192
Cummins, Jim 2, 7, 8, 13, 18, 33, 37, 79, 130, 132, 133, 166, 179, 187
curriculum 2, 4, 29, 141, 142, 145, 155, 161, 172, 176, 191, 195, 203, 204
  National 51, 70, 173, 175

dimensions of diversity of meanings of speaking a language 41, 116, 123, 130, 131, 170
Duarte, Joana and Gogolin, Ingrid 13, 16
Duarte, Joana and Günther-van der Meij, Mirjam, 2, 3, 4, 7, 10, 135, 182, 194, 201

EAL 52, 60, 72, 73, 75, 82, 83, 84, 85, 88, 89, 92, 95, 100, 116, 146, 152, 166, 177, 200
  coordinator 43, 83, 88, 94, 96, 123, 138, 146, 147, 161

discourse 86–94, 97, 100, 116, 123, 131, 133, 134, 135, 152, 195, 196, 197, 198
  learners 82, 85, 86, 87, 89, 91, 100, 135, 201
  policy 44, 49, 52–53, 74, 83, 93, 106
  teaching/pedagogy 91, 93, 102, 105, 200, 201
education policy 22, 29, 50–53, 72, 81, 106, 138, 140, 141, 142, 143, 144, 146, 173, 197, 198, 201, 202
emergent bilingual, *see also EAL learners*
  notion of 37
  pupils/learners 77, 84, 85, 100, 102, 104, 105, 106, 133, 134, 136, 185
empowerment 13, 133, 164, 166, 167, 190, 191, 192, 199, 204, 164, 166, 167, 190, 191, 192, 199, 204
Eteläpelto Anneli *et al.* 2, 6, 23, 24, 27, 29, 30, 61, 145
ethnography 43, 203
  ethnographic perspective 1, 3, 43, 116
  ethnographic work 1, 4, 24, 44, 45, 49, 50, 196

Foley, Yvonne 22, 202
Fraser, Nancy 135

García, Ofelia and Flores, Nelson 2, 6, 7, 8, 105, 131, 134,
García, Ofelia and Kano, Naomi 9
García, Ofelia and Li, Wei 10, 15
Global South 4, 39
Gogolin, Ingrid 7, 101, 127
Goltsev, Evghenia *et al.* 201

Hall, Stuart 90, 93
Hélot, Christine *et al.* 7, 10, 13, 15, 16, 37, 132, 187
heteroglossia 9
heteroglossic orientation 8
Heugh, Kathleen 4, 16
Hymes, Dell 17

immigration, *see also migration* 21, 22, 126, 127, 186, 203
initiation-response-feedback 57
interactive whole-class teaching 56, 58, 59, 63, 66
intervention framework for collaborative empowerment 13–14, 23, 30, 130

Jaffe, Alexandra 46, 102, 103, 105

Kirsch, Claudine *et al.* 18, 200, 201

'language-as-a-resource' 17, 77, 133, 136
language awareness pedagogy 10, 132, 181, 182
language ideologies 20–21, 25, 38, 46, 80, 93, 105, 123, 129, 130, 145, 194, 197, 203
'language of the month' 82, 94, 95, 96, 97, 99
language portrait 14, 48, 49, 113, 118, 119, 122, 125, 127, 128, 178
language statistics 40, 45, 51, 91, 93, 114, 115
legitimate language 4, 12, 17
Leung, Constant 52, 53, 74
Li, Wei 16, 22, 38
linguistic schoolscapes 44, 49, 94, 98
Little, David and Kirwan, Déirdre 2, 10, 133, 135, 166, 181, 182, 186, 187
lived experience of language 16, 17, 19, 115, 128, 152, 171
Lytra, Vally 22, 52, 157, 203

Mecheril, Paul 4, 21
mediated agency 28–29, 68, 110, 177
MFL
    lessons 19, 43, 82, 84, 85, 107, 184
    policy 44, 49, 53, 120
Menken, Kate and García, Ofelia 23, 194
migration 4, 13, 21, 40, 48, 105, 114, 127, 134, 136,185, 186
monoglossic paradigm 8
monolingual habitus 3, 101, 194, 196
monolingual nation (state) 13, 38, 39,
monolingual norm 11, 12, 22, 46, 101–113, 116, 123, 129, 130, 131, 132, 133, 134, 136, 137, 152, 153, 158, 163, 164, 169, 170, 180, 185, 186, 189, 195, 197, 198
multilingual digital storytelling 132
multilingual pedagogies
    definition of 2, 7, 8,
    school as a place for 18–22, 130, 132
    socioeducational contexts of 8

multilingual turn 8, 10, 38, 119
multiliteracies 187–190
multimodality 48, 58, 170, 172

named language(s) 38, 114, 122, 131
National Literacy Strategy 56, 70

Ofsted 51, 141, 143, 173, 201
othering 126–127

Pantić, Nataša 23, 26, 28, 198
parents' involvement 57, 84, 167, 170, 171, 174, 175, 187, 191, 192
participant observations 43, 45–47
participatory activities 44, 47–49, 81, 113, 116, 127, 132, 136, 157, 159, 169, 177, 178, 184, 191
'pedagogical space' of multilingual pedagogies 35, 129–137, 146, 162, 172, 173, 176, 177, 182, 190, 191, 192, 193, 195, 199, 200
performativity 50, 143, 145, 166, 195, 196, 197, 201
plurilingual learner 179, 185–187
plurilingualism, notion of 37
position of successful learner 12, 105, 106
positionality
    child's *see also* stancetaking 102, 123, 125, 129
    researcher's 4, 49–50
    teachers' 30, 35, 158, 161, 202
Priestley, Mark *et al.* 2, 6, 23, 24, 30, 31, 32, 100, 136, 139, 141, 142, 194, 197
primary school
    and dialogic teaching 17, 187
    and pedagogical repertoire 32–33, 136
    as part of conviviality 134
    linguistically very diverse/superdiverse 12, 13, 16, 41, 50, 116, 130, 132, 133, 134, 136, 164, 190, 191, 192, 196
    pedagogy/pedagogical perspective of 12, 29, 75, 91, 106, 116, 123, 130, 131, 132, 135, 136, 146, 162, 165, 167, 196, 198, 204
professional agency *see also teacher agency*
    definition of 29
    life-course dimension of 29
    subject-centred sociocultural framework of 2, 6, 25–30
PSHE 42, 172

racism 4, 21, 160
reciprocity (in pedagogical interaction) 181, 182, 192

reflexivity 23, 27, 112, 136, 145, 159, 160, 161, 181, 197, 198, 200, 203
representation of multilingualism 48, 94, 97, 98, 127, 128, 134
'river of reading' 111, 112, 113, 167, 169, 170, 189, 200

senior management team 142, 143, 144
social justice 91, 134, 135, 136
speaker(s)
  -centred approaches in research 10, 19, 48, 167, 185
  perspective of the 16, 41, 86, 152, 157, 158, 160, 186, 160, 165
  plurilingual 9, 10, 12, 16, 17, 35, 37, 38, 47, 48, 49, 50, 53, 77, 87, 90, 105, 106, 114, 116, 123, 128, 135, 146, 157, 158, 160, 171, 177, 178, 182, 184, 185, 186
special educational needs 67, 138
spiral-curricular 181, 187, 188, 192
stancetaking 46, 102, 103, 105, 123
subjectivation/subjection 46, 105, 185
subject position 12, 104, 105, 126, 133, 186
subtractive bilingualism 8, 93, 105
superdiversity
  notion of 38–40, 115
  superdiverse voices 40, 113–129, 130, 136, 145, 184
symbolic acknowledgement of multilingualism 94–100, 105, 116, 123, 127, 131, 133, 134, 195, 196, 197, 198

teacher agency
  and professional identity 23, 26, 27, 30, 44, 47, 60, 150, 190, 194, 195, 197
  and professional subjectivities 29, 30, 34, 35, 76, 80, 131, 147–151, 176, 199
  and micro, meso and macro levels of context 23, 24, 25, 81
  and time 141, 142, 146, 162, 172, 173, 197, 204
  and workplace 24, 27, 47, 138–147, 161, 196, 197, 198
  and relationships (vertical/horizontal) 139–147
  classroom as context for 28–29, 34, 54–75, 110
  definition of 32, 100

dimensions of 30–32, 198
ecological approach to 2, 6, 24, 30–33, 139
for social justice 23, 198
general teacher agency 62, 64, 66, 67, 72, 73, 75, 155, 161, 195
teacher agency in multilingual pedagogies
  contextual factors for 34, 35, 199, 200
  features of 197, 202
  framework for 1, 2, 5, 6, 25, 26, 33–36, 54, 80, 81, 101, 129, 131, 137, 138, 162, 176, 199
teacher education 23, 90, 196, 201, 202, 204
  CPD/in-service training 52, 176, 191, 192, 198, 200, 202
  initial teacher education 3, 52, 53, 83, 166, 198, 200, 201
teacher professionalisation 195, 200, 201, 202
teachers'
  language experiences 20, 43, 87, 151–158, 165, 181, 182, 202
  pedagogical motivation 162–167, 190, 191, 192, 195, 196, 197, 198
  professional investment 74, 89, 150, 151
  professional priorities/values 147, 149, 150, 156, 161, 165, 167, 192
  rapport with the children 140, 147, 148, 149, 150, 153, 155, 195
translanguaging 9, 40, 77, 179
  definition of 9
  its anchor points for teacher agency 10–17
  strategic use of 15, 110, 136, 158, 158

'unofficial' talk 76, 80, 81, 180

voice 10, 17, 34, 35, 45, 48, 58, 59, 65, 66, 71, 77, 78, 80, 107, 112, 135, 136, 158, 165
  children's voice in the research process 4, 47–48, 113, 182

Wertsch, James et al. 28, 68, 167, 177
'whole child' 149, 162, 164, 165, 166, 167, 171, 173, 190, 191, 192, 199
whole-school development 166, 186, 187
working consensus 55, 59, 60, 61, 62, 66, 71, 106, 107, 109, 129, 141, 149, 150, 163, 195, 200
workload 145, 146, 161

For Product Safety Concerns and Information please contact our EU Authorised Representative:

Easy Access System Europe

Mustamäe tee 50

10621 Tallinn

Estonia

gpsr.requests@easproject.com